Too Many
Cooks

Kitchen Adventures with

1 Mom,

4 Kids,

and 102 Recipes

Too Many
Cooks

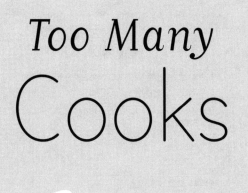

Emily Franklin

voice

HYPERION   NEW YORK

Library of Congress Cataloging-in-Publication Data

Franklin, Emily.
    Too many cooks : kitchen adventures with 1 mom, 4 kids, and 102
recipes / Emily Franklin.
        p. cm.
    Includes index.
    ISBN 978-1-4013-4083-4
    1. Cookery.   I. Title.
    TX714.F724 2009
    641.5—dc22

                                                            2009003452

Hyperion books are available for special promotions and premiums.
For details contact the HarperCollins Special Markets Department
in the New York office at 212-207-7528, fax 212-207-7222,
or email spsales@harpercollins.com.

Book design by Jennifer Ann Daddio / Bookmark Design & Media Inc

FIRST EDITION

1   3   5   7   9   10   8   6   4   2

THIS LABEL APPLIES TO TEXT STOCK

We try to produce the most beautiful books possible, and we are also extremely
concerned about the impact of our manufacturing process on the forests of the
world and the environment as a whole. Accordingly, we made sure that all of
the paper we used has been certified as coming from forests that are managed to
insure the protection of the people and wildlife dependent upon them.

For the six of us and all the meals to come

Contents

Autumn

Winter

Early Spring

Too Many
Cooks

Introduction

This book was born very simply out of two loves: food and children.

And not necessarily in that order.

I love food. I love kids. Well, to be fair, not all kids. I love mine, though. This is true with food, too. I love looking at food at the farmer's market, peering at specialty stores, talking about food, shopping for food, reading about food, but I do not love eating all food—though I'm willing to try. Most of all, I like cooking food. And I like cooking it for my rather large family.

Not too long ago my husband and our four kids and I were out for dinner at a somewhat famous seafood restaurant. This restaurant was located, I should add, on an island known not only for its beaches and for its shells but for its great bounty of fish. We'd prepped the kids for the menu, done the parental reconnaissance mission of scouting out the goods before, and yet still their decry came.

"There's nothing to eat here."

Nothing consisted of scallops and soft-shelled crab, salmon and flounder and red snapper cooked in all manner of ways—breaded, fried, baked, broiled, encrusted with wasabi. *Nothing* went on to include shrimp, mussels, cod, and sole. The plasticky kids' menu offered pizza and nuggets.

Even then with the harried waitress and the tourist masses and the sun-tired kids and the on-vacation-but-still-needing-a-vacation parents, we still said no to the pizza and nuggets.

"We're at a fish restaurant!" I insisted as the kids began to color on their menus with waxy crayons.

"You don't have chicken at a fish restaurant," my husband, Adam, a pediatrician, agreed while detangling the youngest from her fork and asking the oldest not to use his as a musical instrument.

"But what if we want nuggets?"

It's a simple question. And yet the answer is more complicated and deserves a whole essay (which I give on page 29).

"You know what? Order whatever you want." I pointed to the big menu. "From here." Then I said my piece. "Try something new."

The reality is that just because I love food and like to try new things, doesn't mean my children will.

But I could try, which brought me to this question: What happens when you mix the mayhem of motherhood with new foods and recipes?

What happens when, as a family of six, we order from the full menu? Explore the new, the untasted, the untried, the unknown both in our home and out? For one whole year we would introduce new foods on a regular basis with the goal of broadening our culinary landscapes. Twelve months later we'd see about the kids' menus. I didn't announce with grandeur my plans to infiltrate our meals with newness. I didn't say our lives were going to change. They did, of course, but I didn't know this when I set out one night with a coconut and a hammer (more on page 22).

Too Many Cooks is not a cookbook, though it contains recipes. Rather than being a book solely about cooking, this is a narrative of family eating. My husband is a physician and he's got lots of literature about the health crisis affecting kids in this country, but this book is not about cooking rigidly healthy meals, though healthy ones are encouraged. Mainly, I don't have a platform. I'm not here to lecture about local or organic or beef or sweets. This book documents the family fun, chaos, and conviviality that surround mealtime and food while introducing new meals, never-before-tasted vegetables or crackers, fish, fowl, and grains as I show my kids how to order off the other menu.

Too Many Cooks is an "eating book."

I'm not a terrific measurer. I'm not an immaculate chef. But I make good food and can think on my feet, which comes in handy (think: stirring sweet-corn risotto while nursing and running through spelling words for the week after putting in work hours). Friends, relatives, and strangers at the market who see me shuffling through with four children often ask me, "How do you do it?"

Prior to my life as a writer and mother, I was a cook on historic yachts and luxury boats, cooking three meals and a high tea for crowds of up to forty people in a galley smaller than a shower stall. And with a diesel-fuel stove that ran at turns scalding or tepid. If I handled deveining shrimp, making lobster bisque, and creating chocolate pudding cake while caught in rough seas off the Maine coast, surely cooking in my own kitchen would be a lesser challenge. Right?

Not necessarily.

Too Many Cooks is a culinary calendar of days and seasons with my family. As with good food, I am happy to share these moments; the highs and lows of parenting in the kitchen. I can say that cooking for one whiny, picky child is far more difficult and stressful than for forty on the rolling seas. But I do it anyway.

I have long believed that cooking and parenting go hand in hand. Not only because children need food and one of the earliest ways we connect to them is by feeding, but because both are wonderful and messy. At their best, cooking and parenting bring joy, fulfillment, and pleasure. But a bad day in the kitchen—or with a kid—and frustrations (and often a bad taste in your mouth) abound. At the end of the day, you try your best with kids, give them everything you can, and see how they turn out at the end. Who hasn't done the same thing in the kitchen; closed their eyes, shut the oven door, and hoped that when the time comes to reveal the dish, it's recognizable and good?

Too Many Cooks is my quest to create happy, healthy eaters without tricks (if you purée vegetables and add them to brownies, all you're really doing is getting your kids to like brownies, which they probably already do). So this is not about sneaking healthy food into sweets. In fact, this is not about sneaking anything. This is the opposite—a bare-all. A culinary centerfold, if you will.

Back at the seafood restaurant, when the plea for nuggets went unanswered, the kids wound up with barbecued salmon, crusty cod, and shrimp. No pizza. Nix the kid menu. We endured the bitter battle for the first few minutes and then, when the plates came, we shared and tasted and tested. That was the beginning.

As a working parent, I know there is great variety to how people with children tend to cook: some in fits and starts, in snatches and on the run, some slow-cooking and bringing out recipes their own parents used. This book is not a judgment on how other people cook. I have friends who shop exclusively at organic markets and insist on local produce. I have others who don't give much thought to food, shopping at big chain stores and whose idea of cooking is pressing the Start button on the microwave.

But no matter how we cook or what food means to us, we need to feed our families. The kitchen is a microcosm of family life, and eating together is the most universal of gatherings. I want to teach my kids to explore new ideas and tastes. Some they will adore, others they will revolt against and hope never to have again, and some will just roll off their tongues but implant deep within their growing minds. Part of the reason for this book is the actual food—I hope they'll appreciate curries, recognize rhubarb, have opinions about onions and leeks, roasted cod, and fingerling potatoes. The other part—the biggest part—is being together.

I have said what this book is not: not a self-help guide, not a how-to manual, not a soapbox from which I will preach about only one sort of food or one specific way to parent. I didn't want to write one of those books. If you read this and take with you a recipe or a parenting tip or some nugget (ha!) of truth that helps you, that's great. If you only read, relate, and smile, that's fine too. All I'm asking is that you try it.

A Note About the Recipes

The recipes in this book were all made for my family, so please be aware that each recipe makes enough for at least six people of varying appetites, sometimes with leftovers. In addition, though I specify just "olive oil" in the recipes, this should always be extra virgin olive oil (except in the hummus on page 116, which does well with standard olive oil rather than virgin). Butter in all recipes may be salted or unsalted unless otherwise specified (I know, I'm breaking culinary laws). As you read, you'll probably see that my cooking style, like my parenting, tends toward flexibility rather than arbitrary rigidity. I'm not trying to incense the perfectionist cook or baker, but rather document my style in the kitchen and out. While I am not here to force anyone to eat any particular way, I wish to disclose that I try to buy organic when possible and choose local products when feasible. This book is nothing if not an ode to our motto of "A Little Bit of This and a Little Bit of That Keeps You Healthy," so while I adore hearty quinoa grains and am mad about my greens, I might also indulge in a fried Twinkie if the time and place called for it.

Happy eating together!

EMILY

Additionally, this is a work of nonfiction—that is, all of this really happened (and continues to do so). I have changed the names of my children for their privacy.

Late Spring

In Which India Is Introduced

You'll like it. It's really good. Trust me. When people say these things to me, I feel inclined to disagree even before I've tasted whatever it is they're offering. Perhaps this is due to years of my mother trying wholeheartedly to convince me that eventually I'll love headbands (still don't, though a navy-and-sky-blue striped one is on my dresser just in case) or maybe this is because none of us likes to feel that something is being forced on us and we must enjoy it. So considering this, I've developed a different tactic with my kids.

Depending on what I'm serving, I blend it into the meal or keep calm about the concept of trying new dishes. I don't load the offering with hidden pleasures or glam it up, but I don't downplay it either. Just honest.

It's May and warm, though the humidity hasn't yet seeped into everything, so I can still use the oven without feeling overwhelmed. I've planned Wild Coho Salmon with a very simple teriyaki glaze, broccoli, and maybe some brown rice if I get a chance and it doesn't burn like it did last time when I forgot about it (see page 14).

At breakfast, Julia eats her cereal as though she's paying for it by the mouthful.

"You'll have to hurry up," I tell her. "We have to take everyone to school."

"Not Will," she informs me.

"No, not Will." Will is eight weeks old at this point and not ready for name tags and circle time. He is in the stage my older brother calls "the potted plant," which means he can sit in his car seat or in my arms or just about anywhere just doing his job of being a baby. "But everyone else has to go to school. And I still have to nurse."

Nursing has become the family's dictum of time. Forget clocks. It's all about the feeding. "When can we leave?" "As soon as I'm done nursing." "When's dinner?" "Right after I'm done feeding Will." "Can you play baseball?" "Not until I'm done nursing."

Jamie, all limbs and bright new grown-up teeth, charges in, energy for twelve people at eight in the morning, jousting with a baseball bat. "What's for dinner tonight?" Jamie is eight years old, intensely verbal and analytical and while open to trying new things on an intellectual level, has gut reactions that range from funny and sweet ("I thought this looked like the best dessert in the world. Turns out, it's just gross. But thanks for trying!") to revulsion ("This sauce is killing me, Mom."). Prone to spewing facts (for example, when Adam and I were talking about Fidel Castro playing for the Washington Senators, Jamie piped in with, "It's funny to have a dictator play pro baseball. Especially because of all the communists." We were surprised, but also amused by his pronunciation of communists as "com-*mune*ists"). Sometimes, Jamie makes up these facts, other times he's completely correct. He adds wisdom and gusto to each meal.

"Don't swing the bat, please."

"What's for dinner?" Daniel, full-cheeked, with wire-rimmed glasses and café au lait hair, echoes his older brother. It dawns on me that we are speaking of a meal that is ten hours away, and yet my response has the power to elicit joy or ruin the remaining eight minutes before we get in the car.

Six-year-old Daniel is the kid who is at turns maddening and heart-melting. Loving and filled with mischief, he is as likely to scream and turn red at the thought of eating peas as he is to suddenly develop a taste for all things Cajun ("Oh, man, are these Cajun fava beans good."). Daniel causes the most disruptions during family dinners with his various desires—some rational ("Please could I have the sauce on the side?") and some irrational in the way that only parents truly understand. ("I only want it cut in triangles, but not that way—and not on the red plate. And with nothing touching it. And if you make me eat peas, I will die.")

"Salmon," I tell the kids and take the paper-wrapped parcel from the fridge. I bring it over to the sink, explaining to the kids what I'm doing. "See? You always want to wash the fish before you make it, right?"

"What kind of salmon?" Jamie wants to know. "The normal kind?"

Sip coffee. Unwrap salmon. Check on baby in bassinet. Julia still eating cereal piece by piece. Soon it will be soggy and she'll want a replacement bowl that I refuse to give. Mean Mommy. "Normal with olive oil and sea salt?" I ask.

Jamie shrugs. "I don't know. The kind we had when you told me that story of how Uncle Nick made you eat rocks."

This is how he navigates—I am meant to follow. Just like the way some people remember events by what they wore or what song was playing in the background, Jamie associates meals with stories. I think back. Got it. "No, not that kind. The kind that tastes like Chinese food."

Kids have so much associative memory; they see the outside of the doctor's office and start to bawl, or have a warm bath that signals it's time for bed, but what about with food? We get a chance to start fresh with kids, to help attach good feelings to good food. Theirs is a memory slightly more malleable than the grown-up mind, not yet worn by years of resistance.

When trying to have them taste new things I sometimes pick a food—or a category of food—that they already like (like Chinese food) and pair it with the new thing. When I first made the salmon for them, I called it "Chinese salmon" and sure enough, teriyaki sauce, rice wine, scallions, a touch of brown sugar, and it smells like we're bringing brown bags back from Peking Cuisine down the road. Does this always work? No. But I think it can help. Too much originality can be overwhelming for them, so I'll often make only part of the meal new—reliable vegetables, known-entity grain, new protein. Other times I throw parental caution to the wind and serve it all up and wait to see if there's glee, gluttony, or groans.

"What are we having with the salmon?" Daniel runs his palms along the counters, tracing a pattern only he can see while I rinse the fish, pat it dry, eye the baby again and do a quick visual to make sure all the lunch-boxes are in their pre-game position by the door.

"Broccoli and brown rice."

"Are you gonna burn it again?" Ever-verbal Julia, three years old with a tangled mop of blond-brown curls, wants to know. She stares at me through her thick round glasses. She has the most changeable palate. From very early on she's shown a preference for more adult food. However, her texture issues are also complex—no cooked fruit ("too mushy"), no raw carrots ("too sour") and while she might try a new food and adore it one night, the next day she'll often rage against it.

"This cereal is soggy now. I want more of a different one."

"No," I tell her. "No more cereal. You can eat what you have there or be done."

"Then I'm done." Julia grimaces as I take the blue bowl from her. What was once bran flakes is now a pile of brown mush, like rain-wet leaves at the end of fall. I wouldn't want to eat it either.

"Well, you burned it last time," Jamie reminds me. He motions for Julia and Daniel to watch him. "Remember she danced around like this?" Jamie takes a place mat from the table and waves it above his head, doing a combination march and dance—my homage to the smoke detector, which likes to beep very loudly at the slightest hint of heat.

I smile. "I did burn it and I did do that dance, but who remembers why it burned?" My face is flushed from wearing long sleeves in the thick, warm air.

Daniel raises his hand, already trained for kindergarten, then remembers he's not in school and puts it down. "Because you were nursing Will. And you forgot."

I forgot. Breast, baby, bottle of water, kids quiet, I had settled into my uncomfortable work chair and multitasked my way into a pile of unintentionally blackened rice and an obnoxiously persistent beeping from the detector. Cue the image of me, holding Will, who wasn't yet sated and therefore crying, while fanning the air under the smoke detector with an ABC-patterned place mat. "This time I'll watch it more."

The kids ready themselves with the season's extras—sun block, plastic shoes that let in air and an inordinate amount of playground sand, baseball hats—while I whisk together soy sauce, teriyaki, a few splashes of rice wine vinegar, a bit of brown sugar and anything else I see around that might suit the impromptu marinade. I pour it on the deep coral salmon, admiring the way the rich brown begins immediately to seep into the flesh. This type of marinade works well with bluefish, too, also with monkfish—it requires a sturdy base. The scallions I'll slice and add later. I drizzle a bit of sesame oil on because I see it in the pantry looking stout and lonely in its spot next to the other oils. Shove the whole thing, foil-covered, into the fridge, wash hands, and pick up the baby for a quick feeding top-off before we leave for school.

As I put the Pyrex dish into the extra-chilled lower shelf in the fridge, I see tonight's new item—mango lassi, made locally by Dahlicious. I picked the bottle of it up at Whole Foods thinking I'd chug it between school pick-ups and drop-offs, but never got around to it. Its small container is similar to an old-fashioned milk bottle, but plastic with a pleasant orange safety seal and label. I debate showing the kids now. No. I'll wait. We're rushing, and I don't want to give them any preconceived notions about this drink.

"OK. Everyone ready?" I ask. Baby in car seat by the door. Other kids reasonably clothed. Not filthy. Dinner to some degree started. Baby sated for now. Partially started novel waiting on the computer upstairs if I find the time today.

"Uh, Mom?" Daniel says, his brow furrowed.

"Come on, we're going to be late." Suddenly we need to leave—if only parenting came with its own set of emergency codes like in medicine: Let's leave—STAT!

"Mom!"

"Daniel—come on!" It's always a wonder to me how I can go from relaxed enough to explain fish prep to suddenly worrying about traffic and being late for drop-off.

"But Mom." Daniel's voice verges on whiny. The skin on the back of my neck starts to prickle.

I am reduced to barking one-word orders. "Daniel. Now!" I open the door, holding the car seat in the crook of my elbow and beckoning the rest of the brood out with my head.

"Mom!"

"I mean it, now, come on." I hate hearing my voice like this—surely my eyebrows are arched, my mouth taut—I sound drill-sergeant demanding and all we're trying to do is get to school. I vow to soften my tone.

Daniel stamps his foot. "No, but . . ." I shoot him a look. He raises his golden-retriever-colored eyebrows and adjusts his glasses. "Because you have to—"

Calm but stern mom voice takes over. "I do not have to do anything. You don't have a choice right now. I make the choices."

"OK, OK." Daniel steps out the door and onto the small back porch we use primarily to hold strollers and muddy cleats. His shoes continue to spill a small trail of sand as he walks, remnants of yesterday's playground outing. "Fine," Daniel acquiesces. "If you want to go out with your breast hanging out, I guess that's *your* choice."

Enough said.

After drop-offs but before the baby needs to nurse—again—I wash and slice some scallions, sprinkle them into the salmon dish in the fridge. While I have my hands wet, I wash and cut up the broccoli. So maybe I didn't remember to buckle my personal produce into my bra, but I do remember to cook the rice and remove it from the heat before burning. I make two cups of brown rice, the short-grain kind, which I find to be slightly sweet and sticky—in a good way. The roundness of the grains works well with sauces and soups. I buy it in bulk and keep a jarful by the stove.

The rice simmers away, the fish is prepped, and the broccoli is all ready for roasting.

With some crayons scattered on the table and others rolling onto the floor, Julia colors a "larnry fish with a big hat and the letter A." Despite numerous attempts at finding out what "larnry" means, I still am unclear. It sounds like another word for cranky, which would be a nice addition to my vocabulary. *How are you today, Emily? Actually, I'm a little larnry. Not enough sleep.*

Jamie practices piano, and Daniel disappears upstairs only to return with half of a broken plastic horn I thought my husband, Adam, chucked out months ago. *Sqwaaak!* The noise is jolting. I suffer through it a few times until I've poured most of the marinade from the salmon and put the dish into the oven. *Sqwaaak!*

"Daniel?" I say in a tone that is meant to imply "enough of that noise." I could bring the mango lassi out now to show them, but the noise is too much. It might make everyone *larnry.*

"What's for dinner?" Daniel's shoes have regained their sandy contents and he contributes to the household décor by spreading the grit around the hardwood floor while we repeat our conversation from this morning. He does a mental checklist of the foods. Salmon. Rice. Broc. Nothing bad there. "OK. But when?"

Say it with me: "When I'm done nursing Will." This buys me an indeterminate amount of time as opposed to saying dinner will be ready at six and tiny tantrums erupting when it's not.

Thirtyish minutes later, the broccoli is ready, the fish sits on the stovetop ready to be served, and the rice is—

"Hey, Mom, good job with the rice! It's not burned!" Jamie uses the voice of parental or teacherly encouragement, the kind one might use with a toddler taking her first steps. I smile at him. Jamie grins back with his new front teeth. They are bigger than the others, and when he smiles, he looks like an advertisement for childhood—at turns delightful, growing, mismatched—awkwardly beautiful. I stare at him for just a few seconds, amazed at the incredible tumbling-past of time. Amazed how the same eyes looked at me from his blue bassinet, the same one Will is outgrowing now.

"Mom?" Jamie claps his hands to re-Earth me. His wide eyes wait for my response. When Jamie was an infant, his head seemed disproportionately big, his eyes large. His pediatrician father thought he looked like E.T.

I lift the lid on the rice with a pair of metal tongs. "Thanks for noticing. I managed to save us from more noise." I point to the smoke detector. *Sqwaaak!* Daniel punctuates the conversation with his broken toy.

"OK. Enough with that," I say, simultaneously dropping the horn in the trash, and adding, "Time to wash hands for dinner."

I save enough food for the grown-ups to have later after the kids are in bed and, when all is calm, the bellies full enough, the afternoon crazies settled, I go to the fridge. The mango lassi. Right.

"Hey, guys?"

Four faces look at me. Three with milk mustaches, one waiting for another round of nursing. "What?"

"So, who likes spicy food?"

Daniel's hand flies up. Julia tilts her head, unsure. Jamie explains, "I do, except for jalapeños. I had them that one time with Grammie and I cried because they set my whole mouth and tongue and lips and everything on fire and I would have needed an extinguisher to put out the hotness. But you can't have an extinguisher in your mouth because they don't make them for mouths. But I could invent one."

"Could it be blue?" Julia asks. Jamie nods.

"Anyway, if you ever encountered a jalapeño again, what would help cool you off?"

"A sprinkler," Daniel offers. He probably has visions of the warmer days to come.

"Yes." I nod, as they clear their plates. "But you know what's a really good way to get rid of spice? Milk. It really cools off your mouth."

"So, like, if you have a giant thing of spicy meatballs or something and then have milk it's OK?" Daniel drums the table.

"Yeah." I go to the fridge. "When I was growing up, I ate a lot of Indian food—like curry and chana masala—we can have that another time. But a great way to get rid of the heat from that is a special drink."

Daniel lights up. He nudges Julia. "Like a dessert?" Julia asks, sitting on her knees, her whole body leaning onto the table.

"Sort of. Sometimes when you have Indian food, you have something called a lassi. It's a yogurt drink and it can be either sweet or salty." They think this over for a minute and before they can object or excite, I bring the bottle out of the fridge and show it to them. "So, you can make a lassi, but I saw this one and bought it and you can try it and just see what you think."

"I want mine in a real glass," Julia says.

A reasonable request. The liquid is thick but easily poured. I serve equal amounts in three glasses (about two inches in each). "Now, how does it smell?"

"Sweet."

"It looks like melted Creamsicle."

Daniel looks up. "It smells really good." He smiles, revealing his chipped front tooth, his eagerness. They all sip the drink, comforted by its fragrant mango scent, the familiarity of yogurt.

"So, sometime if we have Indian food can we have a lassi?" Jamie asks.

Bingo. Exactly what I wanted to have happen. Now they can associate a known entity like the lassi drink they know they like with something new like chicken tikka masala or dal. "Absolutely."

"Mom?" Daniel licks his upper lip free of lassi and wipes his hand on his shirt. I check to make sure my breasts aren't hanging out.

"What?"

"They should call it mango glassi because it's served in a glass."

Impromptu Asian Marinade

This makes enough to coat about two pounds of salmon or another sturdy fish, such as monkfish. Additions might include crushed garlic or minced fresh ginger, but aren't necessary. All measurements are approximate—don't worry if you add too much or don't have enough of any one item.

Mix together:

about 1/3 cup of soy sauce	1/4 cup brown sugar
1/4 cup teriyaki sauce	big squirt of ketchup
a few generous splashes of rice wine vinegar	dash of ground ginger

Whisk well and pour over fish to marinate for as long as you like (overnight or thirty minutes or right away—up to you).

Roasted Broccoli

Roasting vegetables definitely increases our consumption of them. Cauliflower, broccoli, carrots, Brussels sprouts, broccoli rabe—they all taste incredible with such simple seasoning and easy time in the oven. I roast nearly everything, but the basics are this:

head of broccoli	cooking spray
good olive oil	coarse sea salt

Preheat the oven to 375°. Slice the broccoli into large-ish pieces, including the lengths of stem that you might otherwise discard or crop. Some pieces will have a flat bottom where you've cut into the core and others will be a simple "tree."

With your fingers, rub a bit of olive oil onto a cookie sheet and arrange the broccoli in a single layer. Spray the tops of the broccoli with cooking spray—or if you're feeling very fit and don't mind the extra fat/calories, you can douse the tops with olive oil, making sure to evenly coat the dense green.

Sprinkle with sea salt. You can cook these straightaway or let them sit covered with a dishcloth for a few hours, then slide the pan in thirty minutes before you want to eat. Leftovers—whole or chopped—spruce up a salad quite nicely. Cook for about 25 minutes, until stems are tender but not too soft and bits of brown have colored their undersides.

Unburned Brown Rice

Brown rice takes a bit longer to make but is worth it for taste and nutritional value. Measure your rice and add double that amount of water. Heat on high until boiling then reduce to simmer until cooked (about an hour for two cups of rice).

Note: *If you are breastfeeding, busy, or otherwise distracted, set a timer!*

Mango Lassi

1 cup milk (any kind— I use 1%)	1½ cups pureed mango (fresh or canned)
2 cups plain yogurt	dash cinnamon
sugar to taste (start with 4 tsp. and add from there)	dash cardamom

Blend all items. Adjust sugar content. Dust with spices if you like. Serve cold. Makes around 4 cups and keeps for a day or so in the fridge.

Note: *You may use mango juice (sometimes easier to find). If so, use ½ cup milk, 1½ cups plain yogurt, and 1½ cups mango juice.*

Milk Feeds More Than
Just the Baby

Question: Why am I, a mother of four, sitting on the floor at dinnertime holding a hammer and about to whack the object in front of me in order to feed my children?

Answer: I thought it would be fun.

Dinnertime, and I am covered in sticky milk. Given the fact that I am three months postpartum, this shouldn't be a huge surprise, but this time the milk isn't mine. No bottle, no jug of organic milk, no sippy cup that has proven labels wrong yet again by leaking. This milk is from somewhere different. But I'm getting ahead of myself, which is what got me into the sticky mess in the first place.

Sunday afternoon chugs in, and Adam and I are doing the weekend marital dance of divvying up the errands. "I'll take the kids to the playground, you do the shop." "We need to return the books to the library before we get fined." "Did you call Dr. Weiss to make the checkup appointments?" And so on. Scheduling becomes intricate ("If you go to the gym at nine and come back by ten, we can take Jamie to the birthday party and still have time to shower!"), a carefully set up suspension bridge designed to utilize our combined strengths and make up for our individual foibles.

In short, I volunteer to do the food shop, which is how I wind up at Russo's, a wholesale produce market open to the public. Outside, pots of zinnias, magenta petunias, and flashlight-bright marigolds are set to one side. Herbs, still uncut, flank a table piled high with bicolor corn. To the left of the entrance are large bins filled with melons: cantaloupe, watermelons, Asian melons, honeydew the color of sea glass. Inside, the array of foodstuffs is stunning: plums and snake melons; round lychees and long, arthritically gnarled fava beans; mounds of fresh cheeses; neat boxes of blueberries, strawberries, and newly arrived blackberries. Below the produce, shelves hold myriad items all grouped by country of origin—everything from chutneys to deep-brown oyster sauce, crackly rice noodles, packets of seaweed wrapped in cellophane, different varieties of Arborio and Carnaroli rice for risotto. I love wandering here and often spend too long gazing at the crazy quilt of colors, planning menus and wishing I had infinite weekend minutes amidst the bright-skinned summer squash and unidentifiable twisty tangles of spiky greens.

It's easy to get distracted with the visual intensity and sensory overload here, which is what is about to happen to me this particular Sunday when I come upon the simplest of items. There, clustered in careful pyramids next to bins of lotus stems and ripe mangoes, are happy, hairy little coconuts.

An image springs to mind of my father crouched over a newspaper with a hammer poised to strike such a brown little ball. In mock horror I realize the kids have never tried a fresh coconut, have never delighted in its hard, toothy flesh, its sweet milk, the swift cracking of the shell when met with the hammer's blow. I pick one up, put my thumb into the dark brown dimple on one end, and immediately shake it. The liquid slosh is somewhat muted. I add it to my purchase.

I will show the kids this nonnative fruit. (Is it a fruit? A legume? Why don't I know this?) I will be the mom who shows them new things. The one who brings them new experiences. The one who, when they look back on their formative years, ushers in the kitchen comforts. Or perhaps just the one who let them take a whack at a coconut with a hammer. With glee, I bring the coconut and the rest of the cart's contents to the colossally long line and wait to pay.

"What's the hairy football?" Julia points to the single coconut that is perched on the windowsill above the toaster oven. It resembles more a reject candlepin bowling ball, one whose holes have been filled.

"It's a coconut, Julia-belle," Jamie says. "Coconuts grow in Brazil and New Zealand . . . not just the tropics."

I raise my eyebrows. "You sure?"

"Yup." He pretends to chuck it at me as I make dinner. "Are we eating it?"

"Leave it." The order is automatic. Then I soften. Fun. This is fun. He's not breaking wineglasses. "You can touch it. But we're not having it until after dinner."

As the plates are cleared, I get the hammer from the top of the basement stairs storage area and search for newspaper. We've stopped our daily subscription due to lack of time to read, figuring we'll pick a few sections to read online, and our Sunday papers have been recycled. Ah, the modern age. I get a cookie sheet instead and place the coconut on top with a tinny bang.

Daniel laughs. "You're gonna kill it?"

"It wasn't alive, it's a fruit," Jamie says, then pauses. "It is a fruit, right, Mom?"

I furrow my brow. "Uh, I think so. Actually, I'm not sure." I like to let the kids know that I don't know everything. That I don't know a lot of things. That it's OK not to know, and saying as much doesn't make you look foolish.

I continue. "Now, when I was little, Grandpa Rick whacked a coconut and it"—I bring the hammer down hard on the coconut as I speak—"cracked open. Except . . ." The firm brown ball stays solid. I whack again. And again. Soon the kids are giggling as I try to no avail to smash it open. Finally in heated annoyance and flusteredness I put the coconut directly on the floor—hardwood be damned—and grip it caveman-style between the soles of my feet. "See? This way I can use"—splutter, smack—"both hands." I bring the hammer down full force, and still nothing. Then once more and—slurp—the thick bark splits, spraying my face and shirt with sticky milk, coating the floor and delighting the kids.

"Check it out!"

"You're coated in goo."

"Can we have it?"

The excitement builds as I try unsuccessfully to use the underside of the hammer to pry open the coconut enough to serve. Proudly, I display a morsel for each child. "Here!" Will watches from his bouncy seat, amused with a drool-spilling smile. He and I are both covered in spit-up. "What do you think?" What I recall from my own first time with coconut is loving the feel of its meat on my teeth. That the *act* of eating it rather than the taste itself was what made it good.

I am often struck by the sameness of days as a parent. How one day seams into the next until months have passed—seasons, even—and your children are a year older, their ill-fitting shoes proof that really that much time has passed. Sometimes in the midst of even the crappiest days, days when I've raised my voice too many times or gritted my teeth or tried to write checks while listening to Jamie's latest story, I feel the ache of wondering if this is the day they will remember as adults. Adam consoles me with this fact: It is about averages. What you do most. What it all adds up to be, the chronicity of actions. So, bad days might stick out. Good days might too. Back with my dad, I remember wishing that the sweet coconut meat had only smoothness, no rough edges, no bits of cracked shell to mar the texture. Who knows why that memory has staying power.

"You can pick off the brown bits," I say.

Daniel, Jamie, and Julia each hold pieces in their palms, ready. Tentatively, Julia sticks the tip of her tongue onto her piece. Jamie gnaws at his with his big front teeth. Daniel goes at it from the side, seeing if he can test without taking in too much. Then they behold me, their sticky, wet mother, and agree, "I don't like it."

"It doesn't taste like anything."

"Yuck."

They are despondent, but the disappointment is ephemeral.

This is what memory is: a fading gleam, rough around the edges, of something you can smell but not taste. Or can almost touch but cannot quite grasp. Will my memory of this match the kids' when they are older? Will they remember it at all?

"So now we know we don't like coconut!" Jamie makes a grand gesture as though conducting a symphony, all arms and hands. Then he puts a hand reassuringly on my arm from his seat at the table. "Just think! You don't ever have to get it for us again." He grins. The others laugh. Daniel picks brown bits out with his fingers. "But it was really fun to see you try and serve it."

Crackling Shrimp in a Coconut Shell

One thing you can do with a split coconut that no one wants to consume is chuck it out, as I did after the kids and I struggled to free the meat with our teeth. Another option, which I did at a later date, is to use the split shells (or half of one) as a serving dish. The flavor from the sweet coconut meat infuses the shrimp and, perhaps just as sweet, there are no heavy dishes to clean. To choose a ripe coconut, shake it; the milk should slosh, and the coconut should feel heavy for its size. These sweet and slightly spicy shrimp crackle when they cook.

1 nail	1 ripe coconut
1 hammer and a screwdriver	

1 small onion, thinly sliced	½ tsp. salt
1 tsp. fresh grated ginger	1 lb. shrimp, cleaned, de-veined (and, if serving to kids, de-tailed)
1 tbsp. sesame oil	
3 tbsp. brown sugar	1–2 tbsp. coconut water
½ tsp. cinnamon	1 lime
½ tsp. chili powder	

FOR THE COCONUT:

Preheat oven to 400°. Drive the nail partway into one of the "eyes" and remove it and repeat in another eye. Drain coconut water into cup for later use. Split coconut in half with the hammer and screwdriver. It doesn't matter if the halves are even—just be happy you did it without thumb injury. Rub insides of coconut with coconut water and put halves loosely together. Wrap in tinfoil as you would a campfire baked potato and place directly on oven rack. Let cook for 1 to 1½ hours or until insides are soft to the touch of your thumbnail.

FOR THE SHRIMP:

In a pan, sauté onion and ginger in sesame oil on medium-high heat until just starting to brown. Meanwhile, make a rub with brown sugar, cinnamon, chili powder, and salt. Coat shrimp with rub with your hands and drop into hot pan with onions. Shrimp will crackle as they cook, and the sugar will start to caramelize. When shrimp are cooked through, remove them and the onions from the pan. De-glaze pan with coconut water, turning heat on high and letting coconut water clean the tasty bits from the sides and bottom. Let liquid reduce slightly.

Scoop shrimp into the coconut halves, drizzle with reduced coconut water, and serve with a wedge of lime for a burst of tang. As you eat, dig out a bit of the coconut meat along with the shrimp.

Note: If the thought of having to hunt and whack your food is too much, feel free to simply make the shrimp in a pan and serve it with:

Lime-Coconut Soba Noodles

This aromatic dish is served room-temperature or chilled. The dressing also works on brown rice. The hot noodles soften the peppers just enough but let them retain their refreshing crunch. Top with toasted sesame seeds or sunflower seeds should you desire an extra crunch.

salt

8 oz. soba noodles

½ cup plus 1 tbsp. coconut water (coconut milk is OK if you haven't got water)

1 bunch scallions

1 cup sliced peppers (red, orange, yellow), uncooked

¼ cup sautéed onions

1 tsp. tahini

1 tbsp. sesame oil

1 tsp. teriyaki

1 tsp. rice wine vinegar

1 big squeeze lime juice

1 tsp. honey

lime zest (optional)

Cook noodles in salted water according to package directions, but use ½ cup coconut water in place of some of the water. When noodles are cooked, rinse with very cold water. Put the scallions and peppers in a large bowl. Sauté onions and let cool. Add onions to peppers and scallions when warm but not hot. Put warm noodles over vegetables. Whisk together tahini, sesame oil, teriyaki, 1 tbsp. coconut water, rice wine vinegar, lime juice, and honey. Dump dressing onto noodles and veggies and toss gently so everything is evenly coated. Garnish with lime zest if desired. Serve right away or chilled the next day.

Blessed Be the Nugget

Blessed be the nugget for lo, though it is the bane of many a waistline and has permanently altered menus across the world, despite its overly cutesy name and it being an advertisement for all things fried, it is an easy place to start.

The nugget. A morsel. Consider if the clever word hadn't been stumbled upon but rather had been marketed as a "hunk" or "wad" or "portion-ette." Or any other mealtime misnomer. Probably the menus across America wouldn't be as plagued as they are now with nuggetification. And perhaps parents wouldn't feel compelled to plate piles of all manner of nuggets for their children.

However, because we already exist in the Land o' Nuggets, the best we can do is use them as a jumping-off point for other foods. They aren't inherently evil, in moderation. The tiny breaded chicken pieces—fried, baked, or otherwise—are just confining. Consider the tale I mentioned in my introduction. You're seaside at a world-renowned fish restaurant and your five-year-old wants . . . chicken nuggets? Oh, but they're called *tenders* here,

Chicken Nugget

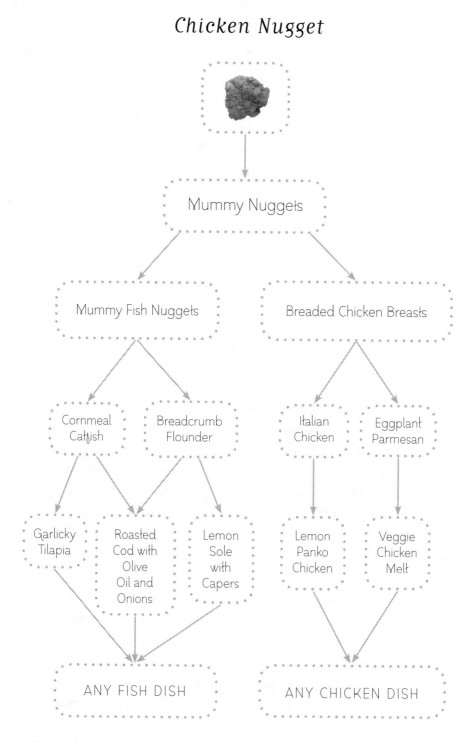

Mummy Nuggets

Mummy Fish Nuggets

Breaded Chicken Breasts

Cornmeal Catfish

Breadcrumb Flounder

Italian Chicken

Eggplant Parmesan

Garlicky Tilapia

Roasted Cod with Olive Oil and Onions

Lemon Sole with Capers

Lemon Panko Chicken

Veggie Chicken Melt

ANY FISH DISH

ANY CHICKEN DISH

as though using such a sweet word—the word of love songs!—will lessen the culinary blow. Or you're at someone's house who has taken the time to prepare Chicken Parmesan from scratch but all your kid wants is a nugget.

We'll get to the diagram in a bit.

"Look, Mom!" Jamie points to a box in the freezer section. "Pizza nuggets!" It's as though we're at the zoo for the nutritionally challenged, what with the pizza nuggets, the ham 'n' cheese nuggets, even the spinach nuggets, which, although they contain some greenery, are just another way of nuggeting all meals.

Now, nuggets are cute, and from the flow chart we can see how they are in fact extremely useful as the launch pad to greater food-dom. What I did was this: When the kids were all under the age of five, I told them I was making (wait for it—annoyingly adorable name approaching) "Mummy Nuggets." I said they would be just like chicken nuggets, but I'd make them so thus they'd have my name. They bought it.

I cut up organic chicken breasts, dredged them in whole-wheat flour, dipped them in egg, then lightly coated them with whole-wheat bread crumbs. I sautéed them in olive oil and, to finish them off, shoved them in the oven while I did the next batch.

I made about 42,000 Mummy Nuggets.

I froze them on a cookie sheet, then once they were solid, stored them in a gallon-size bag so I could grab a handful anytime and bake them in the toaster oven. Easy for me. Easy for them. Mummy Nuggets—not deep-fried, not uniform in their shapes, not pieced together out of odd leftover fowl parts—were accepted.

Now, let's refer back to the flow chart. Before the nuggets ran out, I made the exact same chicken recipe but with whole breasts. When the kids asked what I was making, I responded with, "It's like Mummy Nuggets but instead of little pieces, it's one really big nugget." They ate it with glee. During that meal, I told them that the real name for this dish is Breaded Chicken Breast. I told them that one can order it at many restaurants, and repeated the name. I made sure to serve it again the next week, because while kids remember every time they've been given a shot, every scrape and bruise, they have memories like goldfish about some things—including healthy foods. So when I make new dishes for them, I make sure that after the initial introduction, I reinforce the concept a couple of times.

Then the fun began. Breaded Chicken was easily converted into Italian Chicken (also known as Chicken Parmesan) and easily described as "breaded chicken with pizza topping on it" but then labeled with its true name. Chicken Parmesan begot Eggplant Parmesan. Breaded Chicken also morphed into Lemon Panko Chicken.

Meanwhile, on the other side of the chart, I was reeling in the fish. Mummy Fish Nuggets are simple—cod or haddock or tilapia cut into bits, coated and breaded and served. A hop, skip, and jump later and Baked Cod, Cornmeal Catfish, or even Skillet Shrimp with breadcrumbs are on the table. For the advanced class, the breadcrumbs are gone and dishes are pan-seared or roasted with olive oil and sea salt or slathered with sweet onion puree and a light grating of Parmesan with crisp snow peas.

I begrudge the nugget for its cutesy name, its dominance on the kid menu, its fat content, and its disturbing shape. But I understand "nugget power," how nuggets are worshiped in the temple of kid food. I just choose not to honor it completely. Everyone can view the nugget as they choose. Jamie summed it up by stating, "It's like you want it because that's all there is. But then you see the big menu, not that little one with three things on it that they give kids, and then maybe nuggets just sound boring."

I chose not to fight back, but instead work with the stubborn nugget for a greater good. So Mummy brought the alterna-nuggets to the table and, lo, they were good.

Mummy Nuggets

These are best made in large batches. As per the chart, feel free to substitute in strips of cod, tilapia, or eggplant. Increase eggs and breadcrumbs as you increase the amount of meat or fish. If you are making a lot of this, set up five stations for yourself: one plate (or cutting board) with the raw meat, a plate with the flour, a wide bowl with the eggs, a plate with the breadcrumbs, and a clean plate for the about-to-be-cooked pieces. If you are in a rush, you could skip the clean plate and go right to the frying pan.

2 (or however many) lbs. chicken breasts	2 cups breadcrumbs (you can use Italian seasoned ones, plain, or panko for extra-crispy) to which you have added 1 tsp. salt and mixed with your hand
½ cup wheat flour	
6 eggs (or, if you prefer, 3 whole and 3 whites), beaten	olive oil

Heat oven to 300°. Set up your stations. Cut the chicken into uneven strips and/or pieces. Dredge in flour, tapping off excess as you go. Dip into egg, coating evenly. Dip into breadcrumbs until covered and then let rest on clean plate. When all the pieces are ready, coat a large frying pan with olive oil and, when hot, drop in pieces of chicken. Do not overcrowd. Keep on medium-high heat, turning chicken as it browns. As soon as pieces are browned, transfer to baking sheet and put in oven. Keep frying pieces, adding small drizzles of olive oil as needed. Pieces will continue to cook in the oven, so you don't need to worry if they're not cooked through in the pan. When all pieces are done, turn oven to 375° for a couple of minutes until the chicken is very hot and a bit more brown. Take sheet from oven and serve that night's dinner. Let the rest cool completely, and put into freezer bags to use whenever you want.

Note: *You could use cod, haddock, tilapia, or catfish . . . and feel free to swap cornmeal for breadcrumbs or make the following:*

Cornmeal Catfish

If you need an easy summer dinner or lunch, these fillets fit the bill. Tangy and crunchy, they are delectable as-is, but also when served with the tartar sauce or the Cucumber Yogurt Sauce on page 306.

catfish fillets (6 oz. per adult,
4 oz. per child)

¾ cup buttermilk

1 cup cornmeal

1 tsp. paprika

1 tsp. dried mustard

salt and pepper

olive or other oil for cooking

Let fish soak in buttermilk as you combine cornmeal, paprika, dried mustard, salt, and pepper. Take one of the fillets, shake off extra liquid, and dredge in cornmeal mixture. Repeat until all fillets are crusted. Fry in a bit of oil and let drain on paper towels before serving.

Are You Awake?

Sometimes I cook in bed. Underneath the clean, white duvet with my head on a pillow designed for side-sleepers, I am not asleep. Rather, I am debating the merits of polenta versus quinoa, wondering if quinoa can handle being sweetened the way the corn grains can. With my eyes closed I conjure up the scene—the satisfying plunge into the polenta with the measuring cup, the sound of the cornmeal hitting the metal pot, the pure comfort associated with warming milk, the creamy texture of the final product: warm, sugared polenta with milk. From start (buying the polenta in bulk at the store) to finish (leaving the hot, milk-rimmed pot to cool in the sink), I can picture it all.

Only recently has it dawned on me that my bedtime cooking fantasies aren't something everyone does. My husband, Adam, received this year a fortune in a Chinese fortune cookie unlike any other I'd ever seen. One so true, so relatable, that we framed it.

"Some men dream of fortunes; others only cookies."

I do dream of cookies, but ours is not an exclusive relationship. I also dream of soups, apricot muffins, mango curried chicken, simple granola, and all things edible.

Adam doesn't sleep-cook like I do. He'll sometimes retrace interactions with his pediatric patients or let his mind wander, often settling on a sporting event. He can relive various plays—catches, home runs, dives, touchdowns, putts—as he drifts off, snoring before I am even tucked into a ball on my left side. Down the hall, our four kids are in the deepest of kid sleeps, the heavy kind of slumber that only children know—hair pasted to their smooth foreheads, one with his legs draped over the bed's edge, one with his whole body turned around the wrong way but not caring, another kept in her bed only by a flimsy bed rail whose mesh is torn, her blanket up to her chin, and the baby with his arms flush over his head as though preparing to touch his toes. I rub my feet together and continue.

"What do you think about crispy polenta?" I ask, my hand wandering over to Adam's bare chest as if it were a culinary come-on.

A sleepy voice answers in the dark. "This is what you're asking me?"

I nod, but the gesture goes unnoticed. "Yeah, I guess."

"I'm not even sure I know what you're talking about." His own hand finds mine and grips it for a few seconds before loosening as sleep pulls him back.

"Polenta. You know polenta—the cornlike stuff? The one you liked at that restaurant with the cod?" I'm getting excited now. I prop myself up on my elbows and turn toward him. "I was thinking I could make some of it sweet—like a pudding, but I know that's not your type of thing. So how about crispy polenta?" No answer. "In the oven." Deep breaths. Adam's chest rises and sinks in the warm spring air. Soon it will be time for fans and air-conditioners. "With cheese."

"Melted on it?" Adam resurfaces.

"Yes. Melted, bubbly pecorino on top of polenta."

"Sounds good." This is his final comment before the snores start.

Some people love to shop: skirts, sweaters, belts, this season's handbag, last season's jaunty accessories. Madras, plaid, paisley, patent leather, camel hair. These are words that bring excitement to my mother, my sister-in-law, my mother-in-law. Time in boutiques, on Montana Avenue in Santa Monica, Fifth Avenue or Barneys—all of this sounds wonderful to the fashion mavens, the aficionados of style.

I am not one of those people.

I shop for clothing as though I'm trying not to get caught: I dash in, grab a pair of jeans, sometimes try on a shirt, and sprint back to the car. I like a cashmere sweater as much as the next spit-up-covered mom, but I'm not going to spend my hours browsing. As early as second grade I remember being dragged into Patty Ann's Boutique to buy what was then the height of cool: wide-wale cords, a maroon and navy plaid dress with a ribbon one might tie in a floppy bow at the neck, turtlenecks with hearts or flowers on them, dark jeans. I don't blame my mother for these trips. She was merely doing her job and trying to clothe me in something other than my older brother's hand-me-downs (I still long for his red-and-blue-striped rugby shirt). And the trips were successful—I mean, we bought the skirt or top or shoes and I wore them. But the act of shopping did nothing for me.

Hunting for the right blazer, loafers that pinched, or sweater vests was nothing compared to accompanying my mother on other errands.

I remember when my mother led me by the hand into a then-brand-new store called Crate & Barrel. This was in 1977, and I was five. Amidst wine crates turned on their sides—perfect for storing records!—and glass carafes meant to cradle Dubonnet or sangria were simple table linens, useful gadgets such as corkscrews and nutcrackers shaped like fish, as well as a sense of calm that pervaded everything. We were there for a cheese slicer, which we needed because my older brother and I had used the slicer we'd owned to slice bark. Suffice it to say, the blade was irreparable.

In the store there was no back-to-school rush, no pressure to look this way or that, no arguments over purple tights or brown. My mother showed me several options for cutting cheese; one knife's point was pronged like a snake's tongue and curled at the edges, another had a wire stretched taut between bright metal edges—perfect for wide slices of the aged cheddar my mother melted onto ovals of dark rye bread and topped with a wide round of tomato. We settled on a wooden-handled cheese plane she still owns today.

Maybe we were both thinking of Jarlsberg. Maybe Havarti. Maybe some cheese my five-year-old mind couldn't name that day. But the feeling of being with her, in that store, surrounded by so much cooking possibility, stuck with me. Contained within the shelves there, packed away amidst the plain white plates and jelly jar glasses, were meals as yet uncooked, conversations unspoken, a whole future of smells and tastes and togetherness.

Everything my mom made looked and tasted good, though most of it was so simple—cottage cheese with salted tomatoes (or chunks of fresh pineapple), lunches with leftover cold chicken and a splash of curried mayonnaise for dipping, baked salmon with parsnip puree. My mother could plate matzoh and a few hunks of cheese and a handful of greens and it would seem outrageously special. Watching her cook or, more often, cooking with her, was a quiet comfort with tasty (and sometimes, as when she studied closely the seemingly broken sink spray nozzle and then drenched her face with it, hilarious) results. The kitchen, and kitchen goods, have always been a blend of cheer, comfort, and excitement.

Drop me in Bloomingdale's, Harvey Nichols, J.Crew, or any other clothing store and I'm content to spend ten minutes. If I need something, I'll whisk in, grab the pair of pants I know will work best for me, and exit before the plethora of patterns and accessories overwhelms. But give me a farmer's market down the street, a country store thick with jellies and preserves, the food halls of foreign department stores, or a tiny village's fishmonger and cheese shop, and I can last hours.

Adam knows this now after a chance stop for gas in the Italian countryside. We stopped the rental car before the gauge read empty and filled up in front of what looked to be a small chain supermarket.

"I'm just going to run in for one second and see if they have anything to snack on," I said as Adam fiddled with the impossibly small car.

I did not emerge for more than an hour. I don't need highbrow gourmet shops, just foodstuffs ready for the taking or browsing—supermarkets, farm stands, cheese caves, jam jars, or candied violets. "They have purple dish soap!" I told him. "Do we have that at home?" I thrust a palm-size box of wheel-shaped biscuits at him, my face flushed with excitement.

Do not expect me to resurface anytime soon once I've seen the fruit stalls or waxy wheels of Reggianito, small squares of creamy Pave d'Affinois, the cluttered shelves at the Broadway Panhandler. Just as I felt during the cheese slicer day with my mother all those years ago, being surrounded by anything food-related—kitchenware included—brings me a calm usually reserved for places of worship.

Our kitchen is simple and bright. The house is a Victorian farmhouse, complete with uneven floors, warped glass windows, and some dodgy wiring. Little by little we've redone a few rooms, updated the electrical, repainted, added necessary things like, oh, a shower (when we first moved in, we used a camping shower on the front lawn while the real one was being built). The most modern additions were the linoleum countertops, each one peeling and lined with metal that pricked through fabric, tearing many of my shirts at the waist when I'd lean in. Two years ago we gutted the kitchen, added a deep white sink, a commercial stove (which I justify by actually using), some cabinets, a new fridge, and soapstone countertops that keep their cool in the summer—perfect for rolling pastry dough—and build up a patina over time. The stone started as a grayish green. It's deeper now, dark moss flecked with silver and yellow. The walls are yellow, and—more important—washable. I find a sanctity in my kitchen—a place of comfort and possibilities.

The same kind of peace that I find in bed, at night, with a slight breeze traipsing in through the open windows, the soles of my feet tucked against Adam's warm legs, the children asleep down the dark hallway, proof of the youngest one's silence on the monitor I keep bedside.

So I cook in bed, imagining tapenade-covered crostini; apple streusel cake; homemade granola with enough left over to coat chicken cutlets; easy tilapia; wasabi-pea-encrusted monkfish; and comforting, cheese-bubbly polenta.

"I'm going to make it for you tomorrow." I twist my arm around so I can reach Adam's stubbled cheek.

"Hmm."

His sleep pulls me toward that space in between thought control and dream, in which the meal expands, including tilapia and garlicky greens. I will remind the kids that they have had polenta before, warm and sugary, one night when I was out of virtually everything else. I will explain that some foods can be eaten savory or sweet.

The baby will wake soon and need to nurse, so I pack away the meal, sure that if I try hard enough I might really be able to taste it.

Dreamy Polenta

You can serve this warm and creamy or—as noted here—cooled, sliced, and baked. This crisps the edges and produces a chewier version that suits the simple, white fish well.

2 cups stock (vegetable or chicken)	dab of butter if you like
2 cups water (or milk, or a combination of both)	salt to taste
	olive oil if baking
2 cups polenta (cornmeal)	Parmesan or Pecorino cheese, for grating on top

Boil stock and water together in heavy pot. Pour polenta into liquid, stirring as you go to avoid lumps (although, quite frankly, I like the occasional lump). Heat on high a few minutes or until rolling, then reduce heat to simmer and cover. Stir a few times as it cooks—about 40 minutes. Dab with butter, taste for salt, stir in a bit of milk if you'd like it creamy, and serve as-is or . . .

Season but do not add any additional liquid. Let cool. Remove polenta (which will now move as one mainly solid object) and place on a cutting board. Slice into strips, cut into random shapes or, using a biscuit cutter, make into rounds (you might also do this by forming a log shape and slicing circles from the ends). Rub olive oil onto a baking dish. Place polenta strips/pieces/circles onto oiled surface, dot with butter, grate fresh Parmesan or Pecorino on top. Bake for 20 minutes at 375° or until cheese is browning and edges of polenta are crisp.

Note: *You can double this recipe for a larger crew or reduce for one.*

This dish can also be a wonderful hot breakfast or dessert. Use all milk (no stock) and add a few tablespoons of brown sugar and cream as it reaches the end stages of cooking. Serve with berries or banana slices.

 ## Simple Tilapia

3 tablespoons butter	olive oil
1 clove garlic, crushed	salt and pepper
1½ lbs. tilapia	½ lemon

Melt butter in pan. Add garlic and let sit for a minute, then remove from heat. Wash the fish and pat-dry. Place in olive-oiled baking dish and sprinkle with salt and pepper. Drizzle with butter and garlic. Bake at 375° for about 35 minutes or until fish is white and flaky. Squeeze lemon onto fish right before serving. Serve on rounds of baked polenta or in a bowl of creamy polenta with a side dish of greens.

 ## Roasted Broccoli Rabe and Baby Greens

1 bunch broccoli rabe, ends trimmed	sea salt
olive oil	1 big handful baby greens (optional)

Place broccoli rabe on a cookie sheet rubbed with olive oil. Drizzle more olive oil on top. Dust with sea salt. Cook at 400° for 12–15 minutes, until leaves are browning but not too crispy. When you remove the sheet from the oven, drape with a kitchen cloth until slightly cooler (this keeps them from drying out and gets rid of any too overly crispy leaves, wilting them).

If adding baby greens, wash and pat dry, then add in around minute 8.

Side Note

"The fish is kind of plain," Jamie says.

"It's supposed to be," I explain. I'm not trying to defend myself or the tilapia, but show them that not everything is coated in sauce or comes covered in crumbs.

"But it's also kind of good." Daniel nods while using his fingers. I throw him a look that says, *Use your fork,* but he shakes me off—pitcher to catcher. "It's too crumbly."

"I like the cheese." Julia picks the melted cheese from the top of the polenta slices.

"You need to eat more than just the cheese," I remind her. I look at Adam. He is staring at his plate as though he's seen someone from his past—a high school friend, someone he once played baseball with. "What?"

"Nothing," he says, then bites into the polenta and slides flakes of tilapia into his mouth. "Did I dream this or something?"

I shrug, barely thinking of my nighttime cooking escapade, the mental meandering that produced this meal.

"So it's good?" I take a bite. I smile at my family, at the comforts of cooking and providing, at eating together when no one is screaming or fussing or complaining about the marks the chair left on their ankles from sitting cross-legged at the table.

Julia nods, chewing the vegetables and trying the fish. She eats stalk after stalk of the broccoli rabe—she has an unusual fondness for bitter greens. She might be the only three-year-old to ever chant, "Brussels sprouts, Brussels sprouts, so, so good!" while marching around the kitchen.

"Really nice," Adam says. His face is flushed from playing in the yard. "Even though you know I'm not the biggest fan of broccoli rabe."

Jamie looks at Daniel. Daniel will be the spokesperson for their team. Daniel wrinkles his lips. "Yeah, the broccoli rabe is way too chewy."

"And it's just gross," Jamie adds, looking at me across the table. "Not to hurt your feelings or anything."

Julia and I eat our broccoli rabe, enjoying the bitterness, the salty bite of the stems and the near-sour softness of the florets. Will she accompany me on cooking adventures? Will she find solace amidst the pots, pans, and spices? I put my big hand on her small one, fanning our fingers so they spread like a rare fern. Her eyes focus on mine from behind her thick glasses. "Yum."

Note to self: If making again, throw some regular broccoli in with the rabe so male contingency of family doesn't complain.

The Five Stages

Let me state right off that I'm not one of those parents who believes her children to be flawless. I do not proclaim their untainted personalities to anyone and everyone, and I do not, upon hearing that my child has called someone a name at drop-off, said something rude to a teacher, or refused to do what everyone else was doing, say aloud, "My child would never do that!" Because I know they probably did. That said, I adore and relish my children in a way that is nearly impossible to describe and, being a flawed person who is sometimes guilty of all of the above marks herself, I accept them as they are and want to help them in areas that are challenging. Some areas are more difficult than others.

Take, for example, peas. Peas. Those round little vegetables that always seemed to me to be happy food. They roll! They're brightly colored (unless they are that off-putting putty gray-green from a can)! They are finger food! And so easy to prepare! I have an electric kettle and turn it on, put some frozen peas in a glass storage container, and when the water is boiling, immerse the green balls. In the summer even their shells are sweet. Serve them blanched or raw! Voilà. Side of veggies. Nothing else needed.

Unless of course, you are my six-year-old, in which case what you need is not to have to eat the damn peas in the first place. His eyes widen with terror when he sees the mass of them in the bowl. He scans the counter for proof of another green vegetable. One that would be just for him. I am not cruel, so if we have some roasted leftover broccoli or a steamed stem or two, I'll sling those his way while the other kids enjoy their peas. I am not, however, a short-order cook, and the rule of the house is that you can eat what's in front of you—or not. My husband, the pediatrician, and I, the experienced mother of four, are confident that one skipped meal does not a starving child make. "If you're really hungry," we tell them, "you'll eat it. And if not, that's fine." This is not Dickensian drama—no sitting at the table into the wee hours of the morning until the porridge is finished. But neither is it up to the kid to decide on the food all the time. So, for now, it's back to peas.

"I'm having broccoli, right?" Daniel's hair is golden-retriever blond, his cheeks red from running around the yard. We played baseball for a while this afternoon until he yelled at me about how I was pitching. Granted, I am a much better catcher than pitcher. But still, there are rules. For the past fifteen minutes he and his older brother have been chasing each other in a game that can best be described as tag-wrestling, in which the goal appears to be getting very out of breath while attempting to yank a sibling to the ground.

"No broccoli," I tell Daniel. "Just peas."

Adam comes into the kitchen with a barrette in his hair and a baseball glove on his hand. He doesn't find anything unusual about this. Perhaps he's forgotten the hair ornament is there. He is over six feet tall and doesn't have that much hair left, but the sparkly blue heart clip does him justice. I decide not to mention it.

"Come on, Daniel. Let's play outside a little bit and we'll deal with dinner later," Adam says.

It would be remiss for me not to give a bit of background here.

If there were an Olympic category for shit-fit throwing, Daniel would medal. Gold. More than once. He is, not to brag, the king of the shit fit. This is not because of some mean streak. He's not a child who wants to do wrong or seeks to cause trouble. I used to be a teacher, and I'm well versed in those kids. Daniel just can't control his responses. He feels everything. And feels it intensely. Deeply. Profoundly.

Sometimes this is very pleasurable. Example: "Mummy? Do you know how much I love you? Bigger than every sky sewn together with outer space and all the oceans. Also, I want to live near you and Daddy when I grow up, and I'll have you over for dinner or maybe just to read to me even though I'll know how to read by then. I mean, I'll be eighteen! Or maybe forty-two. But still." Clutches my hands and pulls himself into my belly—"I never want to be far away from you because I" *kiss, kiss* "love you!"

Other times, less so. Example: "You cut my sandwich?" [volume increases] "I never asked you to do that!" [more volume] "I hate having sandwiches cut. And you know that!" [at top of lung capacity while thrashing body and turning red] "This lunch is horrible. The worst in the history of the world and there is *no way* I am going to even touch that with my hands, not to say even put it near my mouth!" [and also, the nice lady from the preschool whom you are trying to friend-court is sitting with her pleasant child at your table, trying not to notice but looking aghast]. "If you were trying to kill me, which I guess you are, this fish is the worst way to die!"

Daniel can throw a fit on a train, plane, automobile, or in any social setting—birthday party, school, play date, fancy brunch, soccer field. Much of the time these outbursts are predictable and, also predictably, getting better (read: shorter) as he matures. However, the peas have him doing the slow boil.

In fact, Daniel's reaction to knowing he's going to have a big pile of peas just like the rest of his family is very similar to the five stages of grief.

The first stage is denial. Disbelief takes over and he shakes his head at the warmed dish I'm preparing. "I just can't believe it. I can't believe you're making me eat peas!" He mutters to himself, confounded and confused. "I don't get it. I can't believe this."

As the rest of the family filters into the kitchen from outside, the energy in the room shifts. The dinner is really happening. Daniel moves into stage two—anger. "Come on! I hate this! Look at my plate. I have way more peas than Julia does, and she likes them!" He stomps his feet and glares.

We sit down at the table and begin to serve the rest of the meal—simple roast chicken with rice. Plunging forward into the third stage, Daniel tries to bargain. "OK. I have a deal. I'll eat six"—he looks at me and at Adam, then already counters himself—"No—twenty. I'll eat twenty carrots if you don't make me eat the peas."

"Daniel," Adam says, "you don't have to eat the peas." Daniel looks relieved, but then in seconds knows there's a catch.

"But if I don't, can I still have more of something else?"

"No."

This is all Daniel needs to be bumped right into stage four—depression. He sits forlorn, staring at his plate, unable to sample even the foods he does like because he's so upset by the peas.

Jamie butts in, ever the helpful older brother. "I'll eat them. I mean, they're just round balls."

Julia scoops hers with a spoon. "If you don't like them, just don't eat them."

Will sleeps through most of this, dozing in my arms and then Adam's.

We pass the rice and talk about spring, about the unfurling leaves and temperatures. The way it still feels part like the season past and part like the hot season ahead, and how fun it is to hear baby Will's new babbles. The kids tell us about their art projects and their friends at school and then Daniel moves slowly into the next big phase—acceptance.

"Will Will have to eat peas soon?" His voice is calmer now, but still shaky from his crying jag. Daniel touches his baby brother's cheek.

"A few months," I say. "Right, Ad?"

Adam nods. "We'll start food probably around Mummy's birthday."

"In the fall," Jamie announces. "October."

"How many do I have to eat?" Daniel's watery eyes plead his case.

Adam and I do the parent check-in, only our eyes meeting.

"How many do *you* think you should have to eat?" Adam asks him, preparing the scoop for Daniel's plate.

Daniel breathes out hard, thinking. "How about twenty?"

There's a school of thought that suggests parents ask their kids what punishments they think they deserve, feeling that often the kids are harder on themselves than a parent wants to be. I am not advocating this necessarily, but neither do I think it's a bad thing to have to eat twenty peas when normally Daniel maintains a pea-free diet.

"Here's some milk," I tell him. "You can always sip milk after each bite to make the taste go away."

Daniel nods. "I know." He has gone from denial to exploding with anger to bargaining, then sliding into a soft depression, and is now completing the cycle by opening wide and chewing his way through acceptance.

"So what do you think?" I ask as Will wakes up and stretches his whole still-new body across my legs. Maybe Daniel will surprise us and adore the peas. All that shit-fit for nothing.

One by one Daniel puts the peas in his mouth, doing food math as he goes. "I ate six, so there's fourteen left."

"I like peas," Julia says, and shrugs her small shoulders.

"Me too," Adam says. "Growing up, we had peas all the time."

"Well," Daniel says as he collects another four and pops them into his mouth. "I'm glad I didn't live there."

Sometimes it's difficult to believe (my own denial) that Daniel is capable of throwing such huge fits. I could just as easily go through the stages of grief each time he does it—that burst of anger when I know it's actually happening, the bargaining of please-don't-do-this-in-the-middle-of-the-parent-breakfast, the letdown of knowing it sucks for both of us, and the acceptance of it all—that my stunning, loving, pea-counting child is who he is: a complex twist of DNA and environment and whose stubborn qualities, while challenging now, will probably make him a very fine adult. I have every hope that as my kids grow, they will gain knowledge of themselves—what makes them tick, what works for them food-wise and in the larger sense—and go from there so that they, too, may enjoy not only what's on the table but what the world has to offer.

"I love you," I tell him, because I always do, even when I'm annoyed or angry or he's just thrown a fit.

He looks up at me with a mouthful of peas and milk. "I know." He swallows. "I love you, too. But I will never, ever, love peas."

Side Note

About two days later I steamed some broccoli for everyone and thought it looked a bit bland on its own. I grabbed some sesame oil and dashed some on top with a bit of sea salt, thinking the rich flavor would be well received. After all, I once made garlic green beans with sesame oil and red pepper that were enjoyed by all, even Daniel, who ate three times the portion I'd offered. However, when the sesame broccoli hit the table, the shit hit the fan once more. None of the kids liked it. As ever, Daniel was the most passionate with his response.

Daniel: This is so gross. [pinches nose] I can't even smell it, it's so bad. Please, please—I'll eat peas if you want! Anything, if you don't make me eat this!

That same night when Adam returned from work and we'd put the kids to bed, Adam and I readied our dinners. Upon greeting the vegetables, his brow furrowed.

"What'd you do to this broccoli?" he asked. I feared he'd have a similar reaction to Daniel's, though, of course, more controlled.

"Look," I said. "We're out of peas."

Adam chewed a stem of the sesame broccoli. "This is delicious!"

Sesame Broccoli

There are no measurements for this—just eyeball and shake.

1 head broccoli, cut into big florets

sesame oil

sea salt

red pepper flakes (if desired)

Steam broccoli until just cooked through. Put into container (or back into the pot in which you just steamed it). Drizzle with sesame oil, sprinkle with sea salt and a dash of pepper flakes. Cover and shake a few times so that each piece is flavored and coated. Serve with brown rice, top with sliced scallions.

Summer

Indiana Interlude—Part I

The only thing worse than traveling with four small children is traveling on a ridiculously small plane with four small children, one of whom demands to be nursed from check-in to landing, and an eight-year-old who has suddenly decided he—

"Hates turkey. I mean, I despise it. Or whatever other word you can think of that means hate, hate, hate this turkey. You know I don't like turkey, and now I'm starving and stuck with it and—"

And we're hit with a sudden bout of turbulence. I try to keep the blanket over my bare breast in the name of being discreet, although with the size of the plane, there is little privacy for anyone. We can hear each bathroom noise, each conversation, each whinge and moan from the front of the plane to the back, where we are.

I lean into the space between the seats in front of where Jamie and I are sitting to talk to Adam, who is in between Daniel and Julia. "I can't believe how small this plane is."

"Didn't you realize that when you booked the tickets?" He turns his head and hunches so I can semi-see him.

"Obviously not." I'm overheated, uncomfortable in a seat the size of a school cubby, and trying desperately not to spray the man in the seat across the aisle with breast milk as Will unlatches to let out a wail. "I mean, I figured, big departure city, major airline carrier, fairly large arrival city . . ." My family takes up one-seventh of the entire aircraft.

"Mom?" Jamie's sandwich lies limp on the tray in front of him as he grabs my hand. "Why are we shaking?"

Like many people, I do not delight in flying. Time was, I had family in three different countries, a boyfriend abroad, and elite status on the frequent-flier front. I learned how—with snacks and a good book—to trick myself into going with the flow of the flight, trying not to think of what might happen on board. We've all read those statistics about airline safety versus being on the road. But still. It would be hard enough not to think of the what-ifs were we on a luxury jet. Or anywhere else that didn't scream "tiny metal thing propelled into the air." Maybe if I had an on-board pedicure or heavy sedation. But not like this. I find having the kids near me both comforting (they are the most grounding and wonderful force in my life) and terrifying (how many arms do I have? How many can I carry at once? Who can swim or unfasten their own seat belts?).

The plane chugs and shakes sideways, then quickly drops. Normally I am a bastion of calm, collected under fire of sudden toddler vomit, blood from a new deep wound, or life-threatening allergic reaction. But now, as the plane's swift and sickening dive gets me, I yell, "I am not happy!"

The whole plane hears me. Adam starts laughing but snakes his hand back through the seats to give me a squeeze. Jamie giggles nervously. The heavy woman across the aisle in the appliquéd sweatshirt glances over, her eyes wide with disapproval. Slowly the plane evens out, and despite massive nausea, I reenter the world of the capable. I reformat Jamie's lunch, grab a few extras from my bag for him, and eat my own meal. After we finished packing last night, I threw anything that could possibly constitute a salad into a disposable cardboard container from the Whole Foods salad bar.

The resulting lunch is perfect for travel—hearty enough, with slices of crunchy tofu and French feta cheese, but light enough, with varied baby greens and leftover haricots verts and diced peppers. I don't feel weighed down.

"Are we landing?" Daniel peers out the window. Scratches and condensation make the view fuzzy.

"We are," Adam says as he begins to gather the detritus of traveling with small children—leaky sippy cup, markers, travel-sized Connect Four, dropped books, and scattered wooden tongue depressors Adam takes from work. We use them in myriad ways: for craft projects, stirring paint, to divide evenly any baked good among three children, as yogurt spoons, or as drumsticks on the tray table in front of us until withering looks from other passengers make us stop. "Is he *still* nursing?"

"Yep," I say, and watch Jamie pick at the remains of his packed lunch. He has eaten the yogurt, the fruit, the broccoli and carrots, the bread from his sandwich and left the turkey lonely on the paper towel placemat. "Indiana, here we come!"

We have our travel routine down pat at this point. The trips by car are no big deal. The in-laws are two and a half hours away, my brother-in-law is in Brooklyn, my mom is on the Cape. Under five hours, and it's pretty simple. Flying takes a bit more prep, but we've flown a lot with the kids—partly because family members are flung about in faraway places like my dad in Italy, family in London, and my brothers in California and DC—and also for a few winter vacations.

This is our first venture into the Midwest. We're on our way to visit our friends Dan and Heather and their kids. Heather and I were fixed up years ago by our editor, who was sure we'd hit it off. Turns out, we're also related by marriage, albeit distantly. Dan's sister is married to Adam's cousin's husband's brother. It sounds made up, but it's true. What started as a fun work friendship has grown deeper over the years: We have worked on books together, traveled together, talk most days, and share pretty much everything. It's a wonderful bonus that our husbands are friends and our kids mesh. The six of us step onto Midwestern ground. There's no foreign language, no passport control, no palm trees. For the kids, however, the routine stays the same.

"Which rental car company are we using?" Jamie wants to know. "Dollar? Hertz?"

"Kertz," Daniel incorrectly corrects as we wait for the shuttle bus. I have Will in the stroller and all the carry-ons while Adam wrangles the three other kids and luggage he's artfully arranged on top of our large rolling suitcase. We shoved a week's worth of diapers into the bottom of the bag, using them as padding for the house gift we bought at the shop up the street. Heather and Dan have small children of their own and might be just as happy to receive all of the diapers as they would the naturally harvested and organically produced wooden olive dish and silver scooper.

"We're not using Hertz," I inform them.

Jamie's satisfied smirk annoys Daniel. "See? Not Kertz."

Daniel swings his sweatshirt and thwacks Jamie across the back. Jamie is poised to retaliate until we are all saved by the shuttle bus's arrival. Despite the No Smoking sign, the interior reeks of cigarette fumes, and the kids proceed to pinch their small noses shut for the duration of the journey to Dollar, where we've rented what is to be known hereafter as "the grossest minivan available." The vehicle runs fine, it's merely stained and smelly, but once we're on the road (after a nursing pit stop), all is well.

"See?" Adam says. "We're on our way. Piece of cake." He has a charming way of seeing the best of each experience, always looking for what went well.

Thinking back to the turbulence, I shout, "I'm happy now!"

We have prepped the kids for the different landscape here, telling them how flat the fields are, how much corn is produced, how pure the land will be, how grounded.

"I thought you said it would be yellow," Daniel accuses.

"Corn is green and then yellow," Jamie says.

"I see blue," Julia says, always on the lookout for her favorite color. It is not the sky she's pointing to but a giant billboard advertising liquor. Hmmm.

"We'll see stuff soon," I assure them, and take a sideways glance at Adam. He reaches into his bag and pulls out a CD. One of our family traditions is to make a CD mix before each vacation or for any other reason. We have Vineyard 2004; Rainy Day Mix; Daddy and the Boys; Sun, Sand, and Swains in Florida 2006; *Ciao! 2006;* and so on. There's always a ride from the airport to wherever our destination is, and picking the songs out beforehand and waiting to hear them passes the time. Plus the kids now have a breadth to their music background and are able to sing everything from the Beatles to Carole King to Green Day to Eddie Rabbitt's "I Love a Rainy Night." This last one is Julia's favorite, and she asked to see a video of it. God bless YouTube for providing the original performance of the song on *Solid Gold,* a show I watched in my youth. Julia watched in amazement as a hairy-chested, gold-necklaced, bearded Eddie Rabbitt sang his song as she sat in my lap mouthing the words. "It's so funny because he doesn't look like a rabbit," she said. This was not one of those overly precious kid moments. Rather, this is her attempt at a joke. I could not explain to my three-year-old that I probably saw that episode (I do take a minute to wonder if in our limited-screen-time household I would let Jamie watch *Solid Gold* were it still on). "I love hearing you sing this, Jules."

"You know what, Mummy? It sounds like he's saying 'I love a Rainy Nut.'"

So the songs play, apples are dispersed as snacks. Soon the Galas are cores and the seventh song comes on, and then finally we are out of downtown Indianapolis and following Heather's directions to the tiny town of Culver (population 1,539). Dan's family has a house on Lake Maxinkuckee, where they spend part of each summer. We'll be there for a week. Heather is a friend, writer, and fellow food-lover, and she's given me enough description over the years of what I might find during our Midwestern jaunt. Heather has told me of corn relish, pickled beets, fresh produce from the farmer who appears at midday in the parking lot "downtown." "You never know what kind of food he'll have," she said, her voice mysterious. "You just show up and see if he's there and plan dinner around that." I have visions of homemade pies—huckleberry, blackberry, and peach—of preserves and local foods I've never even heard of. I realize I am probably imagining a country fair circa 1931, but I'm still anticipating a plethora of tastes.

"I need to pee," Jamie announces from the way-back.

Adam and I check with each other before responding—one of those silent parental conversations that occur only with the eyes. This is the advanced course, after your kids learn to spell. Gestures help, or foreign languages—anything to communicate without the children fully comprehending until decisions are made. However, Adam studied Spanish and I took a combination of French, Italian, and one year of Chinese, so our attempts sound like we're ordering dinner in a food court. "Can you hold it?"

The drive is meant to take two and a half hours. We've been on the road for an hour and are just starting to make progress and the baby is asleep. "Um, maybe a little?"

I step on the gas and begin looking for a suitable place to stop. However, now we've left signs of city life and are, as Heather wrote in her annotated directions, "getting into the middle of nowhere."

"Look, corn!" We point out the first few times we pass a field of the tall greens. There's been a drought, however, so some of the stalks are crisped the color of fireside marshmallows.

"I see corn!" Daniel yells.

"Me too!" Julia says as we pass miles of the stuff. Blanketing the ground in wide fields, the corn stretches on for what looks to be miles of green dotted with the occasional house. Some of the houses match my vision—white-porched farmhouses with a silo or a truck in the drive—and others seem a mismatch; brick ranches with satellite dishes. At the beginning of Route 31 we pass strip malls interspersed with the corn. Scattered into pastures and rows of sprouting soybeans are all-you-can-eat buffets, chain stores, and various restaurants that veer far from the countryside experience I'm hoping for.

"You know what I see?" Daniel asks. "Corn!"

"Corn!" Julia echoes. Will wakes up. Even he is sick of the joke by now.

"Do you need to stop?" Adam asks Jamie.

"Now is a good time." I point to the supersized Best Buy, the enlarged Arby's sign glowing in the just-fading light.

"Nope. I'm fine." Jamie buries his head in a book.

"What's Bob Evans?" Daniel points to a sign in the distance, practicing his reading skills. Judging by the jammed parking lot and shape of the building, it looks like a restaurant, but I just shrug. What do they serve inside? Is it warming trays of gelatinous meat loaf, or am I missing out on a cultural experience?

"I don't know, honey. There are lots of places out here that we don't know."

Strip malls give way to more corn and more soybean fields, and just as we've settled into a whir of greenery and slightly eerie signs touting the Lord (HE WILL GET YOU—EVEN IF YOU DON'T WANT HIM TO) and run-down tire shops (WE CAN FIX YO [sic]), Jamie suddenly rejoins the world of the verbal. "I'm about to go in my pants. Seriously! I need to pee now!"

Kids go from zero to sixty faster than any automobile. "Well . . . ," Adam starts. He looks around at the nothing surrounding us. "I'm not sure we can stop."

It's a strange landscape—deserted enough that we think of pulling over to have our son pee on the side of the road but not desolate enough that we feel we can, what with churches appearing every three minutes, and sudden houses cropping up amidst the crops. Finally I see something. "Look. There. We'll go there." I swing the minivan into the parking lot of "The Pie Shop," figuring that while Jamie goes, I can browse. The door is locked and the place empty despite a few vegetables on offer outside the door. Next we spy a church social.

"We can go there!" I announce with glee. Adam shakes his head. "Because we're Jewish?" I ask and turn in anyway. Folks are clustered in a carport near a small brick church and eating from flimsy paper plates. "We're not eating or anything. He's just a kid who needs to—"

"No." Adam fights laughter and points us back on the highway.

"Um, I really . . . ," Jamie squeals.

"We know." I zoom along until a gas station is in view. "Finally!"

Jamie and Adam hop out of the car and go to the gas station-cum-café and ask, then reappear at the car shaking their heads. "The man said the bathroom is broken," Jamie says and climbs in, brave, his jaw clenched with need.

Adam mumbles to me in the front seat, "And when I asked 'What's around here?' the guy said, 'Dude, you're in the middle of nowhere. There ain't nothing here.'"

Adam and I laugh and I check the rearview mirror to make sure Jamie's not wetting himself, though the state of the van is such that it might blend in. After a few more songs on the CD we arrive in Kokomo and stop for dinner at the legendary Steak 'n Shake. Adam's cousin, originally from Indiana, is fairly obsessed with this Midwest chain of burgers and fries, and we've come to taste the goods. And to use the bathroom, which Jamie runs to and emerges with the merriment that only an empty bladder and a boy on the way to a milkshake can have.

I order a grilled cheese and tomatoes, fries, and a shake so thick it can contain two flavors that don't mix. The vanilla on one side, the chocolate on the other, I manage to snarf a few bites of the buttery food before taking Will to the van to nurse. The kids and Adam remain with their two-flavor thick shakes. Having flown on Sunday, we are eating among the post-church crowd, and I decide this is not the place I want to fight for my right to breastfeed in public. To be honest, the food was a letdown. So much buildup from Midwestern friends, the neat black-and-white checked décor. Maybe I ordered wrong. Or maybe after traveling for hours on end nothing would have suited. We leave Kokomo, strip malls, greasy food, and full bladders and head off into the darkening Indiana night.

The town of Culver is located to the north of Indianapolis and 77 miles southeast of Chicago. Roughly translated, this means it is, as the gas-station man suggested, right in the middle of nowhere. As steady rain falls and Will wakes up again, Julia's tousled head lifts from her car seat. "Is this it?"

"Yes," we tell her. "We're here." Dan and Heather's house is perched high above Lake Maxinkuckee with a view that would be wonderful were it not suddenly pouring. The rain will not let up for the first forty-eight hours and we will become well versed in puddle-stomping across the former military academy grounds, banging on Dan's drum set, doing all manner of beading/coloring/sock-puppetry, and dreaming of grilling out while our bathing suits wither in our suitcases. Clementine, who is Julia's age, and Graham, who is eighteen months, peer out the screen door at us.

"Welcome." Heather rushes out to meet us, covering the baby with an umbrella.

"Did you see any corn on the way here?" Dan asks, and shows us inside.

Heather and I find the farmer in the parking lot on the first nice day. After all the rain (a thunderstorm the likes of which none of us had ever seen brought out the emergency radio, woke the kids in the night with thunder and lightning, and drenched the whole screened-in porch), we are desperate for a sunny meal, and we buy up whatever he has: a rugby-shaped melon, baby-cheek-soft peaches and, of course, corn. "Tonight I'll make the flounder Dan bought," I offer, and Heather nods. It's a simple dish, well-seasoned with salt and pepper and then simply topped with garlicky panko that's been made shiny with olive oil.

"Oh, look at the peaches," I say, fondling them. I bag a few more. The fresh produce is in sharp contrast to the strip malls we passed on the way up. "Out of curiosity, what is Bob Evans?"

Heather offers a wry grin. "My first job ever was at Bob Evans!" She details the outfit she wore for her waitressing shifts and adds, "Let's get these." She palms two green things. "Kohlrabi."

"Just so you're aware, I have no idea what to do with those," I tell her on our way back to the car.

That afternoon we let kids doze in the car, their heads lolling to one side and then the other as we turn to follow handwritten signs claiming

APPLES—TWO MILES and FARM STORE UP AHEAD. This is the Indiana I was looking for; no strip malls in sight. Arrows lead us past more churches, bales of hay, houses that are by turns falling apart and spruced up, and no people. Either the day's heat keeps everyone inside or we are the only ones seeking local food, but we press on.

A gray house to our left is flanked by a rusted pickup and a laundry line, but out in front are two enormous tomato gardens filled with vine after vine of ripeness. A woman in a housedress who speaks no English appears, and we pay her seven dollars for a large amount of red tomatoes and, though she looks at us as if we've eaten fertilizer, agrees and steps into the garden rows barefooted to pluck some firm, unripe ones for us. They are the color of an industrial garbage bin and just as appealing.

"You have it in you for one more place?" Dan calls from the driver's side of their car. We nod and drive in tandem on paved but empty streets past roadside mailboxes, also empty, a few dogs sweating in the tree shade, a horse farm. Just past a cemetery where the graves are horrifically (or charmingly) decorated with masses of tinsel, we turn onto a long dirt road that leads us to a huge log cabin with a farm stand across the drive.

Housed in what is really more a redone garage, Grovertown Fruit Farm is stocked with homemade items and produce. The store's personable owners, George and Betty, let the kids have one small apple each for free as we meander. We scoop up potatoes for dinner or maybe to have cold with lunch tomorrow; fresh wheat bread; and I purchase two jars of preserves— one apple butter and one plum sauce. They will serve me well this winter on thick slices of oatmeal bread or baked onto chicken breasts. Heather buys homemade goat's milk soaps and lotions. We're almost on our way when the farmer directs us to his buddy's place "down the road"—which turns out to be six miles "down the road."

When we arrive, there's no produce in sight. No corn fields. No vegetable cart. "Come this way," a woman says when Heather and I have milled around the empty driveway for a minute or two. She shows us to a room filled with eight freezers. "You got your apple sausage, your bacon, your loins, your pork patties, your ribs." All of this constitutes the Pork Shop, the Yankauskas Family Farm. With fervent appetites and so many items from which to choose, we consult each other about today's meals, the week ahead. Heather has told me about a big Indiana specialty, pork tenderloin sandwich, in which the meat is pounded flat, then breaded and fried.

We buy local bacon and Heather scoops up some pork patties for her mother-in-law. I leave with a recipe for savory pie that says it feeds "four people or two teenage boys."

While the rest of the group goes tubing in the lake and Will sleeps, Heather and I set about making a feast to celebrate the good weather and good friends. All of the produce we've purchased lines the windowsills and counters.

I often cook alone—for downtime, for time management, for efficiency. I enjoy cooking with the kids and love producing big meals for holidays, but the quiet pleasure of cooking with a friend fills me with ease and joy. Heather's swift hands slice peaches for a crumble while the bacon fries in an aged skillet. The summer house had been handed down and is shared by Dan and his three siblings and their spouses, who all contribute to its up-keep. The pots and pans don't match, the décor is a mixture of rustic cabin (exposed wood beams and a hulking fireplace) and '70s-chic furniture that is a bit too authentic to be hipster material. In addition to the low-slung maroon couches, a few wicker-back chairs, and odd bulbous lamps, there are, apparently, bats—but we've yet to see any despite Heather's warnings of doing "bat checks" at night. The kitchen is bat-free too, basic but wide enough to fit a crowd around the circular table that comes complete with an enlarged lazy susan we will never use. The kitchen gadgets function well enough for cooking masses of food, which is what we do; sometimes with-out speaking, sometimes making a joke, talking about work or kids, other times trading recipes; we make do with whatever ingredients we've got and produce a meal to enjoy on the now-dry screened-in porch.

Our Entirely Local BLTs consist of: thick-cut slices of wheat bread the color of wet sand, the ripest red tomatoes, a slathering of Hellmann's mayonnaise, slabs of crisped bacon, and chilled green-leaf lettuce I have washed and wrapped in a damp dishcloth until just before we assemble the sandwiches.

"No tomatoes for me," Daniel requests. Clementine, Heather's daughter, requests the same. We substitute cheese on theirs. A fairly large Amish population is not too far away, and the cheese they produce is made from yogurt. Mild in both taste and color, the consistency is slightly soft while formed enough to make slices. We add that to the kids' sandwiches and the cheese melts just slightly.

On the side we have wide wedges of Decker melon. Shaped like a rugby ball and very large, the Decker melon is related to the cantaloupe, with veins running their course along the exterior skin. Inside, the fruit is a shade of sunset-pale orange, juicy and sweet without being cloying, and incredibly delicious.

We settle into a vacation routine of lingering breakfasts, a morning activity, a late-morning swim, lunch, more lake time in the afternoon, sometimes a trip down the road for food. To shake things up we pile everyone into the vans for lunch at the Original A&W Root Beer Stand in downtown Culver. The restaurant is a drive-in, and to signal service we flash our lights. The waitress takes our order from the driver's-side window and asks if we want a tray to hang on the outside. We have traveled not only to the Midwest, but back in time, it seems. All around us, diners enjoy their meals from within their American-made cars (Heather and Dan's Honda Odyssey is the only foreign car we see, even in overcrowded lots by the Lowe's where we purchased an emergency radio, the only one on the road until we spot one Mercedes—with out-of-state plates).

Fighting a swarm of bees, we eat crunchy but not greasy battered onion rings, Big Boy burgers piled with pickles and onion, even a corn dog—the first the kids have ever eaten. I wouldn't think to have a corn dog. Ever. But here, it feels right to eat meat on a stick, and I chew the sweet, bready coating with delight as the kids experience their first root-beer floats. I hadn't had a float in ages—years, decades maybe—but cheated and had one the day before by myself while picking through a junk shop by the deserted train tracks.

Jamie closes his eyes to the bubbling liquid, the icy smooth froth. It's not just because it's soda, which he is only allowed to have every once in a while, it's because these are without a doubt the best floats in the world. Ever.

Daniel slurps his with abandon. "I'm doing this too fast! It'll run out. Can you hold it so I don't drink it?" Adam agrees, and I shoot him a look. Now is not the time to deprive Daniel by glugging it ourselves. Adam rolls his eyes but doesn't drink it.

"I like it!" Julia shrieks, proud. She doesn't like any other kind of soda and argued with Daniel on the way into town that she wouldn't like this.

It's sugary and junky and so good. Watching the kids consume it, eating the kind of food we rarely do, unites us in happiness and sugar-buzz that lasts until we're back at the lakehouse and ready to nap.

Travel Salad

The beauty of this dish is in the garbage-disposal aspect. Add anything and everything. If I don't have tofu patties, I use roasted turkey, torn into bite-size pieces, or leftover salmon or any other protein to make the meal hearty. Remember to cut pieces into manageable bites so you don't have to worry about cutting while on/in the plane/bus/ car/camel/gross minivan.

1 Morningstar Farms Original Chicken Patty (made from soy)

salad greens—baby romaine, frisée, young arugula, red-leaf lettuce

a few unsulphured, unsweetened Bing cherries

diced red, yellow, and orange peppers

green beans (previously
steamed and tossed with a bit
of olive oil and soy sauce)

a few baby carrots sliced into
thin strips

yellow beets (leftover and
previously roasted)

red onion, cut into ribbons

roasted sunflower seeds

French feta, crumbled

Slice fake chicken patty. Throw everything into a Tupperware container (or pinch a disposable cardboard one from a salad bar) and shake. Drizzle with a drop of lemon juice and enjoy.

Note: *If you prefer dressing, I recommend putting some in a plastic baggie or other small container and adding it right before you eat lest everything get too soggy.*

Peach Cobbler

The peaches in Culver were the tastiest I've ever encountered, even in Georgia. We used very little sugar in this recipe because of the ripeness and natural sweetness, but I suspect at home I'd add a bit more.

big bunch of peaches
(we used about twelve)

1 tsp. vanilla

1 tsp. lemon juice

¼ cup white sugar

¼ cup brown sugar

1 tsp. cinnamon

½ tsp. ground nutmeg

2 tsp. cornstarch

Set your oven to 425°. Slice and pit the peaches. Pour the vanilla and lemon juice on top. Add the sugars, cinnamon, nutmeg, and cornstarch to coat the fruit. Bake for about 12 minutes, in oval or square 9 × 9 baking dish or casserole dish, until starting to bubble and cook.

TOPPING:

⅔ cup flour

⅓ cup slow-cooking oats

1 tsp. salt

¼ cup white sugar

| ¼ cup brown sugar | 6½ tbsp. butter, cold and cut into pieces |
| 1½ tsp. baking powder | 3 tbsp. boiling water |

Mix dry ingredients. Cut butter in, and blend with your fingers until mixture is consistency of coarse meal. Add water until it starts to adhere—add more if you need it. Remove peaches from oven, drop bits of topping onto the fruit and, if you're inclined (which we were—I mean, it is vacation after all), dust with cinnamon sugar. Put back in oven and cook for an additional half hour until topping has risen slightly and browned.

If serving only grown-ups, you might pour a splash of Grand Marnier into serving bowls and scoop the cobbler directly on top. Garnish with cinnamon ice cream or cold vanilla yogurt.

Garlicky Panko Flounder

You can use other whitefish for this if you don't have flounder (cod works well). This is easy and tasty in summer with sides of seasonal vegetables or watercress salad, and also in winter with mashed maple squash or roasted potatoes.

¼ cup olive oil per pound of fish	sea salt
¾ cup panko breadcrumbs for every pound of fish	flounder (about 6 ounces for each adult, less for the kids)
2 cloves garlic, crushed for every pound of fish	ground pepper (black or rainbow peppercorns)

Mix olive oil into the breadcrumbs until panko is not wet with it, but shiny and doesn't stick together. Add garlic and sprinkle in a bit of salt, mixing with your hands. Put fish into a sprayed or oiled pan, season with pepper (there's enough salt in the crumbs), and bake at 400° until breadcrumbs are toasted and fish is white and flaky—about 25–30 minutes.

Indiana Interlude—Part II

Heather, Dan, Adam, and I are kohlrabi virgins. Despite our various years of living in different countries and many years of cooking, none of us has had kohlrabi. Heather and I stare at the stout pale green orbs as if they have been beamed down from another solar system.

"What do you do with it?" I ask, and play a game of catch with myself. I drop the kohlrabi on the linoleum floor but it does no harm to either surface.

"I have no idea," Heather says, her green eyes gleaming. It's not always easy to meet and make good friends as an adult, especially ones who rise above diaper-only talk. Though Heather and I certainly spend a lot of time discussing parenting, we could easily have been friends in high school. We take very good care of our friendship and the bond is strengthened by the fact that our mates not only tolerate but enjoy each other (again, rare), and our children, while not perfect matches age-wise, get along well. She squeezes the kohlrabi. "Haven't got a clue how to cook these. But they looked neat."

Actually, they look pretty grimy. "Maybe you bought them because you pity them," I say as I wash them. The scrubbing does little for their pock-marked complexion, their nubby exteriors. Pale green, like honeydew but not as glowy, the kohlrabi wait patiently for our decree.

"They're part of the cabbage family," Heather informs me, looking it up in an old book.

"We could make slaw," I suggest.

If this vegetable is part of the cabbage family, it is perhaps the offshoot relative that no one wants at reunions. The weird uncle who makes inappropriate jokes. At least, this is what we decide after peeling off the rough spots and cutting the kohlrabi into pieces to roast. I cannot recommend this method (or any other), because it's the first time in ages I've tried a food and thought, Nope. No desire to come back here.

"I kind of like this potato," Daniel says, crunching a morsel.

"It's not potato, it's cheese," Jamie says, biting his portion.

"Do I have to eat it?" Julia asks.

"No," I tell her. "And neither do I."

I am aware that I might have judged this vegetable harshly, and I tell myself I will try it again, in another form—either as a slaw or mashed the way I do with celery root as I learned in England. But not this trip.

For our last meal, Heather fries up the green tomatoes we purchased from the woman's garden. She scoops some cornmeal from a masonry jar and pours it onto a white plate. The gritty yellow grains land on the ceramic like rain, calling to mind the thunderstorms at the beginning of the week, the clap-filled, electric nights we've endured and enjoyed. To the puddle of cornmeal we add some flour, tossing in a good measure of salt and some red pepper flakes and dashes of whatever red spices (paprika, cayenne, chili powder) we have around. After the tomatoes take a lingering milk bath in a metal bowl, we dredge them in the cornmeal mixture and fry them up in a hot skillet. Jamie walks by and wrinkles his nose. "Gross. Green tomatoes." Adam agrees. "I'm not a tomato guy," he explains, feeling the need to apologize in advance for his lack of interest. Heather shrugs. More for us.

Daniel thinks something smells good. I predict Julia will like the taste, always game for foods that tend toward the bitter. Later, after the fried rounds have drained on paper towels, more than three of the green tomato slices will find their way to Jamie's plate. Four for Adam. "These are delicious," Adam says, the crunchy breading slicking his lips with oil. We take turns wondering where the old barefooted woman who had sold us the tomatoes was originally from. Hungary? Italy? Here? I enjoy every mouthful of the fried green tomatoes. Each bite has a crispy exterior and a pale green, near-sour flavor inside that matches wonderfully with the delayed spice from the cayenne. Sure enough, Daniel tries it "because it smells so good" despite the fact that he abhors tomatoes and, against my parental predictions, Julia takes a pile and decides after the first bite that she doesn't like it "one bit."

In addition, we barbecue local pike and make cold sesame noodles with tofu, along with the "weird" beans Heather bought on another excursion to the farmer; a simple salad tossed with maple vinaigrette; leftover cobbler with yogurt; and, well after the kids are in bed, a final root-beer float.

Each set of parents tucks their kids in—Clementine and Julia share one room, toddler Graham upstairs, Will in a port-a-crib in the bathroom attached to our room, Daniel and Jamie in the twin beds by the staircase. All of them are under worn sheets and faded wool blankets, their bodies pleasantly aching from time in the lake and on it, their fingers prune-skinned all the way through dinner. We swam all afternoon, delaying packing until late tonight.

Outside, the walnuts and acorns fall onto the wooden deck from overhanging trees. Jamie has taken to pitching them into the lake and seeing if he can find them while swimming. I sit nursing Will while Heather nurses a beer and nibbles on the roasted fava beans I brought her, knowing she'd love their earthy taste, their deep crunch.

Dan and Adam return from town bearing tall cups filled with the A&W restaurant's homemade root beer. I remember a couple summers before, Heather and I would talk every few days and it seemed she was continually on her way to the root-beer stand. She was pregnant with Graham then and craved the drink something fierce.

"I can't believe I didn't know who Graham was then," she says when I tell her my memory.

"Oh, shit!" Dan says. He points inside to the big room where the fireplace hulks over everything.

"What? What?" Adam and I look for restless kids, something amiss.

Heather shakes her head, understanding immediately Dan's concern. "It's right in there."

Swooping across the length of the room, diving this way and that, is—finally!—a bat.

"Do you want me to . . . ?" Adam volunteers. He missed out on the last bat experience at our house a few summers ago. I'd just had Julia then, and when Daniel called me in to look at "the funny bird" in the living room, I'd been completely taken aback by the bat that flew into my face. Once, in Guadeloupe, I'd had a bat stuck in my hair and had to figure out how to explain what was happening in French when I had no idea how to say "bat," "fly," or "stuck." All I could muster was something that approximated "Black bird live in my long hair for the love of God help me, sir," by which point I was so grossed out I considered shaving my hair (I didn't). When Daniel found the "funny bird," I did exactly what I shouldn't have. Instead of keeping calm and telling the kids it was no big deal, I freaked out, screaming "Bleah! There's a bat in my face!" Then I came to my senses as the thing hurled itself around the house, and I huddled everyone onto the porch. I tried to catch it, but couldn't, and the animal-control people said they'd "get back to me later," so I slithered to the kitchen, got my bag and keys, and left for a few hours. The end result was rabies shots for everyone—six weeks' worth of the whole protocol.

Here we have no choice but to deal with it, so Heather ventures inside and Adam recites the shots schedule to Dan, who wonders if maybe his kids should have the treatment prophylactically since bats are a problem every summer. Pitching a large net as though she's leading a high school marching band, Heather is victorious and runs outside to let the bat fly into the dark sky.

I take a deep breath, as if trying to inhale the whole trip—the kids bouncing on the lake while tubing, Dan swearing at the bees, Heather netting the bat, Adam attempting waterskiing for the first time since puberty. I will leave here with warm memories of summer, fun family photographs, a dislike for kohlrabi, a fondness for corn relish, jams, a new jar of sorghum Heather is sure I will find amusing if bewildering since we don't really know what it is, and that pie recipe from the pig farmer to try at home.

"Well, at least we didn't disappoint you on the bat front," Dan deadpans.

"Plus, there's a lot of corn here." Adam smirks.

"So . . . how 'bout a float?" Heather asks. Dan and Adam fetch the large drinks and we talk late into the night about music and old prom dates—stories of who we were before the kids, before all this. The soda slips down my throat, the richness of the vanilla ice cream mixing perfectly with the mellow fizz, the full-bodied root beer. We are two couples telling stories. Four people choosing to be together after a great, simple meal on this last night of vacation before we head back to our regular worlds. It is not that we want to forget who we are now, forget the whiny time-outs and tiny water shoes lined up by the door, the small but growing bodies we've tucked into bed, but rather that we want to remember who we used to be. Who we are.

Fried Green Tomatoes

green tomatoes	pepper
salt	chili pepper (optional)
milk	vegetable oil
cornmeal	

Slice tomatoes into thick rounds. Place in bowl, salt lightly, and cover with milk. Pour cornmeal onto a plate and mix in a bit more salt and pepper (chili pepper if you like a kick to it). Dip slices into meal and coat on both sides. Heat oil and fry slices (flipping gently) until evenly browned. Drain on paper towels and serve immediately.

 Heather's Weird Beans

We aren't quite sure what kind they are—the farmer said "Eye-talian-o," but they were wide and long and quite tough prior to steaming. You might also try pole beans.

3¼ lb. beans	dash of red pepper flakes
2 tsp. mustard seeds	toasted sesame seeds
splash of rice vinegar	sprinkling of sugar
2 cloves garlic, crushed	salt to taste
½ tsp. freshly grated ginger	

Wash beans and steam in large pot until cooked but still crisp. Toss all ingredients with the warm beans and let stand about ten minutes (or however long it takes you to make the fried green tomatoes). Toss again and serve tepid.

Barbecued Pike

½ cup ketchup	dash of Tabasco
¼ cup white vinegar	drop of molasses
3 tbsp. brown sugar	2½ lbs. pike
dash of lemon juice	1 potato
dash of Worcestershire sauce	

Mix together all ingredients (except pike and potato) and spread the mixture onto the pike. Let it marinate overnight or however long you can.

Prior to grilling, cut raw potato in half and rub wet side directly onto the grill. The starch in it will keep the fish from sticking. Place pike meat side down and grill until slightly crisp. Flip onto skin side and let it finish cooking until flaky—about 20 minutes total, depending on your grill and the thickness of the fish.

Crunchy Sesame Tofu

The kids—Daniel included—loved this. You could use the sauce for cold sesame noodles, as a marinade for tofu you plan to grill or pan-cook, or use it as a dipping sauce for shrimp or cubes of firm tofu.

⅓ cup crunchy soy butter

2 cloves crushed garlic

1 tbsp. tahini (sesame paste)

3 tbsp. rice wine vinegar or Mirin

1 bunch chopped scallions

¼ cup soy sauce

pinch of red pepper flakes or chili oil (optional for extra heat)

1 package extra-firm tofu

1 tbsp. sesame oil

Mix all ingredients except for tofu and sesame oil. Slice tofu into large-ish pieces and marinate for a while (or don't). If cooking on a pan, drizzle pan with sesame oil and quickly cook the tofu on high heat until sauce begins to bubble. If grilling, either cook in tinfoil (using sesame oil on the foil first) or directly on heat, leaving off the sesame oil.

Maple Vinaigrette

This is my fall-back dressing; it works on every kind of salad. Even the kids liked it for dipping.

1 tbsp. Dijon mustard

½ cup good olive oil

approx. ¼ cup balsamic
vinegar

2½ tbsp. maple syrup

1½ tbsp. lemon juice

Put everything into a jar and cover tightly. Shake until the mustard is well incorporated into the liquids. Adjust for taste, adding a pinch of salt if you like or a bit more syrup if your taste swings toward the sweet.

Root-Beer Float

2 scoops plain vanilla
ice cream

6 oz. fresh root beer, ice cold

straw

Not much of a recipe here, but as per A&W's tip, put ice cream in first, then add root beer.

Serves one but, like so many foods, is best enjoyed with others.

Say Cheese!

Reentry from vacation is never fun. Although I am a good packer, I am a terrible unpacker. Left to my own devices, suitcases could stay half-full for a week, gritty sandals housed still in a red duffel bag because I am world-weary and the last thing I want to do after three hours in a rental van, twenty minutes on a shuttle, six hours of airport/airplane time, another hour wrestling with luggage, and the car trip home, is unpack.

That said, I don't like clutter. And more than that, I don't like the post-vacation letdown.

"Why can't we just live in Indiana?" Jamie asks. After every weekend away, vacation, or summer holiday he has asked this same kind of question.

"Because we live here." How is it possible that despite doing laundry in Culver we have managed to return with more loads to do?

"But I want to live there." What starts as a joke for Jamie turns into tears. Lumped in my arms are rumpled shirts, the widow water shoe to the one Jamie lost in the lake, a used-up bottle of sunscreen.

"Vacations are like that. They're supposed to be so fun that you can't believe they have to end. But if we lived there—or in Italy or in Connecticut or in New York or in LA—we wouldn't live here. And pretty soon, those places wouldn't feel vacationy."

Jamie's big eyes are brimming. "But it's just so fun . . . there."

I want to talk about all the reasons why home is fun too, but that would defeat how he's feeling and I remind myself that I'm not trying to change his mind. "We had a lot of fun, you're right. And even I feel kind of blah being back. But you know that's only for a little bit while your brain adjusts. Camp starts soon, and we have the whole rest of summer left." I begin the back-and-forth of shoving laundry in the machine. I've come to the conclusion that the best way to inspire unpacking is to designate one suitcase the dirty-clothing one so that when we haul them in from the car, I can start to unload it right away.

Adam ferries more items in from outside, depositing them in the entryway/mud room. Julia picks up the stray socks I've dropped and the underwear that fell from my arms while Daniel rifles through the bags looking for something. "I need my pen. I don't know where it is." He grunts.

I sigh and say, "Making noises at me isn't going to get the pen to show up." I look around at the masses of grit, grime, wet suits in plastic bags, drawings, ticket stubs, snacks I packed in case the flight was delayed, and announce, "OK—everyone outside while Daddy and I unpack."

"I found the bug spray!" Adam says, cheery. "It was in the back of the car." This is the same bug spray we looked for over and over again in Indiana. "That's the last of the stuff." He surveys the wreckage on the floor in the middle of which Will is drooling, still buckled into his car seat. Adam talks to him as he unpacks. "Hey—look—the cooking gunk survived the trip."

I take the jars: homemade jams and a jar of apple butter that I could just as easily make but that seemed so pure and country-cute I had to buy it. "What the hell is sorghum anyway?"

Adam shrugs. "I have no idea. But it looks like tar." He gives me a worried look. "You're not making it tonight, are you?"

I shake my head. No cooking tonight. Instead, we will settle in, do the laundry (I admit to not taking the time to even think about separating white from colored loads—more like a jumble of everything), sort through the piles of mail, and try to remind ourselves of what life is like . . . here.

A few days later Adam hooks up his camera to the television and we have a photo slide show from our trip. We watch Julia jump off the dock, Jamie tubing, Daniel swimming independently, and Will lying next to Adam on the giant porch swing. Heather and I are on the porch looking at the sunset and Dan and Adam are in the boat; all the kids romp around together. It already feels distant, having settled into our familiar routine. Back to work for Adam, the long days of summer to fill with the wading pool and the perpetually half-enthusiastic sprinkler in the yard for me with the kids. And a deadline looming for a novel I've yet to finish.

"When will we go to Indiana again?" Julia asks. She's freshly bathed and wearing only pajama bottoms to be like her brothers in the heat.

"We don't know," Adam tells her.

"Maybe another summer," I say, and go off to finish making dinner.

Everyone sits around the table waiting for the mystery pie. "OK, remember the farm we went to?"

"With the apples?" Daniel asks.

"With the corn?" Julia wonders.

We have a shirts-at-the-table rule so all the kids put theirs back on, but only Julia's is right-side in. "The other farm."

"The one with the dogs," Jamie guesses.

"I took the recipe from that pig farmer and altered it a bit." I glance at Adam; he grins and shrugs.

"How bad could it be?" he asks. "I mean, it smells good. And it's got pancakes in it."

"Pancakes?!" The kids are aflutter.

"Not pancakes—just batter."

Hesitantly, I take the pie from the oven and put it on the stove to serve it. While the pie isn't what I would normally make, it is very tasty. The batter has puffed up and the cheese is melted but not stringy. I substituted ground turkey for the ground pork and it worked out fine.

"I like it!" Daniel scoops some into his mouth and then regrets the speed. "Ow!"

"It's hot." I eat mine.

Adam tries his. "It's like pot pie."

"It is." I chew and swallow. "We still have the sorghum to look forward to—not that I have any idea what to do with it."

Jamie and Julia eat their dinners and Daniel cools his mouth with milk. "Have some vegetables," I say. We pass the carrots and green beans around the table and, though it's always good to be home, I long for a root-beer float.

Culver Pie

The farmer's recipe is titled Impossible Cheesy Pork Pie. I think she might have meant "impossibly" since it's very cheese-filled. Or she could have meant it's impossible to refuse because it is quite addictive. Adam stood picking at it after the kids were finished, and I found myself doing the same while I transferred leftovers to a container.

Nonetheless, it's a quick and easy meal to which you can add lots of veggies; we tried it again with peas mixed in, as well as leftover corn from a few local ears we'd steamed. Should you desire, the recipe is easily doubled.

1 lb. ground turkey (I used all white meat, though half dark would work too)

1 large chopped onion

salt and pepper (optional)

1 cup shredded cheddar cheese (I used a sharp one)

½ cup Bisquick

1 cup milk (I used 1%)

2 eggs

Heat the oven to 400°. Cook the ground turkey and onion in a pan, salt and pepper to taste. Put in greased pie plate. Sprinkle with cheese. Mix rest of ingredients and pour on top. Bake for about 30 minutes or until tester comes out clean. If adding vegetables, add them before the cheese.

Hot and Really, Really Bothered

After camp Julia is tired and cranky, and because of scheduling other pickups and a work phone call, there is no nap to be had today. She flops onto the floor next to Will, who is sleeping in his car seat, and wrinkles her face.

"I am *ho-ot*." She makes the word two syllables, whining on the second note.

"Me too, Jules. It's summer."

"No, it isn't."

"Yes, it is," I counter, not stopping to wonder why I'm debating the season with a three-year-old who is determined to disagree with everything I say. "Should we cool off in my room?" The master bedroom is the room with the most-functioning air-conditioning unit. We generally rely on fans and the thick walls of our old house to keep the warm air out. This is partly successful in summer and very successful in winter.

"No. No. No."

I don't dignify this with a response but instead stare at the calendar and realize we have two doctor appointments at times we can't make, still haven't made a teeth-cleaning appointment for me, and wonder if anyone will notice if baby Will only wears white onesies, as they are the only ones that currently fit. The other hand-me-down ones are in the attic, where it is even hotter than downstairs.

"*Mummmmmy.*" Julia uses my name as a sentence. (Life or term?) "I want to do something."

"Like what?" Sweat beads at my hairline. My hands are filled with notices and handouts, paintings curling at the edges; every day a pile of papers that threatens to overtake its allotted counter space next to the fruit bowl.

"Like go swimming."

I could state why this isn't realistic—we don't have an in-ground pool, the sprinkler's broken, I don't feel like dealing with wet, twisted bathing suits and breastfeeding while keeping an eye on the wading pool. Instead I just say, "We can't." Then I offer this: "Want to take a cooling-off bath?"

This piques her interest for all of four seconds. "No." She wanders around the kitchen in her own way—a combination of dance and tai chi. "Can we do a cooking project?"

Her curls are in full glory in the summer heat. We've been at 90 percent humidity for four days straight and like the lawn, all plants, and the apple slices the kids forgot on the porch yesterday, I'm beginning to wither.

"I'm not sure today's the best day to cook something." I wipe sweat from my hairline and use my T-shirt to mop up perspiration pooling under my bra. Sexy is not a word that springs to mind. "It's too hot to use the oven." I hate feeling as though I am the one always saying no—no to this behavior, no to this project or that, no you can't use my shoes to dig for worms, no you may not eat your brother's Halloween bag full of candy, because it's nearly dinner and because we could have grown a baby in the time that the mini Snickers and Lilliputian Bit-O-Honey have been sitting on our shelves.

"I'm not hot anymore." Julia begs to differ yet again. She displays her slim, summer-browned arms for my approval. "See? Not sweaty at all."

I think about it and get some cereal to snack on while I think. The yellow box of FiberOne sits in front of me as Julia pulls a chair over from the table to the counter, readying herself in case I agree. I chew the cereal, thinking I should be hired to do an ad for FiberOne because not only am I won over by its claim to 57 percent of all daily recommended fiber, it is also the world's best cure for any—um—blockage. Plus it's low in calories and tastes good (to me—Adam thinks it tastes "like bark," which is in fact what it seems to be). After nine months of pregnancy-induced constipation I was desperate and grabbed a box, figuring it couldn't hurt. Now I'm a convert verging on zealot. "Try it—it will really work for you," I coax parents, friends, my agent, the guy in front of me at the supermarket checkout. "And it's good!" Praise be.

I eat it every day but have yet to cook with it. Until now. Cooled by the milk in the cereal, I nod to my daughter, who is waiting for a definitive exclamation point on my earlier "no."

"Maybe a quick project." I open the cabinet and grab the adolescent-size metal mixing bowl from its family nest.

"Yay!" Julia clasps her hands in glee and scoots the chair over to make room for me at the counter. "A cooking project." She watches me gather ingredients from the high-up shelves. "Only"—her hands are spread out in Libra-balancing position, an exaggerated question stance—"what could we make?"

"Can you get the muffin tins?"

We have forty minutes before we need to leave the house to get Daniel. Factoring in a nursing session and a required work e-mail, this just might work. True bakers might blanch at the less-than-perfect measuring Julia and I do, but her face says it all—streaked with whole wheat flour, her cheeks are flushed. With two hands she grips the long wooden spoon, stirring batter as I change around my grandmother's recipe (which she changed around herself a few times).

"We're putting cereal in the muffins?" Julia giggles and tips the Fiber-One box over—some in the bowl, some on the counter. With the heel of her hand she crushes into powder some of the spilled ones.

"We are!"

"Grammie would laugh," Julia says. She spent an afternoon with my mom the day before and has Grammie on the brain. My mother would approve of the cereal-as-baked-good idea; she likes to wing it in the kitchen and passed the spontaneity on to me. I used to stand beside my mom, stirring and sifting and chopping right next to her, all while listening to advice—or advice the way she gave it, which was advice with a healthy dose of opinion thrown in: Don't get your ears double-pierced (I didn't); invest in good shoes (they last longer); chevre and lamb make a great combination; and if you're ever stuck for a meal, slather whatever good jam you have on some chicken and bake it. All valuable tips. Watching Julia and my mom together is primarily joyous—they laugh together, do craft projects, have involved conversations about colors and books. They are free with each other in a way that perhaps mothers and daughters can't ever be.

"She doesn't like barrettes?" my mother had asked during their last visit. Translation: Why don't you make her wear them? I shrugged and waited for my mother to try to tame Julia's hair, to coax it into bobby pins or elastics as she'd done to me as a kid—hair back from your face, Emily; don't touch your hair at the dinner table; look how nice your hair is bluntly cut—but she didn't. She just pushed Julia's curls out of her eyes and held her hand as they walked down the porch steps.

It is easy to pick at the peeling layers of mother-daughterness, to tug at what came before, what still exists now. Every once in a while I make butterflied deboned leg of lamb and slather it with herbs and goat cheese, and I recall my mom's hands doing the same thing. I hear her voice explaining why it's best to use your hands and not a spatula. She taught me practical things, such as how to prune hydrangeas for fullness and how to choose root vegetables, as well as more emotional things: what to look for in a partner, how to communicate with children without sounding like one, how to love unconditionally, and how to embrace being a parent in the best way you can—improvising as need be. That said, she still overcooks her vegetables. But you can't have everything.

"Look, Mummy, the batter is only a little lumpy now," Julia says. Her cheeks are Gala-apple ripe.

"True," I say, and wipe my forehead. My mother insists we need central air. I open the window a bit wider.

I am sauna-hot now from stirring and rushing and preheating the oven. The baby starts to cry. I hand Julia the milk, forgetting for a minute that she is three and not particularly well suited to pouring from a full gallon container. "Wait. Here." I slosh a bit into a measuring cup and turn the rest over to her. "You just stir a bit while I get Will, OK?"

I go upstairs where it's a bit hotter and get sweaty Will in his onesie, his warm limbs and pink lips a welcoming source of even more heat.

When I'm back, Julia says, "I can do it." Methodically, carefully, she pours with a wobbly hand, and measures the flour as best she can, and I don't correct her. When the batter's done to her satisfaction, I put the baby down, spoon the glop into the tins, and hope for the best.

We are not disappointed.

10-Minute Unplanned Bran Muffins

Very much adapted from my grandma Ruth's recipe, which was slightly adapted from her *Fanny Farmer Cookbook* (1964 edition)

I don't have time to sift things into one bowl and then sift into another. I know that I could go to baking jail for this, but trust me, the muffins are good.

1 cup milk (I used skim, and it makes no taste difference)	1 cup flour (whole wheat, if you're asking)
1 cup FiberOne cereal	3 tsp. baking powder
2 overripe bananas	¼ cup sugar
1 egg (which is all I had the first time I made these, but I think you could use two)	½ tsp. salt

Pour milk over the cereal. Mash the bananas. Add the remaining ingredients and mix everything together. Stir only long enough to have everything blend. Let stand for 8–10 minutes or however long it takes you to change diaper/send e-mail/sing song/divert toddler/explain who Nixon was, or any other kid-related issue. Grease muffin tins, bake at 400° for 25 minutes.

Makes 12 normal-size (read: not giant, bakery-size) muffins. If you want the bigger kind, double the recipe or make fewer.

Note: *I added a handful of chocolate chips the first time (yes, they melted all over Julia in the heat, but she loved it) to entice and then the next time made them without and it went over fine. You might also use dried cranberries or whatever interesting dried fruit you have around.*

Bar None the Best Bar

Back when we brought Will home from the hospital for the first time, I was not only hazy from lack of sleep, I was ready to indulge. Sure, I wanted to eat healthy foods for my new baby and recovering body. But I was also longing to be sated with sugar. Prepared to burst with butter. My postpartum treat came in the form of thickly cut apricot bars made by one of the physicians in Adam's office.

"What are they?" Suspicious of all cooked fruit, Adam put the oversize Tupperware container down on the soapstone counters. I peered inside, hoping for something gluttonous, perhaps chocolate. After each of the kids was born, a gracious friend dropped by with foods that got me through those first days home from the hospital. With Daniel it was corn chowder and giant chocolate-chip cookies, courtesy of Heather. After Julia came home, my friend Liz arrived with black-bean soup made bright by orange wedges. In the heat wave that followed Jamie's birth, I existed on mint-chocolate-chip frozen yogurt and turkey sandwiches.

"I'm so glad they're not something I'll eat," Adam said as he leaned down to smell the baked goods on offer. He loathes all manner of cooked fruit—pies, cobblers, jam—sad, but true.

"You sure you don't want to try them? They're apricot bars. How bad could they be?" I said, reading the note that explained the origin of the bars. They are essentially shortbread with apricot slices baked into the center, held together by lots of butter. In my sleep-deprived state, I tried one and was rewarded by the flavor and the texture—just crisp enough but not crumbly.

Adam screwed up his face and waved me off. "No. Don't make me. Please!"

Instead, he proceeded to work his way through the Cowboy Cookies that my friend Heather (a different Heather, also married to a Dan!) kindly made and dropped off for me a few days after being home. Everyone tried the cookies and loved them and, selfishly, I stowed the last few away in a drawer so as not to tempt Adam (and to keep for my late-afternoon pick-me-up) and which he managed to find and devour anyway.

"Hey—at least they have oatmeal in them," he'd said in his defense.

Will is looking especially big today, getting ready for another baby milestone—turning over—and it's making me wistful. I decide to relive those sleeplessly murky early days of his life by making those apricot bars with the kids.

"Mush the butter," I tell Daniel, who has washed his hands thoroughly and has them stuck in the metal mixing bowl. "You want to incorporate it into the flour."

"What's *incorpralate?*"

"Incorporate," Jamie announces from the table, where he's sorting through his baseball cards, putting them in an order that makes no sense to my untrained eye. "You know, like when a company is incorporated."

"Yeah." I throw more flour into the bowl. "It means to include or add in—he's adding the butter to the flour or the flour to the butter, whichever way you want to say it."

"I want to do it," Julia says. She yanks a chair over from the table, scraping the wooden floor as she goes. I keep meaning to replace the pads on the chair legs, but every time I do it, they pop off and now I'm concerned that Will might find one with his tiny wandering hands and eat it, so I let the floor be scraped. Someday the kids will be grown and the house will be immaculate and I will wish they were home to scrape and mess, so I try not to mind.

"Julia, get off me!" Daniel elbows her, and she winces.

"I want to do it!"

"Get off me! I'm the one doing this. You can't."

Knowing that a full-blown sibling war is mere seconds away, I take the bowl away and leave Daniel floured and buttered while I talk. "Listen, this is supposed to be fun. What's fun about yelling and poking people?"

This is, of course, meant to be rhetorical, but Jamie can't help himself. "Well, it would be fun if you were yelling and poop came flying out of the ceiling and then a giant . . ." He starts cracking up before he can finish. Daniel laughs too. The bathroom words have begun to invade everyday conversations, but now is not the time to deal with it. Will starts to fuss from his bouncy chair. My breasts will leak in a minute.

"OK, Daniel, you've had a turn with this. Let's wash you up—"

"But I—"

"Wait. Get washed up and then you can be in charge of cutting the apricots. We need lots of apricots for this. Julia, let's wash your hands and then you can finish the butter and flour and mixing part, OK?" She plunges her hands into the mixture without washing them and I shrug. You can't have everything.

"Should I get a blue knife?" Daniel asks. He differentiates between the blue-handled ones, which are the kind we use at dinner and which are safe enough for him to cut with, and the knives that are only for adults, the ones kept in the block on the counter.

"Yes—and a cutting board."

He takes them over to the table, jockeying for space with Jamie's baseball cards, and I explain to him how to cut—in strips. "Like this?" He takes his job seriously, and I nod. Julia and I roll our hands in the dough, adding in the cinnamon and the baking soda, and then Will loses it completely and I leak two wide bull's-eyes through my purple T-shirt. It really is like the early days home from the hospital! "OK. We're done," I tell Julia, and hastily wash her up. The dough would benefit from a more thorough incorporating of things—I want it to resemble coarse meal—but I don't have the time.

We have an electric kettle on the counter—a wedding gift that my husband was convinced we'd never use but which I assured him I would (and do, daily)—and I turn it on while wrestling squirmy Will from his seat. He is a bulky baby—bigger than any of the other kids were—and I look forward to when he's coordinated enough to wrap his legs around my waist to help with the carrying. The water heats up fast and after Daniel puts all the apricot pieces into a Pyrex measuring cup, I pour the boiling water over them to let them soften.

A few minutes later a fight erupts over baseball cards, and our nice little activity is nearly ruined. Only Will saves the day by barfing milk all over me, causing the other kids to laugh and forget how annoying brothers can be.

"You got covered," Daniel says. "Eww."

"Do you need a cloth?" Julia asks and fetches not a dishtowel but one of our good dinner napkins. I take it anyway because the gesture is so sweet.

"OK," I tell them, "I'm going to change, and then we're getting these bars in the oven."

"Can we have one now?" Daniel asks.

"They're not even cooked, idiot," Jamie says, and I give him a look. "What? I didn't say anything."

I ask him to take a break in the other room for the mean word, and I go change. Jamie's been on the marble system—that is, every time he does what he's asked without talking back (or being mean to his brother, for example), he gets a marble to put in a small jar. When the jar is filled, he gets a reward—ten minutes of extra screen time, a song downloaded, something small. Eventually, the bad behavior decreases. Sometimes I think I'd like a mommy jar—I make dinner or agree to tie someone's shoes or make the bed or make a deadline or say yes to a work project I don't have much interest in or make lunches so Adam doesn't have to, I get a marble.

Will gurgles on my bed while I slip into the third shirt of the day, wondering how he is already out of the newborn clothing, grown too large for the 0–3-month size, and nearing the end of the 3–6-month size. I thought this—our last child—was supposed to stay tiny and babylike and seem small. Jamie informed me two days ago, "In ten years, I'll be away at college already!" to which Daniel added, "And I'll be driving Julia to school." "Or I could drive," she suggested. The teen and adult years loom, and I know from my own challenging and charming memories that there is satisfaction to be found in those years too, but . . . but the tiny socks! The milky baby smell! The new fluffs of hair! The wondering about who they will be! The babbling and absolute adoration that greets me each morning from the crib. This is the cruelty of parenting: to try to do such a good job raising your kids that you are eventually out of a job. I console myself with thinking that even though I will be made redundant, there will be new pleasures to be found. Will gums my cheek, and I hold him to my chest as I reappear downstairs for the final stages of the cooking.

"I'm patting half of the dough down," I tell them. Julia joins me. We scatter the slightly mushy apricots on top and then put the rest of the dough on top of that. "They're ready to bake." Jamie resurfaces to let me know he understands that "idiot" isn't an OK word but with his Red Sox hat on at an angle over one eye, he also lets me know that he's his own person. I take a brief moment to look at the flour-covered floor, the chair scrapes, the buttery handprints on the counter, the slew of baseball cards and stray apricot pieces, and the four—momentarily—quiet faces. Sometimes I want to savor them, hold them in the small spaces of time the way we do with each ephemeral bite of special food, stop the rest of the world from intruding. And as I begin to frame this moment in my mind, their voices and present-tense selves all overlap:

"Well, I'm going outside."

"I'm playing in my fort."

"I can't find my Crocs."

"When are these bars gonna be ready, anyway?"

"Soon," I tell them, and pick up the baby. "Soon enough."

Later on: "Daddy, you have to try this!" Daniel squeals with delight. With his dirty, buttery kid hands he pries off a crumbly piece and holds it out to Adam. For the same reason I accepted Julia's cloth napkin as a burp rag, Adam opens his mouth (albeit reluctantly) and tries it.

"Not bad," he says, and gives me a look. "It'd be really good without the apricots."

"Then it's just butter and sugar," I tell him.

"Exactly."

"And germs. We put germs in here." Jamie makes himself laugh.

"Wheat germ," I say.

"You didn't even make them," Daniel insists to his older brother.

Immediately, Jamie is on the defensive. "I was here."

"Doing baseball cards." Julia talks, her mouth occupied with apricot.

"You can't 'do' baseball cards, Julia."

"Anyway, what do you guys think?" I point to the bars. They are not as neat as the ones I was given. Those were precisely cut, perfectly packed by one of the doctors in Adam's office who is a very good baker. Ours are rough-hewn, a bit on the sandy side, but—

"Delicious," Jamie says.

"Like sand, but good," Julia agrees.

"We made these!" Daniel wants another one, but I shake him off. He fake pouts.

"Really"—Adam leans down, pretending to bite Julia's bar—"they're pretty good." He looks at me. "If you like that sort of thing."

He asks me what I think of the bars. To be honest, my memory of them is better than the reality of what I'm eating now. Feeling the rich crunch in my mouth from the bars or smelling the impossibly sweet new baby smell that coated my skin upon Will's arrival—both will fade. It is hard to let go of small things; particular tastes, smells, infant newness. I feel lucky, grateful, but also experience a loss somehow, a meal I can't have again, the food that lingers on the palate but can't be replicated. Will is changing so rapidly, I hardly have time to drink him in.

I pack up the bars and place them on top of the fridge for later. Maybe going back isn't the answer, but I will give in to the need to do so sometimes, just to find out if my tastes have changed.

Buttery Apricot Bars

The bars Adam's colleague gave me were ones she'd made based on snacks she'd had in Australia, or else she read about them in a magazine on the way to Australia—who can remember such things when sleep-deprived? What follows is the recipe that approximates them. Thinking back, right home from the hospital and famished, I probably would have enjoyed a flip-flop rolled in confectioners' sugar. Having regained a bit of sleep and sanity, I can safely say that this recipe will more than entice—best served with a cup of unsweetened tea or coffee or, if you prefer, cold milk.

1 cup dried apricots, chopped	1 tsp. baking soda
	1/2 tsp. salt
1 1/3 cups flour (a mix of all-purpose and wheat is fine)	1 cup brown sugar
	2 sticks softened butter
1 1/2 cups rolled oats (not instant)	4–6 oz. apricot preserves
3 tbsp. wheat germ	

Heat the oven to 350°. Cover the apricots with boiling water. Set aside for a few minutes and drain, reserving liquid. Grease a 9 × 13 dish with butter. Mix the dry ingredients and cut in the butter. Press half of the mixture into the pan and cover with the chopped apricots. Take a teaspoon of the hot water that was used to cover the apricots and use it to loosen up the preserves. Drizzle the preserves over the crust and chopped apricots. Press the other half of the dough on top and bake until golden—about 40 minutes. Let the dish cool completely before you cut into squares or rectangles.

Full Arms

"Where do kings keep their armies?" Jamie asks me as we wander around the local farmer's market. I don't go as often as I'd like, mainly because the market is held on the day when Adam works very late, but also because it clashes with naps and pickups. But it's warm today, and soon the summer will slide by, so I feel compelled to stock up. The other kids are home with a sitter while Jamie and I are enjoying the last minutes of our one-on-one date, having spent the first part of it playing catch in a nearby field. I make sure to spend time alone with each kid, or pair them up in different ways.

"I don't know—where do kings keep their armies?" I ask as Jamie chooses a dozen bright ears of corn, the brightest peppers.

"In their sleevies!" He cracks up, his face flushed with heat, his eyes watering as I laugh. Jamie loves a silly joke, and I adore this part of him that complements his intense, cerebral nature. We proceed to walk around the market using accents from countries no one—not even we—could identify, drawls and staccato, faux-French, England by way of Georgia, and all because Jamie finds it amusing and is so jolly I'd probably dance my way around the market if he asked. And I am a horrible dancer.

"Do we need straaaaawwberries?" Jamie inquires. They are lip-red and local, and I nod. "Should we get some zoo-kini?" He narrows his eyes, pretending to be a spy.

"Yes, and drop the top-secret ingredients into this bag." I open our reusable bag, which I remembered to bring this time, and he drops a massive zucchini in. And then another. "Hey, there, pardner, slow down!" I command in Cowboy-ese. He chuckles and throws in another.

I study our wares as we pay up. In addition to the zucchini, we also buy sweet onions, corn, and carrots for our rice bowl tomorrow night. We have a firm commitment to sit down to a family dinner even if it's only twice per week, and tomorrow night's meal will be a "rice bowl," as the kids named it. We roast broccoli and carrots (sliced on the diagonal for optimum roasting surface), make garlicky green beans, set out a dish of shredded cheese, cubes of salmon or tofu or beans, anything we have around and, with a bowl of (unburned) brown rice, we let the kids add their toppings. Julia has discovered anchovies and sardines (from my bowl), so she adds those. Tomorrow we'll sit on the porch with our rice bowls, the kids vying for a seat on the couch because the old wicker chairs are breaking. The rice bowls are always good for using up odds and ends of produce or protein, and they also help the kids learn portion control by serving themselves and feeling in control of what they add—or don't.

Jamie holds a few rhubarb stalks, the magenta stalks bright in the sunlight. "Will you make rhubarb pie or something?"

I can't face making dough that day, so I think of something else. "Grandma Bev and Papa Haha had the biggest garden—"

"At the Cape, I know," Jamie says. "Did they have these?" Jamie jousts with the rhubarb.

"Yeah, they grew everything—even asparagus for a few years. The grown-ups would send the kids out to pick stuff for dinner." Grandma Bev had a stack of wide, shallow baskets that made excellent sun hats (or Frisbees when empty) and we'd each take a station—my little brother digging in the dirt for potatoes, my older one yanking tomatoes from the vines. I liked to gather the sweet peas, often eating them as I went. We'd pull cucumbers from the vine, peel and seed them, blend half of them with buttermilk, yogurt, onions, and lime juice, and make cold cucumber soup topped with the other half of the cucumber, cut into rounds for texture.

"Let's get some cucumbers," I tell Jamie. "We'll make soup."

"Cucumber soup?" He makes a face.

"Gazpacho. And it's cold!" Around us golden retrievers and mutts waggle through the throngs of people, nosing up to the crates of corn, bumping into Jamie's rhubarb. He pulls it away and sniffs the electric-pink stalks. "So, maybe we could make pie?"

"Maybe Grandma Bev's rhubarb sauce." I raise my eyebrows. "It goes on vanilla ice cream."

"Oh, yeah!" He acts as though he scored a goal.

"Let's add this to our bag," Jamie suggests, holding up a loaf of cinnamon swirl bread the size of a Wiffle bat.

"Let's not," I say. "My armies are full," I say, making him laugh again. He puts the bread down, slides the rhubarb into our carry sack, and then slings an arm across my back for a few seconds. Then he lets go.

Soon we're home with the other kids; Will awake now after his sleep while we were at the market, Daniel wanting to make something, and Julia needing to pee because she keeps holding it too long to messy results and it's Tuesday and Adam's working late and I need to nurse and I have seventeen pounds of zucchini that I don't need. No one actually likes zucchini all that much. Jamie will eat it sautéed with some summer squash and Adam, if pressed, will do the same with perhaps some grated Pecorino on top, especially if I stick it under the broiler, but even I don't love it.

"What do kings do with these?" I wave two arm-size zucchini around in the hot kitchen.

Jamie shrugs. "Play baseball?"

I am tempted to say sure. Then Daniel pipes in with, "Make muffins."

Which is how I come to be grating zucchini and having the kids ready the rest of the ingredients for what will turn out to be, in everyone's opinion, awesome, amazing muffins. At the same time, I have Daniel chopping the fresh green and red peppers so we can throw together a chunky gazpacho that Julia started eating when she was thirteen months old and still likes now. Even Adam, who isn't friends with tomatoes as a rule, eats tons of it when the summer months roll in.

"I have the dill," Jamie says, pulling bits of it off and dropping it into what is now a big bowl of Farmer's Market. We throw the muffins together, with Jamie taking notes on one of Adam's prescription pads so I don't forget the recipe, Will on my hip as I spray the muffin tins, Daniel sprinkling some wheat germ into the batter, and Julia spinning around the room. The riddle is how to pause these moments, the days when they are this age, and, knowing it's impossible, adding ingredients, cooking, baking, enjoying, tasting, and taking notes. We slow down, stack the dishes in the sink, and sit together, waiting for the meal that comes next.

 ## Country Gazpacho

This chunky, hearty gazpacho can be eaten right away or savored over the course of a week. The combination of tomatoes really makes a difference. I like to keep the gazpacho hearty and the vegetables identifiable, but if you prefer a smoother soup, puree half of it or all of it. All of the measurements are flexible: add more tomatoes, fewer onions, green peppers, or more dill—up to you. My version is more like a liquid salad with sunbursts of colors rather than a traditional soup.

2 large cucumbers	3 peppers (one red, one orange, and one yellow)
1–2 fresh larger tomatoes in season (plum/heirloom, or any local)	2 onions
	2 cloves garlic
1 pint cherry or globe tomatoes	bunch of fresh dill

1 can diced tomatoes (not the kind with basil in it)	splash red wine vinegar
	2 tbsp. cold water
1 28-oz. can good-quality whole peeled tomatoes	½ cup good olive oil
3 tbsp. lemon juice	sea salt and pepper
1 small can tomato juice	2 tbsp. Worcestershire sauce

Peel the cucumbers, slice them lengthwise, and scoop out the seeds with a spoon. If you use an English cucumber, the skin is thin enough to keep on. Chop up the larger fresh tomatoes and halve the cherry or globe, seeding casually (meaning, using your thumb, get some of the seeds out but don't be fanatical about it). Put tomatoes into a large bowl. Cut the peppers, cucumbers, and onions into bite-size pieces and add to the bowl. Mince the garlic and add it to the vegetables, stirring gently by hand. Chop a handful of dill and add it (you may use leftover whole sprigs for garnish). Add can of diced tomatoes, reserving the liquid from the can. Cut up the whole canned tomatoes, and add. Stir lemon juice, tomato juice, vinegar, water, and olive oil into the mix and salt and pepper to taste. If you want a more liquidy soup, add some of the reserved can juice. Otherwise, keep it thick and add the Worcestershire sauce, mix with a spoon, and cover in the fridge for a few hours. The soup will pick up flavor as it sits (the next day it will be great). Add drizzle of olive oil to each portion if you like, and serve cold.

Croutons

old French bread or any other kind of bread you have	olive oil
	sea salt

Cut bread into strips and then into oversize cubes. This is a rough-cut job, not meant to be exact. Place on a baking sheet in single layer, drizzle with olive oil, sprinkle with sea salt, and bake at 300° until toasted—about 15–20 minutes. Let cool. Serve on top of gazpacho.

Zealous Zucchini Muffins

This can be doubled—or tripled or quadrupled—easily for those who are a bit overzealous in the growing or purchasing of zucchini. Feel free to make it into bread rather than muffins, but cook for about an hour.

2 cups grated zucchini	2 eggs
1½ cups whole-wheat flour	¼ cup wheat germ
1 cup white flour	1 cup milk
1 tsp. baking powder	½ cup sugar
½ tsp. salt	½ cup unsweetened applesauce

Mix all ingredients. Scoop into greased muffin tins. Cook for 40–50 minutes or until tester comes out clean. Makes 6 honking-big or 12 regular-size awesome muffins.

Grandma Bev's Rhubarb Sauce

My grandmother insists that the hardest part of this recipe is growing the rhubarb. This is great for an ice-cream topping, mixed with yogurt, or simply eaten by the spoonful in place of applesauce.

1 pound fresh rhubarb (yields 2 cups cooked sauce)	sugar

YOU CHOOSE:

Tart = 1 cup sugar : 4 cups fruit	Sweet = 2 cups sugar : 4 cups fruit

Split the rhubarb stalks. Cut into ½- to ¼-inch pieces and put into a large bowl. Add sugar to bowl. Let sit for at least one hour, but preferably several hours or overnight. This draws the liquid out so you never need to add water—that's why this sauce is so full-flavored. Stir occasionally. Pour the rhubarb and sugar mixture into a cooking pot and bring to a boil. Take away from heat and cover. Let stand for a few minutes until soft. When the mixture is cool, blend it well. Enjoy now or can for later in the year (Grandma recommends putting into pint jars and freezing it).

Serve over vanilla ice cream (or on top of peach cobbler).

Dog Days at Dogana

Four hours into the nine-and-a-half-hour flight and it looks as though everything we brought on board has been thrown into a giant blender and spewed out into our rows of seats. We are, of course, herded toward the back of the plane, sequestered as though our big brood might scare off the masses from ever flying with Alitalia again—which, quite frankly, we might.

My father and stepmother, Min, moved to Italy years ago from London, restoring an old pig farm, Dogana, into a glorious house with sheep and horses and vegetables and a caretaker named Julio and into which we will all descend as soon as our plane lands. Which—as far as Adam and I are concerned—cannot be soon enough. The kids are in various stages of undress: Daniel with his socks and shoes off asleep on my lap, Jamie with one shoe on, the other hidden under our flying detritus, his sweater on the floor that Julia uses as her pillow. She is tucked, like all good carry-ons, under the seat in front of me. She likes to have her own space, which I understand and agree with, however she has left me with no room for my legs or feet. I am doing my best to avoid feeling pins and needles throughout my entire body what with a baby and kids thoroughly inhibiting the idea of personal space. Adam has Daniel's feet and Jamie's head coming at him from either side but is quite happily snoring away while I dream of landing, of seeing my dad, of doing the first big food shop with my stepmother.

I should say right here that Min and I have a complicated past. My parents divorced when I was a teenager, so I never grew up with a step-parent, and we more than stumbled over the emotional terrain.

My father and I have always been close. While his postdivorce dating was at turns humorous ("You're dating someone who chants?") and horrifying (it's not easy for any child to see his or her parent lonely), none of it was as difficult to deal with as his marriage to my stepmother. I found her cold. She found me sarcastic. To be fair to us both, she is old-school English and not supereffusive and I have a tendency toward verbal snark and, because I was seventeen at the time, this often came across as cutting in tone. I liked to write and read and hike. She was into fashion and preferred swimming. The one thing we had in common—my dad—was the one thing on which we couldn't connect. I resented the physical distance—they lived in Europe while I'd moved back to the States—and she had to put up with being cast aside every time I arrived in town, dressed for a hike with my dad. The first time we ever truly connected was in the kitchen, and it's the place we still find the most ease together.

"I'm dreaming of arugula," I tell Adam. Spicy, leafy, fresh arugula. "I think I'm going to buy pots of anchovies!" I picture the small glass jars in the Dogana kitchen—cylinders of salty oil packed with anchovies or tuna. Perfect for salads or pasta sauces. We buy them at a small, dark store two villages over, up a hill, past a field of bulls and an unfortunate waft from the fertilizer farm that makes the breeze turn, for one-eighth of a mile, into pungent manure land. But the anchovies!

He shakes his head. "No, not anchovies," he says with his eyes closed. "Gelato."

Dogana, the name of my dad and Min's farmhouse, is comprised of a main house and a studio in which Min paints and in which Adam and I will sleep with the younger kids while the others stay at the main house. To get to the house, we must first drive a couple of hours from Rome, twist and turn the car up and down hills and, finally, turn onto an unmarked dirt road that winds through fields and past cloud formations that resemble sheep or a few donkeys, until at last we're in front of Dogana. Set back from the dirt road, and fenced to prevent the dogs from bothering the sheep or being gored by the local *cinghiali* (wild boars) at night, the house is flanked by a rocky pasture on one side and a small orchard on the other. The driveway is circular and noisy with local red chipped rocks that the kids enjoy chucking into the air to make the dogs go wild. Beyond the house is the pool—one long rectangle that overlooks a field of wild white horses that is behind the studio. Past a tumble of fruit trees is a shaded one-room cottage where my dad does his work when he is not at his office in town.

"Town" is about a fifteen-minute drive away. To call Farnese a town is to give it a bit more grandeur and size than is warranted, but this being Italy, the foodstuffs are fantastic. There's a small shop that sells cereals, a few vegetables, milk, and various dry goods; a tiny but delicious restaurant; a church; and a gas station with one pump perched precariously on the hill that winds past my dad's office and to the place that serves—in our family's collective opinion—the best pizza in the world. However, this being Italy, the ovens have to heat all day, which means that only at nine o'clock at night are they able to serve said pizza—perhaps not the most opportune time for a kid's meal, but they rally—Julia talking nonstop, Jamie digging into his pizza, Daniel trying his and resting his head on the table.

Last year, our trip to Italy was divine despite being plagued by a heatwave. We kept cool in the fresh-water pool and had the kids take siestas with us in the afternoon heat. Min and I would assemble large lunches on the cement table near the house, and the kids would fill up on fresh-cut salt-crusted bread, slices of prosciutto, and tons of cheese.

"I love ricotta salata!" Julia had said, her *l*'s more like *y*'s. I yuve it!

Daniel couldn't get enough salami. Adam—never a fan of tomatoes—ate them at every meal, amazed at their taste. "They don't even taste remotely like the ones at home."

That's what Italy was—ultra-tasty, ultra-hot, ultra-good.

This year, we arrive with the kids a bit more together, and instead of falling apart when we land, they are holding their own amidst the long queues and bags bumping them in the aisles.

"Mom," Daniel says, still holding an empty cup of orange juice—this being Italy, it wasn't from concentrate but rather freshly squeezed blood orange juice. Never mind that the flight crew forbade us from using the portable DVD player, the iPod, or any other "devices with this the electricity batteries" [sic]. At least we had good food. Good, that was until, "Mom—can you hold my cup?"

I am holding a sticky Julia, the two of us squeezed into the aisle as we all wait to deplane. "Sure, but why?" I ask Daniel.

"Because," he musters. He hands me his drink and vomits all down the front of his shirt.

Oh, because of that.

We make it through baggage claim with the kids singing their own songs. At home, Daniel has been singing "Dancing in the Street," only now that we're in the huddle of people waiting for a rental car, he has substituted his own words so he sings, *Summer's here, and the time is right—for pooping in my pants!* Meanwhile, Julia has wriggled free of my arms. Thanks to Jamie, who shared his Little League cheers, she is chanting loudly, to the tune of Queen's "We Will Rock You," *We will we will, you know what. Kick your butt. All the way to Pizza Hut.*

I am proud to be an American mother.

Almost one in the morning and we are outside running in the pitch-black with the kids. The time change has messed with our sleep cycle, and the kids are all wide-awake and ready for anything. Adam and I, based on our past trip with them, have decided to keep them up as long as possible on our first night in Italy so they'll adjust faster. We let them flit like the bats above—ducking into my dad's lap or into the kitchen to see Min or out toward the fields until they suddenly tire out and stumble toward us. We're on oversize outdoor metal furniture, comfortable on waterproof beige cushions, taking sips of limoncello and listening to figs fall from the nearby trees when the sheer weight of their ripeness causes them to land with a thud on the ground. The limoncello is made locally—at first taste sweet, then deeply sour, then as the alcohol hits, the tongue goes back to the sweet notes. There are two kinds here, the regular and the crema— the ultra-rich, creamy limoncello is a dessert and a drink all in one. It is the color of French butter, heavy cream tinted with subtle yellow, and we sip from square shot glasses as the kids propel themselves back and forth through the night gardens.

My dad cleaned up from dinner. It is the only meal Min will make alone during our stay. After all the years and subtle—or not-so-subtle—digs at each other, she and I finally made our peace in the kitchen. The peace didn't happen all at once, more a slow drizzle that started in the middle of an argument when Jamie was a newborn. I'd grabbed a snack from her kitchen in London and she'd snapped at me and I'd bitched back—one of those arguments that is really an argument about everything else. All those emotions bundled into a croissant or something along those lines. We'd had a dinner party that night—some of my dad's and Min's friends, some of Adam's and mine—and while she'd bought much of the food, I'd cooked it. I assembled monkfish (which is possibly the ugliest of fish) with an orange and ginger sauce and she prepped the scallions. When the dish was a hit, she'd asked me to write down the recipe. It was the closest physical proximity we'd ever had. Though we continued to falter in our relationship, we had finally found common ground. The next time, it was an impromptu dinner in the English countryside fashioned out of chicken breasts I'd flattened with the side of a wine bottle and stuffed with local pears, feta, and red peppers. Again, Min wrote the recipe down on a scrap of paper and tucked it away, its own little white truce flag. We spoke about food preparation calmly, nicely, and used cooking to segue into conversations about her painting and my writing.

This trip, Min and I will shop for fish and meat, venture to the greengrocer, and send the kids to the garden with Julio (who speaks no English but manages fine with gestures and enthusiasm) for large, nubby carrots and sweet egg-shaped onions. We will cook together sometimes side by side, other times at far ends of the open kitchen. We do not press our luck.

"Nice night," my dad sighs and Adam nods. It is hard work to get here but worth the trip. I go to the fridge for one more salty anchovy and return to find the kids sprawling on the lawn.

"We're tired now," Jamie announces, his breath heavy from exertion. Daniel flops onto his grandfather's lap.

"I'm going to see Mini-Min!" Julia says, and toddles off to the kitchen to do just that. She emerges with a piece of orange and I take the little ones to Min's studio that is also the guest cottage so they can go to bed. My dad and Adam get the bigger boys settled upstairs.

We all eagerly await gelato. Even if Farnese, which is a long drive from Rome, had nothing else, we would be sated with this gelato bar. Last year, Daniel charmed the owners, ordering every day in Italian, and developing a taste for Mele Verde—green apple. It's a funny flavor to want as a kid, what with the *caramello* and vanilla, the chocolate cookie, the *fragola*—rich strawberry. Julia got plain chocolate every day and as her cone lost its battle in the heat, she licked and licked, amazed at her simple good fortune of being allowed yet another round of gelato.

"Ready?" Dad asks, and we all pile into the cars. We need two cars to fit all of us, so the boys put their booster seats in the back of the ancient red Land Rover that looks as though it should be on safari and our generic Italian stick-shift rental that came with a sticker that boasts WE HAVE A RADIO!

In town, Min orders *affogato*—espresso with a scoop of vanilla in it,

Dad has two flavors on one cone, Jamie goes for strawberry and vanilla, Julia has her usual chocolate, and Daniel gets . . . an entire five gallons of green apple. Because the town is tiny and because my dad and Min stand out as the only foreigners, they've become friends over the years with nearly everyone. Knowing that Daniel's favorite was not always available, my dad asked if they'd make it, which the owners did, but in a quantity suitable for a football team, not a six-year-old. Daniel's eyes are wide as plates when he's shown the amount. "For me?" The owners laugh and scoop some onto a cone for him. Adam goes for coffee and caramel, and I get my usual. It's called *fiore di latte* and, try as we might, we cannot translate it properly. To me, it is the ultimate vanilla with a hint of flowers, but with the texture of a soft marshmallow. Dotted in the soft mellow sweetness are bits of crunch—crystallized sugar.

"This is the best!" Jamie eats his with one hand while playing foosball at the outdoor table. Daniel, a vision in melting green, enjoys every lick while Julia is immersed in chocolate we will later wash off in the pool.

Adam thanks my dad and adds, "This is like the only time in my life I'll ever be able to eat gelato twice a day and feel justified." We feel the indulgence is warranted, though, with the heat and with the company, the comfort of being with family but out of the normal realm.

The kids try the banana yogurt ("good") and chocolate cereal ("really good") that Min picks up from the shop in town (despite having gone in for lettuce). They try tuna soaked in olive oil and served with roasted peppers ("OK—can we swim now?"). And fresh blackberries picked from the bushes in front of the house ("So good! You have to try this! Quick!"). They even get Adam—a staunchly anti-berry person—to try them.

"Come on, Dad," Daniel insists. "You always tell me to try it, right?"

Adam nods, his mouth betraying his willingness. Julia pricks herself on the thorns but bears the scratches to see her dad's response.

"I went for a walk yesterday," I tell him, "and I ate them the whole way up the road and the whole way back."

Jamie plucks a handful and gives them to Adam. "Here are six of them."

"Six?" Adam's concerned.

Jamie shrugs and looks at Daniel. "You always have us eat like that—you know, 'Here are only six green beans' or something, so you have to have this amount of blackberries."

Adam puts them in his mouth, first one at a time and then more, smiling. "All done!"

The kids are impressed. "Daddy ate blackberries! Daddy ate blackberries!" They fend off the jumping dogs and rush inside the gates toward the house to report back to my dad and Min.

"Aren't they good?" I ask Adam, and pluck one for myself. "See?"

"No," he says, and the smile is replaced by a grimace. "I still don't like them."

Monkfish with Roasted Peppers, Bacon, and Zucchini Ribbons

This is a variation of the fish I made in London that caused some begrudging bonding between me and my stepmother. It also caused Adam to reconsider his prior disinterest in monkfish. Monkfish is not pretty to look at. In fact, it's fairly frightening alive (think horror-movie mouth, complete with sharp teeth and icky tail), and not much better raw (it can be a bit slimy and veiny). So if monkfish proves off-putting, you might try cod or haddock. But honestly, if you can get past its exterior, monkfish is delicious.

5–6 oz. monkfish per person (for kids, about 2–3 oz.), washed and patted dry	1 large zucchini, washed and trimmed of its ends
sea salt	¼ cup olives, preferably a mix of black and green, chopped
pepper	two handfuls cherry tomatoes or globe tomatoes (red or yellow), washed and split
olive oil	
1–2 thick-cut pieces bacon per each piece fish	
2 peppers—red, yellow, or orange	

Heat oven to 450°. Season monkfish with salt and pepper. In a large pan, heat a bit of olive oil and sear the monkfish, cooking it without moving it for about 3 minutes. (If you don't have a big enough pan, work in batches.) Drape one or two pieces of thick-cut bacon over each piece of monkfish in a single layer and place in hot oven in pan.

Over an open flame on your stove (meaning no dish, no nothing, just you, the veg, and the flame), use tongs to roast the two peppers until they are blackened on all sides. Stick the roasted peppers into a bowl and cover with plastic wrap (or alternately into a brown bag that you close by rolling tightly) while you work on the sauce.

While the fish and bacon cook, slice lengthwise ribbons of zucchini with a vegetable peeler or mandolin, season with salt and pepper, and set aside. In a pan, heat a bit of olive oil and throw in the olives for 2 minutes, then add the tomatoes for a few minutes more until just starting to crack from the heat. Set aside.

Remove peppers from plastic wrap (or brown bag). Their skins will slip off easily. Discard any black bits and slice the peppers thin. Open oven and throw peppers and zucchini ribbons around the fish; the bacon drippings will flavor the vegetables during the last few minutes the fish is in the oven.

When bacon is crisped and fish is cooked through (about 10 minutes for each inch of fish—so about 25 minutes, usually), remove from oven.

To serve, spread a bit of tomato-olive sauce onto plate with spoon. Place fish in the center of this and use the zucchini ribbons and peppers as an edible garnish, placed here and there around the plate.

Unbelievable Umbria

Italy is one long, prodigious meal punctuated by conversations, walks, and swimming with the kids.

Our dinners at Dogana are delectable: pasta with *gigantes*, thumb-pad-size white beans, anchovies, split tiny tomatoes in red and yellow, and peas. With gelato for dessert.

Arugula with syrupy aged balsamic, ricotta salata scattered with figs. With gelato for dessert.

Chicken with local apricots and plums. With gelato for dessert.

Wild boar ragu over freshly stretched pasta. With gelato for dessert.

Our lunches are long, lovely events. Daniella from up the road brings *marmelatta di prugne*. Italian prune plums are smaller and denser than the plums we see frequently in the States. Shaped like very large eggs, these are the plums that are dried into prunes. Sweet, with yellow insides and bluish-purple skin, they have freestone pits—that is, they come away very easily from the flesh. My dad and Min have the trees in their yard, but Daniella's property has more, and she's taken the time to collect and simmer them into perfect jam. "I make jam," she says. "And a mess!" she adds. The kids cannot get enough, slathering it on bread, on slices of cheese, on leftover chicken.

These and the figs make an incredible filling for tarts and pies. The fig trees are literally bending with the weight of the fruit, so my dad and Julio take a saw to one of the limbs and sever it in order to save the rest of the tree—it was splitting at the trunk's base. Each fig is palm-size, and so ripe that all one needs to do to eat it is apply a bit of pressure to the sides; the fruit bursts open and can be eaten just like that, in the heat of mid-afternoon on the terrace while the kids take their siestas. Alternately, we squeeze the figs onto crackers and dot them with crème fraîche or simply scoop a spoonful onto hunks of Pecorino. The dogs, Inca and Maya, make themselves sick on the once-forbidden fruit.

Min and I work side by side in the kitchen. The stainless steel counters are offset by the old wooden table that hulks the room—wide enough to have serving dishes in the middle of it while still keeping room for twelve to eat. To the left, a gaping stone fireplace with stone mantel; to the right, a cupboard filled with glasses; tucked behind, a pantry for dry goods—rows of pastas and sauces, cereals, flour and sugar in canisters, fizzy water, and dog food. From the sink and counters, a view to the patio and studio, and farther, the fields. Min gathers fruit from the bowl Julio carved from a fallen tree, and I hunt for mustard in the fridge to make a salad dressing.

Min slathers figs, plums, and fresh halved apricots with vanilla syrup we made with a cup of sugar and water and a few split vanilla beans. I squeeze some lemon juice on the top and add a bit of amaretto, and Min puts the whole thing into the oven for a few minutes to broil. I wash the vegetables Daniel picked in the garden and make salad while I watch Julio's wife, Pina, as she and her Italian friends swarm the stonewalled kitchen carrying huge cans of tomato sauce, jugs of local olive oil, tins of ancho-vies, fresh whole tomatoes as big as softballs, and mounds of cheese. Pina and her crew roll out fresh homemade dough while outside Julio and his twin brother, Mario, get the beehive oven going. The kids watch in awe as the flames are stoked higher and higher. "*Molto caldo . . . molto!*" they say over and over as a warning not to go near. The dough is thin as a pillow-case and is ladled with sauces, cheese, fresh basil from the garden, and doused with olive oil. Some are topped with mushrooms, some with ancho-vies, and some are topped only with chopped fresh tomatoes. Each uneven, rectangular pizza slides into the oven and cooks in two minutes. In a whir of housedresses and rapid-fire Italian, the women from inside cluster around the pizza as it's slung from the oven and onto the concrete tables outside. Min and I slice the chicken, bring out a bowl of salad, and have the kids ferry plates and napkins. Everyone—my family, the farmers, Julio and Pina, and some neighbors and friends—eats the crispy crust and melted cheese, relishing the crispness of the garden salad while we listen to a one-man band my dad asked to play outside. He clangs cymbals, beats a drum with his right foot, makes other noise with his left, simultaneously blows into a harmonica and plays a banjo. It's a cacophony rivaled only by the pure simplicity of the food—such bright, clear notes from the tomatoes and olive oil, the ripe mozzarella, the salty anchovies.

"Great band," Daniel thumbs to the man. I sit with Julia on my lap, my dad to my right. Later, Adam will photograph the boys as they run through the golden-hued field as the sun sets, and the sprinklers will turn on, drenching all involved. For now, we savor the crunch of the crusts and the fruit's sweet finish.

"I could eat twelve pieces of this," Jamie mumbles into his mushroom slice.

"I think you have already," Adam says.

Breakfast—a croissant or leftover bread with jam, some muesli with milk—is a minor happening, often taken outside on the oversize chairs or perhaps while following Julio down to the chicken coop to feed the hens and geese, or if the sun is already scorching, on the shallow steps of the nonchlorinated pool. Bees love the fresh water, though, so we have to keep Julia away from them. The dogs jump in, wanting to steal Jamie's ball, and we chase them until we're all tuckered out.

* * *

One day we go to swim in the Mediterranean, another day to Pitigliano to explore the hilly historic town and buy sauces from Alessandro and Helga's *laboratorio gastronomico*—local wild boar ragu that tastes earthy, deep, dark, and perfect over pasta; fig preserves; creamed honey—from the Ghiottornia. Another day Adam and I go out, just the two of us, to Orvieto (and of course, this is the day that Daniel gets stung by a bee). One afternoon we take shovels and head down a dirt road nearby to excavate some Etruscan pottery pieces with the kids, but mainly we just hang out at the house, swimming and reading and playing catch and coloring outside and going for long, shady hikes in the woods with Grandpa and the dogs.

One day we go to "the rocky place." The whole activity consists of driving in the Land Rover down a hill so steep we all lean back to avoid the feeling of tipping over, following a dirt road through a field of very big-horned bulls, and parking—not making eye contact with the bulls—and stepping down another hill. Thereupon we find ourselves on an island of rocks—from boulder to pebble, midsize to palm-size, they are red, they are black, they are white with gray stripes. The kids spend more than an hour moving the rocks around, chucking them into the nearby river, and collecting so many that Jamie's pants are sagging. At Dogana, my dad and Min use the large flat rocks as soap dishes—unique but replaceable.

"Pull your pants up!" I instruct Jamie, but it's no use. The weight of the rocks is too much. Adam, my dad, and I hunt for bookends. I like to find the large-ish rocks—ones with flat bottoms—and use them at home to prop up our many books on the living-room built-in shelves. How we will get them through customs, past the newly imposed luggage weight restrictions, and into the house is another issue.

"Shall we go into town?" Min, ever-elegant in her linen and khakis, is ready for our last shopping excursion. My family and I will fly home in two days. I nod and go with her not into Farnese, but to the next town over, the one that has a hardware store, a big greengrocer, and a tiny supermarket.

Time was, this would have been a chore. Now it is a pleasure. Perhaps when you work on a relationship, which we decided to do—without ever speaking about it (how English!)—the payoff seems even better. We are so far from the ill-will, the sarcasm, but I remember it well. We talk about her art, her latest painting show, my writing, the distinct loneliness and love we feel for and about our art. When she forgets the names of the hens and sheep portrayed on her canvases, when she stumbles over words about the museum show she had recently, I chalk it up to her ever-growing fluency in Italian. When she fails to remember that we need batteries and buys six pounds of meat despite being a vegetarian, I try not to focus on the oddities, but I wonder if something's amiss.

"Are you eating meat now?" I ask her when we've deposited the pounds of beef in the back of the truck.

"No?" she says, but it's a question. She hasn't eaten red meat for twenty years.

"Are you OK?" I ask, and I'm not sure what I'm looking for in her response. She pauses, her hands on the wheel, and nods.

We walk through the cobblestone village streets and talk about food.

"Try and sneak some through," Min nudges. "They won't know."

I am bemoaning the loss of ricotta salata—it's creamy here, spreadable, whereas the only kind I can find at home is crumbly in texture and not nearly as rich. My dad had stopped with us on the way from the airport at a small hut that sells cheese on the roadside. He emerged with a hulking round of the stuff and we've proceeded to work our way through it, steadily, twice-daily, like gelato. "They'll confiscate it—plus, I have the olive oil."

"Wrap it in a garbage bag," she tells me as we pick through green beans. I nod and get back to the business of procuring the lunch feast. It's best to shop early, and since we're heading into town for a final pizza evening, this lunch will be a simple, hearty meal for everyone. We make homemade hummus with sesame, lemon juice, local olive oil, and a dash of lime; we lay out two different breads, four cheeses, salamis, roast beef, turkey, grilled radicchio, tomato slices, prune jam, green beans steamed just for a minute and doused with lemon and butter, wine, mildly fizzy water, and milk.

At dinner in town the night before our departure, the thin-crust pizzas arrive just as Daniel is nearly asleep on the table. Will is already sleeping. Julia has her second wind. Jamie wolfs down forbidden soda. "I love Fanta!" he declares. Adam's funghi is so good he can only murmur, my margherita is incredible—crispy, chewy, cheesy—the three c's of pizza. Julia eats her entire portion, Adam and Jamie adore their mushrooms, Daniel perks up, Dad talks about the trip and how great it has been, and I notice Min barely picking at hers. She's ordered her usual, cheese with anchovies that come arranged like a pinwheel, but she's distracted. I catch her eye but she only looks back, doesn't speak. Is this just end-of-the-vacation blues? Is she full from our outing when I tried figs wrapped in prosciutto and she ate melon wedges? Or is it something else? I think back to our conversations, about the few words she's mixed up, how she'd wanted to use balsamic instead of syrup in a dressing, how she asked if we wanted bread with the pizza. It seems impossible to believe, in this small Italian night, in this even smaller village, that anything could be wrong. But my worry won't leave me alone.

The next morning, the kids drain the banana yogurt, take a chocolate biscuit, and we say our good-byes. Julio, shirtless, hairy, and with a chest like a rolled sleeping bag, comes up from the garden with thick carrots for the kids. He says it best. "You." He points to us all. "Here." He points to the ground.

Min hugs me tighter than ever, crying onto my shoulder, and I kiss her cheek. She palms the kids' heads.

"Soon," I tell her. "We'll see you soon." The kids don't want to leave, but we have to catch our flight. I think of them, swimming naked in the pool the night before, running through the fields when the industrial sprinklers came on in the golden dusk, the languorous meals, all the tastes of Italy.

"Ready?" Dad jingles the keys. He's making the journey to Rome with us, to help us check in and get settled for the return flight. I look at Min. She is in her bright red bathing suit, having already done her multiple laps for the day, and a sarong. Last year when we left, we were already booking a trip back in our minds. Now the nagging feeling of the previous night's dinner tugs at my chest. Is there something wrong? We all hug good-bye again. I hope we will return again. "*Spero che ritorni presto,*" I say, getting partial credit for vocab though not grammar. We drive past the donkeys, the fields, and wish we could have just one more gelato.

"Can we have it right now?" Daniel asks. He has his face pressed to the glass like a puppy. Jamie's head is in his book.

"Just one more time?" Julia pleads.

I shake my head and look in the rearview mirror. Someday I will explain that when something is so good, we will always want one more.

Dogana Hummus

1 can chickpeas plus a bit of the liquid	3 tbsp. lemon juice
	dash of lime juice
1 large can cannelini beans (or other white beans), drained	¾ cup good olive oil
	basil (optional)
1½ tsp. tahini	chopped tomatoes (optional)
2 cloves crushed garlic	salt to taste

Drain chickpeas but reserve liquid. Blend everything else but the salt. Add bit of liquid and salt to taste.

Or leave out the tahini, double the white beans, and add chopped tomatoes and chopped basil.

Rustic Fig (or Plum) Tart

PASTRY:

2 cups flour

½ lb. butter

1 tsp. salt

1 tbsp. sugar

4–6 oz. iced water

FILLING:

2 lbs. fresh plums or
ripe figs, pitted and sliced

¼ cup sugar

zest of 1 orange

1 tsp. cinnamon

¼ tsp. grated nutmeg

2 tbsp. flour

1 tbsp. sugar (for topping)

Preheat the oven to 375°.

FOR CRUST:

Combine flour, butter, salt, and sugar in a medium mixing bowl with your fingers until the butter is pea-size. Slowly mix in water with your hands until dough is soft. Put dough on a floured work surface. Roll out to about a 14-inch diameter. Place on parchment-lined baking pan.

FOR FILLING:

Mix all of the ingredients well. Place in the center of the dough, leaving a 2-inch border around the ends. Fold dough border over plum filling so that filling is encased but fruit is partially uncovered. It should look countryish—that is, not perfect and not fancy. Bake for 30 minutes, sprinkle with one tablespoon sugar, and continue baking another 5 minutes until golden. Serve warm with whipped cream or vanilla gelato.

Autumn

Back to School

Summer's end brings with it a flurry of needs: new shoes, a backpack for Daniel, barrettes for Julia to replace the ones we've scattered around various airports, yards, and cars. We need to use up beets from a friend's garden. We need to visit my mom (aka Grammie Max) and my stepfather, Dick, at their new house.

While Adam schleps the kids to the shoe store, I tackle the beets. We have golden ones and deep red ones. I peel both colors, doing the golden first so that the red juice doesn't bleed into them, and then remember I have carrots in the fridge. The carrots I slice in thin diagonal pieces and roast in the oven on a cookie sheet with olive oil and salt and a bit of fresh rosemary. The beets I decide to slice two ways: the red into thin rounds and the golden into thick matchsticks. I cook both in a large shallow pan in olive oil, sprinkle with sea salt, and when their edges are just crisped and the pieces cooked but not mushy, I turn off the heat. When the carrots are cooked, their sweet and nutty smell wafting from the oven, I plate the tri-colored beet salad and top with Capricho de Cabra, a Spanish goat cheese of exceptional creaminess and bright white color.

The kids, begrudgingly wearing their old shoes until school starts, try the salad. Daniel gets halfway through the first mouthful and sticks out his tricolored tongue, adding, "No way." Julia and Jamie ask for seconds. Adam tilts his head back and forth, considering. He swallows but doesn't ask for more. Will watches, moving toward solid foods but not quite there. I save the rest for myself for later and go to get markers so Julia can "decorate her shoebox."

We drive to visit my mother at her new house for the first time. On the way, the kids wonder if the new place will have room for them to sleep over sometime (it does), what the house is made of (brick), and what Grammie will serve for lunch (unknown).

"I ordered pizza," my mother says after she buzzes us into the entryway. "It'll be here soon."

"What kind?" Daniel stares up at her, unable to check out the new digs until she answers. Daniel is a separatist when it comes to food. My older brother was this way too. He'd keep his peas quarantined from his rice, his chicken a safe distance away from both. Why ruin a food you like by mixing it with another food you also like? In other words, foods should not be combined. Chicken, good; pie crust, good; chicken pot pie, bad. Onion, good; mushroom, good; onion-mushroom pizza, bad.

"Just pizza," my mother says with her eyes delivering the news: This is food with everything touching on top. Dread builds inside me.

My mom gives us all a tour and then the kids wander around checking for toys, buttons, remotes, good places to hide. My mom and her husband, Dick, have only recently left the suburbs for the city, trading a house with a playroom and pool table for a chic downtown locale that comes with a parking space. It's not easy to convince the kids that they've made the best move.

"But it's farther away," Jamie says.

"But it's close to museums and the Swan Boats," we say.

"There aren't toys here," Julia says. She's used to board games and matching games, rolling pool balls across the green felt table and hearing the solid clunk when each ball sinks into a woven pocket.

"There will be," my mom insists. "We haven't finished unpacking everything yet." But there's no denying the house is different; fancier, more adult, with highly polished hardwood floors throughout.

"Hey, check it out! You can slip all along the hallway here!" shouts Jamie in his socks. No rugs and polished floors make for excellent floor skating, which is what the kids do, managing not to need stitches. Will marks his territory by spitting up on any and all surfaces, including the Oriental rug in the living room, and then lunch is served.

When the doorbell sounds, the kids slide to the kitchen.

"The pizza might look a little different," my mother warns, primarily for Daniel's benefit, "but it's very good."

We have red onion and pepperoni. We have broccoli, corn, and mushroom. We have spinach, ricotta, garlic, and fresh mozzarella.

"This one has no sauce!" Daniel points to the "white pizza"—the spinach one. On a floor-skating high he adds, "But I'll try it." He likes it but doesn't reach for another slice, preferring instead to have the broccoli.

"So what do you think of the house?" my mother wants to know.

"It's good." Jamie shrugs.

"And?" She wants him to comment on the drapes in the master bedroom, the light fixtures in the hallway, the tiled floor in the bathroom.

"See how I'm not fussing about all the food being together here?" Daniel bites into a crunchy thin-crusted piece of the broccoli, corn, and mushroom. We nod.

"So, you like it?" My mother means the house, not the food.

"I liked the other one better," Julia says. "There's no playroom at this one."

"This has the disgusting cheese on it," Jamie says. "The kind that I don't like in lasagna. But for some reason, it's not too bad right now."

We eat the pizza, trying out the new combinations of toppings, testing the nooks and crannies of this new house, the next phase of Grammie's life. "Let's play hide and go seek!" Jamie takes off for the guest room, Julia slips into the red bathroom downstairs, and I help clear the table while Adam feeds Will.

"I think it'll be good, Mom," I tell her.

Daniel checks to see if he can fit into the storage closet. He pokes his head out from amidst the lightbulbs and supplies, his mouth ringed with pizza sauce. "Hey, you know, this place is actually really good."

Tri-Colored Beet Salad

This looks beautiful and has a blend of sweet and salty that would be great served with fish or with cubes of sautéed tofu. You might also add in brown rice or quinoa for a hearty side dish or as a main meal.

3 big carrots	2 golden beets
olive oil	goat cheese (I used Spanish Capricho de Cabra)
sea salt	
sprig of fresh rosemary	lemon or lime juice (optional)
2 red beets	

Peel carrots and slice on the diagonal, about ¼ inch thick, so you get a wide surface. Toss with olive oil and sea salt (not too drippy, just a drizzle) and arrange in single layer on a sheet. Sprinkle rosemary on top. Bake at 375° for 20–30 minutes undisturbed. Meanwhile, peel beets. Slice red beets into matchsticks and yellow beets into thin rounds (about ⅛ inch thick). Sautée yellow beets first in pan with a bit more oil and salt until just cooked—about 10–15 minutes—and starting to brown at edges. Then remove yellow beets from pan and sautée red matchsticks for about 10–15 minutes until just tender. Take carrots from oven and beets from pan and arrange on plate with crumbles of goat cheese on top. Serve warm or cold with a squeeze of lemon or lime juice on top right before serving if you like.

Connecticut Sojourn

Instructions for a fall weekend:

1. Go apple picking.
2. Have your overtired six-year-old, in the first eight minutes of the two-hour activity, bag his entire quota of apples and declare he is "done"!
3. Have your three-year-old ask why some of the apples she's been eating "taste mushy." Ask where she found said apples and have her respond, "I didn't need to pick them, they were already on the ground!"
4. Have your father-in-law watch as you and the entire jumble of your family climb down from the bouncy hay wagon. Have father-in-law ask you to "reenact" the dismount three times so he can photograph you "in action" to "get a better shot." Exchange grins with your brother-in-law, who has had to do this all his life, whereas you have only endured it for the decade of your marriage.

5. Feel the sticky hands as everyone tastes their first apple—Galas, Macouns, Empires, Red Delicious, Goldens. The crunch is delectable. Watch as the entire family suddenly scatters like dandelion seeds into the warm wind to find their own special trees for more picking.

6. Ask where your eight-year-old is, only to hear him yell back, "I'm somewhere but you have to find me." The apple orchard is 120 acres large. Run.

7. While wearing world's largest five-month-old baby (WLFMOB) in Baby Bjorn, chase eight-year-old up and down orchard aisles. Speculate whether they are called aisles or some other farm term you don't know. Wonder briefly why you aren't well-versed in farm terms, and ask your husband why. Have him tell you, "Maybe because we don't live on a farm."

8. See brother-in-law walk hand-in-hand with eight-year-old and six-year-old for what seems like a very peaceful moment only to hear, "Do you think it's nice to aim for your uncle's head?"

9. Nurse while standing up with WLFMOB still attached in front carrier. Smile begrudgingly while father-in-law takes photo. Smile into direct sunlight and realize you aren't just sweating in the unseasonably hot weather but that you are leaking milk through your shirt. As father-in-law snaps away, think, "How do you like *them* apples?"

10. Locate eight-year-old having apple-throwing fight with six-year-old brother who is now on his second wind, both of them with enough energy coursing through them to power many wind farms. Instruct them to stop chucking fruit and find rest of family.

11. Hold three-year-old daughter's hand and show her how to twist the apples off the trees rather than pull. "We don't want to hurt them," she acknowledges, patting the Macoun like a puppy. Smirk as she adds, "Even though we're just gonna eat them!"

12. Finally locate mother-in-law crouching beneath overhanging

branches and when you say, "We didn't know where you were," hear her reasoning, "I'm in a fort!"

13. Watch as your father-in-law, armed and dangerous with his camera, tells your husband to "Freeze!" See your partner in matrimony pause with six-year-old on his shoulders and smile for the camera only to be told by his father, "No—wait. Go back to that other apple. Now, try to reach for it. That's right. And again!" Shake your head and laugh at the "candids" and then be told by your father-in-law, "You laugh now, but just wait . . ."

14. Weighed down by WLFMOB, seventeen pounds of apples, three fatigue-heavy children, two in-laws, and bursting breasts, catch the hay wagon back to the cash registers jammed with caramel apples, cider, and lollipops in the shape of pumpkins. Head for the parking lot.

15. At your in-laws' house, proceed inside with seventeen pounds of apples that now feel like fifty and WLFMOB, who is now shrieking.

16. Subject apples to all manner of preparation: baked with brown sugar and raisins; sliced into neat tarte tatins; slivered and stuffed with Istara cheese into chicken cutlets; chunked into hearty crumbles with thick, crunchy topping; diced into whole-wheat muffins; and plain—as-is—for snacks, school lunches, and juggling.*

17. Offer all items to children, only to find they have eaten so many apples while picking they have no interest in the proliferation of pies and crumbles now.

18. Assemble crew for the two-hour-plus ride home. Hug in-laws good-bye.

19. Arrive home and get back to normal life only to find, a day later, a thick envelope in mail.

---

*Until right now, it has gone largely undocumented that my husband is something of a juggler. In fact, I married a clown. That is, Adam's job prior to going to medical school was slathering on full makeup—triangle eyes, overripe red mouth, oversize floppy shoes, and a rainbow wig—all to entertain children at their birthday parties. He may not be able to rewire a lamp, but he can make a mean balloon octopus or any other animal you might desire. So juggling apples is a natural, if bruise-inducing (for the fruit, not us) autumnal activity.

20. Behold: you, hair gleaming in the sunlight with your beautiful baby showing off his just-in two bottom teeth.

The six-year-old, no signs of fatigue, just blond, cherubic, glasses-clad, on his father's shoulders, reaching for the perfect apple. Realize that your father-in-law has captured the same pose as the one you have at your home of said father-in-law with your husband at the same age.

The eight-year-old, long-limbed, beaming as he explores the trees and casts a knowing grin over his shoulder.

Your three-year-old, in hand-me-down jeans, a striped shirt, and mismatching striped sweater she put on all by herself, proudly picking and filling her very own bag while her grandmother hides in a tree-branch fort.

You and your husband with all of your kids jumbled onto your collaborative laps on the hay wagon, and this wonderful heap as you all climb down from the wagon, hand-in-hand in what is, surely, the perfect shot.

21. Smile at the absolute, true incredible bounty of fall.

Autumnal Chicken (Chicken with Cheese and Apples)

Istara is a semihard, slightly nutty, and sharp cheese. If you can't find it, you could substitute any similar cheese, even a good cheddar. For the apples, I used a combination of Empire, Gala, and Delicious (my father-in-law likes to hoard the Macouns), but I suspect any firm apples would be fine. We were out of toothpicks. In fact, I'm not sure we ever had them, so to say we'd run out is not true. But in their place I used chopsticks, which we always have in some kitchen drawer, that I snapped in half and cleaned of any splinters.

olive oil

6 chicken cutlets (you could use breasts, too, but hammer them so they are fairly flat)

salt and pepper

fresh thyme

Istara cheese (we had a block the size of my palm and I used only part of it, so approximate one ounce per person), cut into matchsticks

3 apples, peeled and sliced into crescents

toothpicks

Rub a baking dish with olive oil, season chicken with salt, pepper, and thyme. Place the strips of cheese in the center of each cutlet. Add apple slices on top of cheese. Roll the cutlets from one end to the other and spear with toothpicks or chopsticks. Bake at 350° for about 25 minutes, until chicken is cooked and cheese is melted.

 ### Barbara's Baked Apples

apples

butter

brown sugar

raisins

cinnamon

Core, but do not peel, one apple for each person. Pack hollow inside with bits of butter, brown sugar, and raisins. Add cinnamon if desired. Bake in dish at 350° until soft (about an hour), covering with tinfoil if needed to keep from burning.

Serve plain or with vanilla ice cream or yogurt.

 ### Tarte Tatin

5–6 apples

approx ¾ cup white sugar

1 vanilla bean (optional)

butter (optional)

1 pie crust

Peel apples and slice into uniform wedges. Coat pie pan with white sugar (added points if you snap a vanilla stick and let it hang out in the sugar the night before you make this). In concentric circles, add apples, tightly packed together and all facing the same way. If you're going for fancy, do this very neatly. If you're thinking, To hell with order, and want to serve this as a "rustic tarte tatin," then you can be a bit more freeform. Dot with butter if desired (I've tried it both ways and both produce smiles). Bake apples in glass dish for 15 minutes at 425°.

Cover apples with simple pie crust dough—I use a combination of vegetable shortening and butter in mine so you have flakiness and taste, but you can also use frozen puff pastry. Bake for 25–30 minutes or until crust is evenly browned and apples underneath are bubbling in the caramelized sugar.

Transfer to a rack and let cool for 10–15 minutes. Hold a platter or other flat serving dish on top of pie plate and in one swift motion, invert the pie plate. Serve warm or cold, with cream on top or without.

Side Note

Julia, like her father, does not like much cooked fruit but declared the chicken "really yummy" and has asked for Istara cheese many times since. Daniel and Jamie liked their "apple pie" chicken and Adam liked his, too.

Adam does not like cooked fruit in any form, so he declined the invitation to sample the tarte, apple muffins, a crumble, and a pie. However, I mushed up the leftover apples and baked them into whole-wheat bread and he ate that and liked it. You can take any whole-wheat bread recipe and add in some pureed applesauce—it adds moistness and slight sweetness. If you have a recipe for any quick bread, you can leave out the oil and use applesauce (or this purée) instead.

Will is too young for any of this but enjoys playing "watch Mummy drop the apples on the floor" and loves playing apple catch.

Wedding Vows

When Shakespeare wrote that sonnet about the marriage of true minds, he left out the line about committing to sharing a palate for the next however many years. Long after the ceremony is over, food lingers on. Adam and I have a mixed marriage. We're raising the kids to be one religion, but food-wise, Adam and I still have our own stations.

Curries, prawns, spicy noodle dishes, and all manner of vegetables were commonplace for me growing up. We were as likely to eat murg makhni and naan as we were to eat noodle pudding and brisket. I knew about beets. My mother made saag paneer from scratch, crêpes were the birthday request for years, Brazilian shrimp dishes were commonplace. That said, there were the lean years when both my parents were working and food became more of an afterthought. Highlights included Weaver Chicken Rondelets or prepackaged chicken tetrazzini that sent me to school dreading dinner all day long.

When I first met Adam, we were so in love neither of us could stomach food. A few weeks later, when we were still smitten but finally hungry, I began cooking.

"I cook too, you know," he'd said in the galley kitchen of his medical-school apartment.

"Like what?" I'd asked, not doubting, but curious. Would our tastes mesh? Did it matter?

"Salmon, broccoli, stuff like that." He watched me roast a spaghetti squash. "Is that for us?" Read: Do I have to eat that? I nodded. "Give me a recipe, and I can follow it," he continued.

I grinned. "Oh, a recipe-follower. . . . I've heard of those." I explained how I wasn't the best follower of recipes, not the most devoted in terms of items and amounts.

"How do you know it's going to turn out OK?" he asked, checking his pager and about to head off to his pediatric surgery rotation.

I shrugged. "I guess I don't know that for sure, but I just hope."

This gastronomic leap of faith is in some ways a bit like charging full-steam ahead into love, which is just what Adam and I had done, despite the fact that he was due to practice medicine in rural Ecuador for six months and I had my open-ended ticket to India and Nepal and was due to leave in a few weeks.

Love, like a good meal, did end up conquering—if not all, then most. We accrued eighty thousand air miles; suffered jet lag, typhoid inoculations, rabies shots, and malaria drugs; and eventually cut our trips short and wound up back together—this time in a kitchen we shared.

"What is that?" Adam's face suggested he'd seen maggots roiling in rotting flesh.

"Beans," I said, and stirred. "Curried beans."

"God, talk about putting two bad tastes together . . . are you hoping they cancel each other out?"

I shook my head, inhaling the thick spices I'd heated up while dry to bring out their flavor—turmeric, curry, cinnamon, coriander. "I fully intend to enjoy this." I offered him a spoonful. "You?"

"I'll pass."

Before we married, Adam warned me. "There's something you should know," he'd said over dinner in an Italian restaurant in the Bronx that was so dark we had to squint to make eye contact.

Was he previously married? Wanted in several states? Impotent? Only interested in Cheech and Chong movies? "What?"

"I don't like foods ending in 'Y,'" he explained. He wasn't particularly sorry about it, it was just a fact being stated for the premarital record.

"None?"

"Curry—no way."

"I love Indian food! Oh, no! What else?"

"Name a berry," he challenged.

"Strawberry." He stuck out his tongue. "Blackberry?" Same response. "Blueberry?" He wrinkled his nose. "Boysenberry?"

"No berries for me. Just don't like them."

Visions of sunlit mornings complete with the *New York Times* and fresh strawberries evaporated. So, too, did champagne with a raspberry floating in it for garnish.

"But you like fruit, right?"

Adam nodded. "But just not cooked."

Apple crisp. Tarte tatin. Apricot tarts. Blueberry buckle. "You mean berries cooked or—"

"All fruit. Love it in its natural state. Not at all when it's cooked."

I tried to problem-solve. "If it's because it's too mushy, then you could try having a semicooked—"

Adam cut me off. "No—I've done all that. It's just not for me. Love bananas, not bananas flambé. Love apples but—"

"Apple crisp?" I asked, my voice ripe with hope.

Adam shook his head. Bad prognosis. "No. I'm sorry."

"Oh." I swallowed some water and thought. "But 'fruit' doesn't end with 'Y.'"

"No, but yogurt starts with it. . . ."

"You don't like yogurt? Wait a second. . . ."

Well, against my palate's judgment (but not the rest of me), we said "I do." But I didn't . . . make curries or stock the fridge with ripe berries and thick yogurt. Entire dishes dropped from my repertoire. He didn't like beans, either, or tofu or tomatoes.

And then one day, browsing the aisles and trying to figure out what felt funny (Did I lose a sock? Forget pants?), I realized what was missing was my earlier preferences. Sure, Adam and I had plenty of overlap—butternut squash, all fish, corn, greens (but not hot leafy ones like spinach, only for salads), all baked goods (save for those with fruit), roasted potatoes, eggs, turkey sandwiches, and so on. But we didn't have common ground when it came to my other, pre-Adam, pre-married gustatory life. And while I didn't pine for those dating days, the single times, I missed those dishes.

So I made beans. And my mango curried chicken that had supplied many a memorable night in graduate school—big, loud dinners when my roommates and I would eat on the floor, one night of torrential rain when I'd cooked the curry for a friend who loved it so much he blamed it for the kiss we later shared. And tofu and all the rest. And sometimes Adam ate it and sometimes he didn't. Sometimes he made dinner and sometimes I ate it. Mostly, we ate the same things, but other times, we didn't. And it was OK. He was in medical school and then in residency, working long odd hours and needing fuel before grabbing sleep and trekking out again.

"Try it," Adam said to me one night. We were at a new restaurant in the Berkshires, on a twenty-four-hour vacation while the grandparents stayed with baby Jamie.

"I don't know . . ." I hesitated.

Adam pointed to the mystery item on the menu and the waiter nodded. I had my doubts. "It's dessert," Adam said. "How bad could it be?"

I shot him a look. "What if it was baked apple? Or plum pudding?" Adam grimaced.

"But this is—" The plate arrived. Sweetly scented. Flecked with crystallized bits of sugar in a merry-go-round of colors.

"Birthday cake." I stared at it. "I've just never liked it. Never really even had it . . . I made a deal with my brother growing up that he could have the frosting and I'd have the cake, but I didn't even really want it. Why have cake when you could have pear tartlets or rhubarb pie?"

"Are you serious?"

I studied the cake. It looked pretty. But how good could it be? He thought he'd convert me. I thought I'd abstain. Then Adam handed me a fork.

I was apprehensive because before I met him, I'd never been to a Dairy Queen. Never eaten Lays Potato Chips crumbled over franks and beans. Never tried Hebrew National Salami baked with barbecue sauce. Never really eaten birthday cake.

But now I have.

"Thank you," I tell him when I'm losing my Dairy Queen virginity. We're with Heather and Dan and our combined brood of kids. I take a scoop. "So, this is a Blizzard."

Heather cracks up. "I can't believe you've never done this. This is my youth right here. The Dilly Bar."

"Do you like it?" Adam asks me. The kids, their faces smeared with imitation chocolate sauce, soft-serve vanilla, "cherry" crunchy topping that needs quotation marks because it's definitely not real cherry, wait for my response.

I wipe my mouth on a waxy paper napkin and feel the sugar glee kick in, the same as the birthday-cake high. Adam tried berries in Italy. Maybe I'll be able to have him eat cooked fruit one day. "I do!" I tell him.

Mango Curry Chicken

This chicken can make things messy (either by curry stains or by inspiring surprise kisses), but it's worth it. Sweet and spicy, this is best served with papadums—very thin crunchy wafers often made from lentil or chickpea flour—which you can make or buy. If you don't have mangoes, substitute in peaches (fresh or canned) or fresh apricots. This dish picks up heat and flavor as it sits, so you can enjoy leftovers—cold, on salad or rice—the next day.

1 onion, chopped

1 shallot, chopped

1½ tsp. oil

1 tsp. minced fresh ginger

4 chicken breasts, cut into smallish pieces

2 tbsp. curry powder

¼ tsp. cinnamon

2 tsp. turmeric

1 ripe mango, stoned and sliced (or one can)

2 tbsp. brown sugar

1 can peaches in juice or syrup

salt

In a large heavy-bottomed pot, sauté onion and shallot in oil until translucent. Add ginger and chicken and continue cooking until chicken is beginning to brown. Add curry powder, cinnamon, and turmeric. Add remaining ingredients, including syrup or juice from peaches. Continue to heat on medium-high until the fruit is cooked and sauce is slightly reduced and bubbling. Salt as desired.

Aftertaste

News that the kids detest a certain food travels quickly. Their whole bodies register their discontent, their limbs showcase the unkind tastes in their mouths. In this case, I have made "the most disgusting chicken ever," but they are suffering through it because it's dinner and because their father and I are suffering right along with them. The dinner stinks. The green beans are overdone. The potatoes not done enough. The chicken is as billed. But while the food is terrible, at least we are together. This will be a small grace in the face of the bad news we have to share with them.

"I really, really hate this," Jamie moans as he forks through the red sauce.

I'm not quite sure what I meant to make. On the one hand Italian, on the other hand perhaps slightly Indian, this is not a dish I will document for generations to come. Just as well.

"It is what it is," Adam says, and eats a bite of his.

I knew the meal would turn out like this. I had one of those midway-through-the-prep revelations where I shook my head, sure of the impending grossness, but kept on going anyway. I was positive as I sloshed the crushed tomatoes into the pot that we'd all be disappointed by the taste—or texture— just as I was sure on our very recent trip to Italy that something was wrong with Min. I'd noticed changes in my stepmother. How she searched for words that seemed to elude her. That she wasn't painting. That conversations had an otherworldly quality. ("I would like a branch," she'd said during dinner one night and pointing to an array of food. It seemed poetic but made no sense.) How she hugged me so fiercely upon our departure that it was as if she were trying to anchor herself to something she couldn't name.

When I cook, I go in with great intentions, all good hopes that everything will turn out well. With the bad chicken, I knew it wouldn't. I had the same hunch about the test results my dad and Min were finding out in London.

"If this is what's for dinner," Daniel says with his mouth twisted, red sauce slicked to his upper lip, "I'm done."

Adam and I ask them to stay at the table. We look the kids in the eye and ask them to sit so we can all talk. Before you give your kids something new to taste, there's a charge in the air, a jolt that tells them that they can't go back. Once you try chocolate or sardines or sushi, your mouth can't un- know it. I know what we have to say and that they will be unable to forget it, either.

What we tell them is this: Min is sick.

"Like, how sick?" Daniel wants to know.

"Very sick," I answer. "She has cancer."

Jamie thinks, his brows wrinkled. "But cancer is really bad, right?"

Adam nods. "Some of the time it is. Other times there are lots of treatments for it." Adam and I have sent Min a big bunch of flowers, all white, after her latest surgery and I try and picture them by her bedside. I wonder if she is imagining painting the blooms.

"And which kind is hers?" Jamie's eyes are dry, but his mouth is pinched. His plate is growing cold. I feel as though I should be providing them with something ultracomforting now, some gooey mac and cheese from the oven, something sweet to follow. When we were kids, my parents used to make us hamburger, macaroni, and peas as comfort food; the sweet and salty tastes were always soothing. But there isn't anything that would ease the tension in the kitchen, no dish that would be untainted. "Is it the bad kind or the curable kind?"

I speak slowly, carefully, but honestly. "Min is really sick. She has a kind of cancer that can't be fixed."

"Where is she sick?" Julia asks. She differentiates between sick in the nose (a cold), or the eye (conjunctivitis), or knee (scrape).

"Min is sick in her brain."

This detail solidifies for Jamie the gravity of the situation. We have not involved the kids from the very beginning, waiting instead for a proper diagnosis, a real prognosis they can understand. We do not say "metastatic" or "brain tumor."

"And is she going to get better?" Daniel's sadness is palatable.

"No," I say. "She's not going to get better."

Jamie does the math for his siblings. "But if you don't get better"—he starts to cry: wide, plump tears that land in his bad chicken—"then you die."

I nod. "Yes."

I believe that this is the gentle way of telling the kids. Adam deals with grief at work quite often, and we'd discussed when and how to let the kids know that Min is dying, that there will be a loss for all of us. I want to give them not only a chance to prepare for the loss itself (and the loss of the magic they experienced in Italy with her and my dad), but give them a place in which they can talk about their feelings.

As with food and other topics of conversation, Adam and I try to parent with simplicity and openness.

"I don't want her to die." Jamie and Daniel are crying, and Julia doesn't know quite what to do. My whole body feels sad, and I'm nauseated from the meal and from the news. Adam's eyes are brimming and so are mine.

"Me neither," I say.

We sit there for a long time; talking, not talking, hugging, and staring at our unfinished plates.

Hamburger, Macaroni, and Peas

This reminds me of eating on the deck of my grandparents' Cape house. It reminds me of eating on the floor of the den and in the yard with my brothers. And also of meeting my sister-in-law, who was by rights skeptical but then won over by this Franklin family tradition. Legions of roommates, college dorm mates, kids, uncles, aunts, and house-guests have been treated to this simple fare. It may not be elegant, but it works, providing comfort in a bowl at least for a while, even if you have to remove the peas for people who detest them.

1 box elbow macaroni	1 bag frozen peas
1 lb. ground meat	salt

Salt water and cook pasta according to box directions. Drain well. Sauté meat in a pan, then drain fat. Add meat and peas to pasta and cover for a few minutes to cook the peas enough so they're done but still have bite. Season with salt. Serve in a bowl with a spoon to your nearest and dearest.

The Beatles Live in Our House

We are a nation of Beatles lovers. As a kid, I used to listen to my parents' albums, watching on the record player as the apple on their Apple records spun around and around, the speakers sending words and melodies that lodged in my being and never left.

"*Let it be! Let it be!*" Daniel shouts rather than sings. He makes the song into a command rather than a plea. Daniel runs from the kitchen, where we've got noodles boiling, to the living room, where Jamie is clearing off the sideboard.

"*Let it pee,*" Jamie sings back. Bathroom humor hasn't yet lost its appeal.

"Is the kugel done yet?" Julia slides on the floor in her tights while Adam schleps the extra table up from the basement.

"Not yet," I say. "Soon you can help, though." As it's nearly Rosh Hashanah, the Jewish New Year, it's time to bring the family recipes out again. Over time, the kugel has morphed, changed like a folk song, altered for taste (I never liked the canned pineapple that Grandma Ruth used), and kept for tradition (I like the cornflake crunch my grandma Bev and mom put on top). I let the kids take turns bashing the bag of cornflakes. "Roll it," I instruct, "don't smash it." We add cinnamon and sugar to the bag and let it sit on the sidelines until we're ready to sprinkle it on top.

"*Let it peeeee,*" Jamie sings again, stretching the word and looking for our reactions.

"Jamie . . ." Adam's voice is a warning. He's very sick of the farts and poops and pees. I'm only mildly sick of them.

Jamie smirks. "Fine. Let it pea. Like as in the vegetable."

Daniel overhears. "*Let it pea, let it pea.*"

Julia giggles while she wriggles herself under Will's play mat. "*Let's eat peas, let's eat peas.*"

Daniel responds with, "*Don't eat peas, don't eat peas,*" each word perfect in pitch and just like the original save for the legumes. "No, wait, here it is: *donate peas, donate peas.*" He smiles, solving some agenda in his mind. "Because John Lennon would like that, like you're donating peas instead of just not eating them."

The kids know more than their share of Beatles history, often spewing their trivia in public. While grocery shopping with me the other day, with her little legs in the front part of the cart, Julia belted out lyrics to "Two of Us," which were met with appreciative smiles from the other shoppers, until one kindly woman approached and said, "Oh, you like that song?" Julia nodded.

"It's by a band called the Beatles," the woman informed her while I plucked yogurts from the refrigerated shelves.

"It's *by* Paul McCartney," Julia explained, her hands gesturing widely. "He wrote it about his wife, Linda." The woman looked agog. Then Julia clearly felt as though she'd somehow put this woman down, so she gave her some encouragement. "He sings it with John Lennon and the other Beatles, though!" Yeah, good try!

We went home and had lunch together, and I couldn't stop reaching for her hand, this rather heartbreaking yet funny moment of my three-year-old singing, *"You and I have memories longer than the road that stretches out ahead."*

Now the noodles are out of the water, still hot, and Daniel adds the soft cheese. We'll add more ingredients after the cream cheese melts a bit. "This doesn't look like cream cheese," Daniel says, studying the package. In the background, "Hard Day's Night" plays and Jamie hums along as he zips through the kitchen on his way to the dining room, where Adam is angling then unangling the tables, trying to make room where there isn't any more.

"It's called Neufchâtel," I say when Adam appears. He looks worried. I assure him with, "It's just like cream cheese." I shrug. "Look, I was at Whole Foods, they didn't have normal cream cheese, and I didn't want to go back. It'll be fine."

You don't want to mess around too much with traditional foods, but at the same time, I don't like feeling confined by them either. So I've done a graham-cracker top, I've done low-fat this and that, and this year, rather than a big brisket or a giant bird as the traditional main course, I'm going with wild salmon. "Tell it to calm down," Jamie joked when we put it in the fridge. We host Thanksgiving, and I don't like the idea of duplicating that dinner, so honey salmon feels special enough and big enough to fill us all. I combine half a cup of soy sauce and half a cup of honey, mix it very well, and adjust from there until it's the correct balance of sweet and savory.

This year, rather than going to my in-laws', we have everyone congregating at our house—aunts and cousins and parents and grandparents—meeting in the middle. Someone will bring honey cake, another traditional food but a new recipe, and my mother-in-law will show up with her arms full of chocolate-chip cookies, which are not at all traditional at Rosh Hashanah, but when is a chocolate-chip cookie a bad idea?

. . .

Daniel sings along with the music, changing into a thoughtful voice when "Here Comes the Sun" begins. "This is a different version of it. Really, the Beatles sing it. This is someone else."

"This is Richie Havens," I tell him. Recently, Julia was asked to bring her favorite music to school and brought in a disc of the Fab Four. She proceeded to explain to her preschool class that she liked the music very much and when asked by her teacher to pick a favorite, Julia responded with, "I like 'Twist and Shout' and 'Bungalow Bill,' but the Beatles aren't playing anymore." When I picked her up, the teacher relayed this information to me and Julia added, "They can't play anymore because two of them died." Her teacher raised her eyebrows and nodded.

"She knows her stuff!" the teacher said. It's one of those comments a parent can interpret either as "Wow" or "What the hell are you teaching your toddler?" I think the kids may be working some of their thoughts about death and Min in with the band's history.

I pour some honey into a cup and mix in some soy sauce. "Is that Chinese salmon?" Julia asks.

"Sort of," I say. During Rosh Hashanah, the tradition is to eat apples dipped in honey, to symbolize everyone's hopes for a "sweet" new year. We'll recite the blessing for eating tree fruits and say a prayer over the apples and honey. The honey salmon will help symbolize the Jewish New Year, and we'll make an apple cake for dessert. God forbid there be only one dessert on offer—no, not for this big family of eaters. Two, three, six, that's better.

Adam wipes off the extra table and has Jamie assist in moving chairs. We have eighteen people coming for Rosh Hashanah dinner and we have to arrange our space to accommodate the kids, the adults, the endowment of food. I station Daniel at the table with a cutting board and a bowl of peeled apples for him to cut, and I have Julia organize the napkins, choosing which ones we'll use, admiring how carefully she folds each one. For centerpieces we have bowls of ripe apples left over from our apple-picking adventure.

"I found cream cheese!" Adam says with his head in the fridge. "You want it?"

To hell with recipes. One nice thing about kugel is that it can tolerate any number of additions. "Sure!" I cut it into pieces, add it to the already-melting Neufchâtel, then add in some 1 percent cottage cheese. To counteract any benefits of the lower-fat cottage cheese, I add butter and egg yolks, because it would completely go against tradition to make a nonfat kugel. I'd tried once, and it was better suited for bricklaying than for eating.

"Should we put the table this way? Or like that?" Adam displays various ways of seating, and before I can decide, I need to go back to the kitchen, where the apple cake is in progress.

"Either way is fine!" I yell to him.

Daniel adds some spices and sugar to his diced apples and keeps singing "Yellow Submarine," complete with backing vocals so he echoes himself—"*Sky of blue . . .* sky of blue *. . . and sea of green . . .* sea of green!" We borrowed videos from the library of the Beatles performing, and the kids were rapt—concert footage, interviews, *Help!* and *A Hard Day's Night*. Daniel and Julia watched the animated *Yellow Submarine* movie over and over, devoting their allotted thirty minutes a day of screen time to the odd animation and eerie vocals. Jamie is so creeped out by it he can't even be within earshot of the warbly music. Daniel and Julia think it's hysterical. They are quite possibly the only two human beings on the planet who understand this film, including Paul McCartney.

"That dinosaur thing is smoking," Julia said yesterday when we watched it. The grotesque creature puffed away on-screen.

"Yeah, he'll die soon because of it." Daniel nodded, his eyes glued to the television.

"George Harrison smoked."

"Uh-huh, but he didn't die from that."

* * *

The apple mixture is ready. We set half of the cake batter in the Bundt pan, put the apple streusel topping in, layer more cake batter, then put a full lining of apples to the top of the pan, which we'll invert when it's thoroughly cooked.

When the cake is in the oven and the salmon is marinating, the broccoli cut but not yet roasted, the squash and cranberries ready on the baking sheet, Brussels sprouts on their own pan, and the kugel cooking, Adam plays the piano. "Yellow Submarine" swirls around us as the kids use spatulas on upturned Tupperware as their drums. Daniel is the lead singer. Julia is on variable percussion. Will is a roadie, moving items this way and that. I run the video camera and sing. Jamie sets up extra drums, using phone books for depth of sound and the wooden floor, too. For about three minutes, we are a vision of song, of family, of sweet things not just to come but already here. Then Will grabs a spatula, Daniel gets annoyed, Jamie loses it, Julia loses interest, and I check on the food, but Adam keeps playing.

"You know," Julia says to me in the kitchen, "when the Beatles stopped playing it wasn't because John Lennon got killed. It was before then. He told his wife that he was just tired of being in a band."

"Oh yeah?" I laugh as I test the kugel for doneness.

"Yeah," she says, peering into the other room where the discarded drum kits and stray phone books are left. "Sometimes you just get tired of being a Beatle."

Adam's chords continue to fill the house as the food cooks and the kids disperse. I still have that vision of the apple going around and around on the turntable when I was a kid, the same kugel in the oven now, and I think about the way songs and food can be altered and preserved, these melodies that become part of tradition.

Apple Streusel Cake

The moist cake is a tasty match for the crunchy streusel. This was perfect for a special dessert and even better for breakfast the following day.

FOR THE STREUSEL:

4 apples (I used 1 Golden, 2 Granny Smith, and a Macoun)

1¼ cups packed brown sugar

¾ cup flour

½ cup butter, cold and in pieces

2 tsp. cinnamon

1 tsp. allspice

FOR THE CAKE:

¾ cup butter, softened

1¼ cups sugar

3 eggs

3 tsp. vanilla extract

2 cups vanilla yogurt (I used low-fat—anything will work)

3¼ cups flour

1½ tsp. baking powder

¾ tsp. baking soda

¼ tsp. salt

Grease a tube pan (a 9- or 10-inch works fine). Peel, core, and slice apples into small pieces. In a mixing bowl, combine the remaining streusel ingredients with a fork until crumbly. Add in chopped apples. Set aside.

Cream the butter and sugar until light and fluffy. Beat in the eggs, vanilla extract, and the vanilla yogurt. With mixer on low, add in flour, baking powder, baking soda, and salt until just blended. Pour about half of the batter into the pan and sprinkle with half of the streusel mixture. Cover with remaining batter. Top with remaining streusel mixture. Pat the streusel down gently so it really sticks into the batter. Bake at 350° for about an hour or until tester comes out clean. Let cool for ten minutes or so and then invert onto serving plate. Serve warm or cool.

Sweet New Year Salmon

Buy fish according to the group you are serving—the six pounds of wild salmon I purchased might be a bit much for every day.

honey	salmon
soy sauce	salt and pepper

Use a ratio of two parts honey to one part soy sauce, stirring the two until very well blended. Rinse and pat dry the salmon and season with salt and pepper. Pour the honey-soy sauce on top and let marinate for at least five hours. Drain the excess liquid from the pan before baking. Bake at 425° for 8 or so minutes per inch. My mother-in-law likes her salmon cooked through, but others prefer medium—do as you like.

Kugel (Noodle Pudding)

There are as many ways to make kugel as there are Beatles songs. You have to try them all and see which ones stick. This is this year's variation, which we all enjoyed. We had a big crew, so this is a large recipe, but kugel freezes very well and is happily received as dinner or brunch food at a later date.

Cook and drain:

one 12-oz. package wide egg noodles	one 18-oz. package egg noodles

Add:

½ stick butter to coat noodles while still warm

Then add:

8 oz. Neufchâtel, in pieces   8 oz. cream cheese, in pieces

Let these melt at least partially. In a different bowl, mix:

⅔ cup sugar   6 egg yolks

8 egg whites, beaten   8 oz. cottage cheese
until fluffy

Add the mixture to the noodles and gently turn until fully incorporated. Pour everything into a well-greased big baking dish and cook for about 35 minutes.

Remove and top with:

2 cups crushed cornflakes
mixed with ¼ cup brown sugar,
1 tablespoon white sugar, and a
few dashes of cinnamon. You
can have kids crush the
cornflakes in a bag (either by
hand or with a rolling pin).

Put baking dish back into oven for about 30 more minutes, or until a knife comes out clean and top is golden brown.

Honey Cake

This year Adam's aunt Ann brought the honey cake. Moist and nearly breadlike, this is a wonderful snack, a good dessert, and an all-around delicious treat that truly does bring sweet thoughts of a New Year to mind. The coffee brings out the honey's sweetness.

3½ cups flour   2½ tsp. baking powder

1 tsp. baking soda   ½ tsp. salt

¼ tsp. cream of tartar	⅓ cup oil
1 cup sugar	1 tbsp. lemon juice
1 tsp. cinnamon	1 cup warm black coffee
3 eggs, separated	1 cup honey

In a large bowl, combine flour, baking soda, baking powder, salt, and cream of tartar. Make a well in the center and add sugar, cinnamon, egg yolks, oil, and lemon juice. Add coffee and stir. Add honey and stir. In a separate bowl, beat egg whites until stiff. Fold into the other mixture. When combined, place into greased 10-inch tube pan and bake at 350° for an hour.

Happy Birthday to Me

We're en route to Martha's Vineyard, a small island off the coast of Massachusetts, for an off-season birthday weekend. The island is a special place for us, and even though we won't be swimming or riding on the oldest carousel in the country (it closes after the summer rush), we are celebrating my thirty-fifth year exactly how I want to: together.

Piled into the car amidst canvas totes bursting with board games and sweaters, the kids are awake, save for Will, for whom this trip marks the passage into the next phase of babyhood: When we return, he will start on solid foods—my heart aches at the thought! How can he go so quickly from a curled-up ball of milky warmth to this alert boy watching his siblings eat?

"I'm hungry," Daniel intones the minute we're in the car. We make it to the bridge before we pass apples (still left over from our picking excursion) to the backseat, where the following conversation is occurring:

DANIEL: It would be a bad idea if a skunk and a lion got in a fight. The lion is strong, but the skunk smells so bad.

JAMIE: I have an immunity to skunk smell.

JULIA: Chipmunks put acorns and nuts in their cheeks and hide them.

DANIEL: Probably the lion would win.

JULIA: I've never seen a skunk.

ME: Yes you have, Jules.

JAMIE: You have to bathe in tomato juice if you get sprayed.

ADAM: Really? I thought it was vinegar.

And so we approach the ferry boat and drive the car on. Upon arrival, we try to go to the ice-cream shop in town, but the season is so over they've got only two flavors left. Instead, we head to the beach, taking in the wind and waves, hefting Will in the front carrier while the other three charge ahead, collecting sand in their shoes, hair, and hands. Sand that will linger long after the weekend is packed away. The Vineyard holds for me and for Adam a magic that started before we met. He grew up coming here and has warm associations from his own childhood. At the same time, I was here with my family, chasing my brothers (and later, my brother's cute friends), babysitting to earn money as a teenager, and with my mom and little brother for the whole summer after college. And then, one Labor Day weekend Adam and I met. Adam had accepted an invitation from his college suite mate and I had accepted a similar invite from the college suite mate's twin brother, with whom I'd gone to high school. We met, we married less than four months later, and now when we go back to the island, we feel that rush of excitement, the peace of having found each other. And the kids love it too, enjoying their vacations here with us, with grandparents, or for an off-season weekend like this one.

Adam and I have brought a gourmet picnic for our dinner, which we consume after the kids are tucked into their unfamiliar bunk beds. Adam and I sit with our cheeses; baguette; pâté; and various spreads, meats, and roasted vegetables all arranged on the coffee table as we talk about the island, about the kids, about birthdays. This is a loose re-creation of our honeymoon meal, which we also ate on the island. Now we experiment with the local champagne mustard and some *marmelatta di peperoncino*, bright red and tangy, that we brought back from Italy. It is jellied, spicy, and delicious with the Gruyère, and even better with the Vacherin Mont d'Or, an ultracreamy cow's milk from Jura, France. The chicken-liver mousse is fantastic, rich and deep on the tongue, though I refuse to go anywhere near the aspic layer on top.

"Aspic is just gross," I say to Adam.

"Maybe the kids'll eat it," he suggests, but rolls his eyes. We save some of everything for them.

The next day they test the Pont l'Eveque cheese from Normandy, heady and thick, and so pungent that only Julia says, "I love it." The boys grimace. The Brebis Abbaye de Belloc, a sheep's milk from the Basque region, is a hit with Jamie. The cheese is nutty and firm, the color of clarified butter. "Can I have the whole thing?" The whole thing is more expensive than his upcoming orthodontist appointment, and besides, we need to share, so I say, "Just leave some for everyone to have." We keep picnicking, all of us clustered around the table at our little seaside condo on loan from Adam's aunt and uncle.

We take leave of the food when the sun comes out—bright and warm very suddenly after lots of midday rain—and rush out to the yard to play football. Jamie and Daniel, overenthusiastic about the weather turning, shed their shirts and manage to stay warm by running around tossing the ball to me, to Adam, to each other, to Julia, while Will does his version of crawling on the lawn. His version entails pulling his entire body weight by his arms, seal-like and proud of his efforts.

Back inside, Julia scoops the liver pâté into her mouth and nods. "Hmmm." One positive. Daniel agrees. Adam finishes the rest of the spicy marmellata, the one I wasn't sure he'd even try, and wishes we'd bought more. The following day we poke around town, finding books and browsing, swapping who is holding whose hand every so often, pausing for me to nurse Will, and resting in an oversize barn-cum-homegoods-store when the rain starts up again.

Just like on our honeymoon, the days on the island slip by too quickly. The last morning, with bare bones left in the kitchen, we offer the kids the college staple of cold pizza for breakfast. They revolt in horror.

Outside, the Sunday weather has officially cleared, but our ferry is delayed, then canceled, then switched for another one leaving from a different port. We have enough time to grab some food, finally. Clad in bright sweatshirts, the kids are a vision of birthday cheer. We celebrate at breakfast with oversize pastries or breakfast sandwiches—cinnamon twist for me, apricot Danish for Daniel, a doughnut for Julia, eggs and bacon on a bagel for Jamie and Adam, and for today only breast milk for Will—all of us warmed by the heat from a wood stove.

"I made you this." Julia hands me a card. Daniel and Jamie get the ones they made from Adam's stash of gifts and I read them, my whole body filled with love and awe.

"I feel really lucky," I say to them, and to Adam, I nod and say, "Thank you."

"This is the practical gift, because you're always saying you don't have any," Adam says, and hands me a box.

The bowls inside are white with tiny blue designs, the perfect size for serving side dishes, and the size I always mention that I don't have. "And this is for fun"—he gives me a sweater that doesn't look right on me—"but you can exchange it. And this is sentimental." Adam's wonderful card I read twice and grin knowing I can reread it whenever I want. It's attached to a portable DVD player he borrowed from my mother. "Press Play," he says. I do, and instantly my grandparents are on the small screen, describing how our family came to this country, where they grew up, how our history became the present. The interview is too long to watch now, but to have it means so much. My eyes well up.

"Thank you so much."

The kids are being as patient as possible, except for Will, who wails despite having been nursed, rocked, and held.

"We should head back to the ferry," I say, and we gather the brood.

We drive our car into the line and wait. Then we wait for what feels like ten hours but is really only four actual hours, and are then told the ferry still has no space for us. We've used up word games, trips to the bathroom, songs, naps, talking, rounds of which brother can poke the other more, and all while being in a bumper-to-bumper line waiting to leave the island. Our honeymoon-style picnic long since eaten, we have little to offer except sighs.

When we're finally—five hours later—on board a ferry, with overly tired kids, worn-out parents, and a fussy baby who wants to attempt to crawl, we have to give the kids dinner with whatever we have left over. "Could be worse," Adam says. "At least we don't have to feed Will food."

"Not yet," I say, remembering that when we get back, it's time for baby cereal. It's an odd feeling—this transition from such a feeling of purity, of giving my baby only food from my body, and knowing I'm now going to start him on his own culinary path. Part of me is sad about this, not about his needing more than what I can provide for him but that he is moving into the next phase of babyhood, and part of me feels excited—who knows what kind of eater he'll be! His likes and dislikes, his appetite for overripe pears and cooked carrots, it's all waiting to be found out.

"We weren't set up for dinner," Adam says when he sees the odd selection of things we have stashed in the cooler. Our picnic remnants seem dejected and far removed from the glamour of the gourmet feast we had just days before. Gone is the delicious nutty cheese, nothing remains of the baguette, the plum jam, the thinly sliced smoked turkey.

"Here," I say to the kids. I bought precisely point sixteen of a pound of the stuff at a whopping $1.44, so at least financially I am not invested in how the taste test goes.

The ferry churns through the whitecapped autumn water. Jamie reads aloud. "What is Kashkaval Bulgarian sheep milk?"

"You might love it!" I say, trying for brightness.

I watch them test it. Another year, another trip to the Vineyard, more hands together, holding one another, holding cheese that is . . . "A big piece of yuck." "Ew!" I serve up pieces of leftover chicken we've kept in the cooler. "Chicken breasts," I say.

"What's on them?" Daniel is dubious.

"Crema di carciofi," I say. Italian creamy artichoke spread.

"How about crema di car-yucky?" Jamie says, and pushes his food away. "I'm full."

"Me too," Daniel whines.

"I have to pee," Julia says.

"Happy birthday," Adam says. And it has been. I know that when we get back, we'll have to unpack, get ready for school, food shop, pay bills—the usual routine. Will will try his first food and another birthday will be tucked under my belt. But right now, we're all on board. Adam and I trade off wrangling Will, trade off bathroom ventures, food mishaps, and end-of-the-weekend sleep-floppy kids who want to be held, but "not like that, like *this*." We clean up the picnic and show the kids the scenery as the boat chugs surely to shore.

Artichoke Spread

Bake onto chicken breasts or spread onto crusty bread.

4 artichokes	sea salt
olive oil	anchovy paste
minced garlic	dash of lemon juice
dash of white wine	

Steam the artichokes—eat the leaves. Clean the hearts. Cut and sauté the hearts on low heat in a pan with the oil, minced garlic, wine, and salt.

When the artichokes are cooked and everything is coated and soft, add a squeeze of anchovy paste and lemon. Pulse a few times in the food processor and eat on crusty bread or bake onto chicken breasts. Ignore comments from children who do not enjoy it.

Note: *If you want to use jarred artichoke hearts, do so, but drain and pat dry before proceeding.*

Soup's On

Adam is using our only female child to stomp down the leaves in the recycling yard waste bag. He, Daniel, and Jamie are raking and shoving the leaves into the sack and then, when the bag's about to burst with fall's shedding, Adam picks Julia up by the waist and puts her in the chest-high bag to make more room. She finds this hysterical—and it actually serves a good purpose.

I've been inside, sliding some lentils around in a pot with a few other items and now emerge to nurse Will on the porch steps before taking a turn with the rake. Julia collects a bouquet of bright leaves for me, carefully carrying them over. "I got these for you," she tells me, her hair illuminated in the sunshine.

"Thanks, Jules," I tell her. "These are so colorful." These are the last of the good fall leaves; soon the only ones on the ground will be the raggedy brown ones. The sign of winter coming, of gray days and lost mittens. I hold Julia's bouquet in one hand, the baby in the other, and watch with half horror and half amusement as Jamie's current armful of leaves goes not into the brown paper bag but onto his brother's head.

"Hey—stop it!" Adam says to Jamie. He hands over the big rake as punishment.

Daniel returns Jamie's favor, and the yard is a wrestling pen complete with Julia as the mini referee.

"Daniel's not being fair," she says. "He took leaves from the bag."

I take this as my cue to check the soup.

A couple of hours later, I'm back in the kitchen about to serve lunch.

"How'd the soup turn out?" Adam wonders, poking his nose into the oversize pot. He goes to the fridge, spies a naked chicken, and comments, "That's not cooked."

I raise my eyebrows and nod slowly. "Um, I know that. The chicken's for dinner—it takes two seconds to make." He doubts me with a turn of his head. "Fine—not two seconds but not long. I'll do it later. With apricots and sage?" He shrugs.

Adam and I do the last of the darting back and forth from the leaf-filled yard to the inside of the house while Will enjoys the last few minutes of his nap and the older kids wash their hands in preparation for a meal. They appear to be competing for who can have the most yard in their hair.

"The bad news is this," I tell them, "if there was a competition to see who could create a food that looks the most like vomit, I would win with this soup." I stir the clumpy mess. "The good news is that it tastes really good."

Adam, loath to eat *a* lentil, let alone a bunch of them, dutifully shovels a mouthful in. "Hey—it's really good!"

"Thanks!" I beam.

"And, actually, it's good news all around—even if it does look like throw-up. I mean, you'd win that competition. If you're entering a competition like that, you don't want to come in third. . . ." Adam stands up to get Will from his crib. We can hear Will babbling away. With a dull plastic knife, Julia cuts up some herbs to aid with the chicken later, and Daniel asks if the sage and rosemary is from the leaf bag. Later, I'll rub the chicken inside and out with the sea salt, make a sauce with apricot preserves mixed with teriyaki, and we'll eat the crispy dinner with leaves still tucked into the kids' hair. But for now we have lunch.

Jamie tests the soup and serves himself a giant bowl. Julia nods that she likes it and wants it for lunch. Will looks around but says nothing much in the way of words, and Daniel—who was saying no before he even walked into the room—agrees to eat a spoonful. Everyone watches as he winces and slides it into his mouth.

"Try it and you may, I say," Adam says, quoting *Green Eggs and Ham* and causing the oldest child to roll his eyes.

Daniel looks like the Godfather of soup, hands on the table, his shoulders squared. "OK," he says, his hands in a deal-making gesture. "I'll have it."

Gross-Looking but Very Delicious-Tasting Red Lentil Soup

½ tsp. each turmeric, cumin, and coriander	6 cups good chicken or veggie stock
1 finely chopped onion	1 dried bay leaf
1 chopped shallot	1½ tsp. dried mustard
2 cloves garlic, mined	1 dash chili powder
olive oil	½ tsp. lemon juice
2 cups red lentils (they cook quickly and turn to mush)	sea salt and pepper to taste

In a large pot, heat the turmeric, cumin, and coriander dry. Stir until spices are fragrant—about 1 minute. In the same pot, sauté onion, shallot, and garlic in some olive oil. Add red lentils. Cover with stock. Add bay leaf and bring to a boil. Lower heat to simmer and cover the pot. Let cook for about 25 minutes. Stir and add the dried mustard, chili powder, and lemon juice, salt and pepper to taste. Let cook more, adding a bit more stock, depending on how thick you like the soup. (Adam likes to be able to have a fork stand up in it.)

Note: *If you like, serve this on a small pile of greens, such as arugula or baby spinach; the greens will wilt, color the soup, and taste good.*

Rosemary-Sage-Apricot Crispy Chicken

There are few scents as homey as a chicken roasting in the oven. This dish can be prepared all at once—in which case you slather the chicken with the sauce before roasting and baste a few times while it cooks—or add it afterward. The second way provides a crispier skin but the first way is delicious too, and you have the satisfaction of knowing the meal's done as soon as it comes out of the oven.

3 tbsp. teriyaki sauce	1 roasting chicken (I use a 5–8 lb.)
⅓ cup good apricot preserves	1 bunch sage
1 tsp. olive oil	1 stem rosemary
salt	pepper

Heat oven to 450°. Mix teriyaki, preserves, olive oil, and a bit of salt with fork and warm (in microwave or on stovetop) until a bit thinner.

Wash and pat-dry roasting chicken. Place on roasting rack breast-side up. Pat-dry bird again. Carefully tuck a few sage leaves under the breast skin and into the cavity. Do the same with the rosemary stem. Rub inside and out with salt and pepper. Place in oven for about 15 minutes until skin is browning and starting to crisp.

Lower oven to 350° and let cook for about 75 minutes, depending on size, until juices run clear. If you are doing the easy method, at this point, you pour the sauce all over the chicken and baste a couple of times as the bird cooks. If you want to have a crispier chicken, keep the sauce warm in a saucepan and pour it on when the chicken is fully cooked or serve heated on the side.

Words We Can't Pronounce

The day before Halloween, I pick Daniel up from kindergarten with an unnamed treat in my bag. I tell him I have something to share with him and he beams from the backseat, but I can't read the name on the wrapper. This is because I do not speak nor understand Icelandic.

"So you don't even know what it is?" Daniel is incredulous. "But you know a lot of foods!"

"Not this one." I hold the foil-wrapped parcel in my palm. It is heavy for a candy bar. "A friend of mine gave it to me." I tell him about my friend and fellow writer, Steve Almond, who wrote a book called *Candyfreak* that details his lifelong obsession with all things Wonka or otherwise. The night before I was at a book reading, and Steve was there. He is the only person I know who is never without candy and, since the publication of his book, he hardly buys it anymore. People just send him things and he either eats them or gives them out. I pulled from my bag one of my own candy favorites—a Curly Wurly. Normally, I would never part with one, since they are hard to come by here, but my dad's recent trip to London has served me well. He came back with lots of goodies—Branston Pickle to put on our cheese sandwiches, Jammy Dodgers to try later, Lemon Curd for toast, and lots of Curly Wurlys.

Steve and I brokered a deal. I would give him my braided, chocolate-covered Curly Wurly and in return I would get . . .

"This?" I held the brick of foil and turned it over.

Steve shrugged. "It's Icelandic."

"I know." Having spent a bunch of time in Iceland, I have a fondness for the country, its people, and its food. Back before I had kids, my father and I went on a hiking trip to Iceland. Most days we trekked six to eight hours and were ravenous. The food was simple and stunning and tasted wonderful the way all things do when you've been very active. Sure, the landscape is odd and startlingly diverse—at turns black volcanic rock and lush green moss—and of course the people are great. But the food! For breakfast we had smoked salmon, cheese, and brown bread with tomatoes. For lunch we had thick-cut bread with more fish or cheese and dark jam with cucumber slices on the side, and for snacks or nearly at every meal, I had skyr. Skyr is a thick yogurt, similar to Greek, but very high in protein and naturally non-fat. I loved the creaminess, the smooth texture, the comfort of flavors—it was served plain, and we would mix a drop of raspberry jam into it.

For years, I waxed poetic about skyr to anyone who would listen, and one day Adam returned from our local market with the good news that they were stocking the stuff. I worried when I rushed over and bought it that it wouldn't live up to my memory. The last time I'd had it was when Adam and I went back to Iceland a few years earlier for my birthday. While I balked at the price (Who pays nearly three dollars for a cup of yogurt? Answer: I do), I bought it anyway and once the kids had seen me loving it, they asked for a taste. The packages come with a foldable spoon that is secured in the top and come in a choice of flavors—vanilla, strawberry, plain, and blueberry, which is my favorite. The kids scarf down any and all of them. Then again, they've wolfed down other Icelandic items—like Matarkex, which not only has been in production for seventy-five years but also holds the impressive claim of being "the second most popular biscuit in Iceland!" Keep in mind there are only 301,000 people in an entire country that is only slightly smaller than the state of Kentucky (whose population is well over four million). All I'm saying is, they know a good biscuit and an even better dairy product when they see it. Or make it.

"So, is it chocolate?" Daniel is hopeful and asks to hold the candy bar. I unbuckle and go to the back of the minivan, where he's strapped into his booster. Pulled over on the side of the road underneath trees shedding their leaves, we examine the wrapper. The foil cover crinkles, the purple and white gleaming in the sun. "What does that say?"

I shake my head. "I just don't know."

"Call your friend. Maybe he knows."

I could call Steve, but I know from our brief conversation last night that I shouldn't have high hopes for this confection. Culture dictates the sweet tastes of each country—Germany loves chocolate and fruit mixed, England loves its Cadbury and Turkish Delight, and Iceland loves its black licorice. I, however, can't stand the stuff. I want to prepare Daniel for potential disappointment. "Danny, I have to say, this might not be that good."

He shrugs. "But it's candy, right?" Translation: How bad could it be?

I nod and take the bar from him. "Let's smell it."

We do, and Daniel spies the chocolate covering when I open it. We break off a thick, chewy piece that scatters chocolate flakes onto my pants, the car floor, Daniel's thighs. We place the pieces into our mouths. I am the first to break into it but try hard to keep my revulsion to myself as Daniel considers it. The chocolate coating is fine; it's the dark black raw, unprocessed licorice that perhaps only those in Reykjavík could love.

"Blech! Eww!" Daniel looks for somewhere to spit out his bite. I hand him a crumpled-up napkin.

"Yuck!" I shudder and show my true feelings. The taste is so bad, I cannot think of words in English or any other language to describe the foul taste and the ongoing aftereffects. "You know there's a vegetable called fennel that kind of tastes like this?"

Daniel looks horrified. "Well, don't make it for me."

"I usually don't like it at all, but I had it once in London with Grandpa and it was sugary." Daniel perks up. "So maybe I'll make it soon?" He shrugs.

"Your friend gave you something gross." Daniel cannot face putting his tongue back into his mouth where the bad taste lingers.

"He did. But it's not his fault; he didn't know how it would taste."

"Usually candy is so yummy." Daniel wipes the last of his distaste onto his sleeve.

"You know who would love that bar?" He looks at me in disbelief—who could love such a thing? "Grammie." My mom loves black licorice in all forms—Good n' Plenty, black jelly beans. "And Aunt Kathy. She even eats black jelly beans!" Daniel grimaces. "And Grandma Ruth." My mom's mother loves it too. Clearly, the gene skipped over me.

"Can I have something regular when we get home?"

I tell him sure and think that maybe it's not such a bad thing to have a candy bar turn out to be disgusting. Maybe having Daniel (who is the kid who has snuck Halloween treats into his bed thinking I wouldn't somehow find the wrappers, who always wants one more piece) know that not all things labeled candy are sweet and pleasing to him is OK. "Isn't it funny," I tell him, "that kids in Iceland probably would love to have that whole bar?"

"Yeah," he says. "Probably they'd choose to take it to the movies as their one special thing."

When I pull the car into the driveway, we race inside the house and search for something—anything—to take away the remaining yuck in our mouths.

"Milk?" Daniel tries it but it doesn't work. "I can still feel it in there." He describes it with his fingers, roiling them around squidlike.

"Here." I hand him a roasted fava bean.

He gladly accepts, chews it, and smiles. "Now, these are really good. Spicy! But you know I kind of like spicy."

I crunch away on a few of the beans hoping their toughness won't crack a filling, relieved to be rid of the noxious taste. It's always good to try new things, even if all you come up with is the knowledge that you won't ever trade your best candy for someone else's. Later that night, I write Steve Almond an e-mail:

> *I believe Bono summed it up when he asked the questions, "Did I disappoint you? Leave a bad taste in your mouth?" The answer, sadly, is yes on both fronts. That was possibly the worst tasting candy I've ever encountered.*

In the morning, I find Steve's reply:

> *I never promised you a licorice garden.*

Crunchy Snacking Beans (Roasted Fava Beans or Chickpeas)

These fava beans make for a crunchy snack that easily rids the mouth of black licorice remnants. You can substitute chickpeas or play around with other kinds of beans. If you want a mixture of sweet and savory, dust the finished product with a bit of sugar and cinnamon and stick them in the oven for five more minutes. If you want a bit of spice, try a light dusting of chili powder and turmeric in addition to the salt.

1 pound fava beans or chickpeas	olive oil
	sea salt

If using dried beans, soak them overnight in water. Preheat oven to 350°. If you have fresh fava beans, remove them from their pods. If using canned, rinse, drain, and pat very dry. Salt and boil some water, drop the beans in, and let them cook for a few minutes until soft but not mushy. Remove from heat and douse with cold water so you can handle them. Dry completely. With a very light hand, drizzle a bit of olive oil on the beans until just coated. Place beans in single layer on cooking sheet. Sprinkle with sea salt. Cook for 30–40 minutes or until beans are dry and starting to crack. Let cool completely prior to moving the beans or eating them. Store in a glass jar to keep crisp.

Nutmeg-Sugared Fennel

I loathe even the scent of anything anise-flavored, but near-candying the fennel brings out nutty undertones. The kids enjoyed the "crunchy-sugary" but also liked being able to identify the different bulb at the store the next time we went.

1 fennel bulb	½ tsp. sugar
1 tbsp. olive oil	dash salt and fresh pepper
¼ tsp. nutmeg	1 tsp. water
1 tbsp. brown sugar	

Slice the top and bottom ends of the fennel off and discard. Slice the white part of the bulb into strips and plunge into boiling water for 2 minutes. Remove (draining but not patting dry) and place into pan with olive oil and grated nutmeg, and heat on high for 1 minute. Once sizzling, add the sugars and toss to coat, and a dash of salt and a turn from the pepper mill. Add drips of the water to keep the fennel loose as needed. Serve hot.

Note: *This dish is a nice side with creamy polenta and roast chicken.*

A Hard Day's Journey into Night

John, Paul, George, and Ringo are standing on the front porch. They are not about to Love-Love-Me-Do, not about to harmonize and make me swoon with their Mod hair and weeping guitars. Rather, the Fab Four, my fab four, are about to go trick-or-treating.

Jamie, Daniel, Julia, and Will have never been particularly character-crazy. That is, I've not been stitching Mutant Turtle costumes or rushing to the store to plunk down money so my kids can dress up as the latest on-screen superhero or villain. Adam and I keep it fairly old-school, waiting for the kids to think of what they want to be and then trying to make the costumes at home. In past years, these costumes have included a brown owl (Daniel, complete with felt wings), Charlie Brown (Jamie, in a yellow T-shirt on which I drew a zigzag line—he held a sign that read UGH over his head), a silvery blue fish (Jamie) and a fisherman (Daniel), a "blue girl" (Julia, in every article of clothing that is her favorite color), and various members of the Red Sox. As their Beatles obsession continues, the bigger kids announced one morning over buckwheat pancakes that they would be banding together this year, each one dressing as his or her favorite band member. They gobbled up the buckwheat despite my concerns over the dark color of the pancakes, the black flecks, the different taste.

Remarkably, there were no arguments about which kid would get to be which Beatle.

"I'm John Lennon," Daniel said. "I've got the glasses, and anyway, I can sing like he did." The others nodded.

"Since my hair is getting kind of long"—Jamie brushes the front over his eyes—"I'm Paul. Plus, Daniel and I are like the lead singers, because we're oldest." The gentle swoop of his hair is just like mid-era Paul, and he's all charm—blond, but otherwise the pinup boy. Daniel is daring, adorable but with an irreverent streak—who better to play John?

"I get to be Ringo!" Julia slammed her palms on the table as though calling "Bingo!"

"Is he your favorite?" I'd asked, wanting to make sure she wasn't being cornered by her brothers.

Julia's smile tells her true feelings about the overlooked Beatle. "I just like Ringo, that's all," she says, then reconsiders, "And it's easier to carry a drumstick. If I was going as George Harrison, I'd have to use a guitar. George Harrison wrote 'Here Comes the Sun' and 'Something,' which is about Grandpa Rick's friend, and so I will wear a turtleneck and carry a guitar and so that's OK." Julia, while being nearly four years old and quite imaginative, does state the truth. My dad happens to be friends with Pattie Boyd, who was married to Eric Clapton, who stole her away from her first husband, George Harrison, and about whom "Something" and "Layla" and other various songs were written. The kids have glommed onto this fact because, I think, it somehow brings them closer to the Beatles. Anyway, it was sorted: Daniel would be John, Jamie as Paul, Julia as Ringo and Will, by default, would be George.

"Maybe we can shove a drumstick in the Bjorn," Adam reasoned during dinner.

"Will needs a guitar if he's George," Daniel insisted.

Halloween is a Wednesday this year; Adam is home and I am working, but I stop early so I won't miss the fun. Before committing to shepherding the kids around town and nibbling SweeTarts, Twizzlers, and Charleston Chews, we have a simple dinner of easy risotto. I like risotto not only because it is delicious and, despite rumors, easy to make, but also because it has the elements of comfort food while still feeling somewhat special. Plus, you can add whatever you want to it—sweet corn, asparagus in spring, all manner of cheeses, onions, chicken, salmon. Tonight, we're trying salmon, sweet corn, and onion, sprinkled with some grated cheese and served with roasted broccoli.

The myth of risotto is that you need to stand by a pot for twelve hours and stir until your forearms threaten to rubberize. The reality is, it's a dish that isn't complicated and if you make it once, you realize you can make it again. Arborio rice has a greater starch content than your average other rice, and this is what helps make a creamy liquid that is key to risotto. Sometimes I use barley, which tastes hearty and is filling and higher in fiber, but it doesn't produce the traditional creaminess for which risotto is famous. There are other rice varieties used for risotto, Carnaroli or Vialone Nano, but what I have in the house most often is Arborio.

So rather than worry that making rice is suddenly complex, you can sauté some chopped onion and garlic in a bit of olive oil at the bottom of a big pot, add two cups of Arborio rice, and let this cook for a few minutes, until the rice is coated and the onions and garlic are cooked but not brown. Then you can add a cup of good stock and a hearty splash of white wine. This has to be absorbed while you stir, but then once this has happened, you can pour in five or six more cups of stock, bring to a rapid boil, then cover and reduce heat to simmer and *do not lift the cover.* When the liquid is absorbed and the rice mostly cooked (you want a bit of bite to it), you take the cover off and add in whatever you like—fresh corn from the cob (or canned/ frozen), asparagus tips, broccoli florets, shreds of prosciutto, sautéed chicken, peas, mushrooms, mozzarella, or any other item you have in the pantry or fridge waiting to be fashioned into dinner. If you have the time, then by all means you can add the liquid one ladle at a time and relish the slow cooking until the liquid is absorbed save for the creamy starchy sauce.

Tonight, I've cubed and pan-cooked some wild salmon, so I toss the fish into a serving bowl and let the kids use tongs to add the protein to their otherwise vegetably dish. Sometimes I top the risotto with a tiny grating of nutmeg, other times cracked pepper or cheese, or I serve it over greens such as wilted chard or baby spinach. Today, we grate some Parmigiano-Reggiano on top and dig into the salmon risotto.

Everyone has two servings, except Will, who is still getting used to his mushy oatmeal and puréed green beans. The kids are so excited about the upcoming jack-o'-lantern lighting, the beckoning of candy, and illicit school-night darkness, that I probably could have served them anything and they'd have eaten it. Anything, that is, except for peas. Those I believe Daniel would decline even if he were starving in the desert.

After the meal it's time to help with costumes. Daniel and Jamie pull black turtlenecks out of their drawers and Julia finds a dark green one. Guitars are located, both with missing strings. Jamie dons my dad's old suit vest, which we have because I wore it in high school (cringe) when I went through a post–Annie Hall men's-fashion-on-women-is-sexy phase (more cringe), and tried to tailor it myself while wearing it (ouch). It fits Jamie perfectly.

"Let's go already." Daniel poses with his tattered old guitar, knees bent more like Elvis than John Lennon. He strums and sings, *"It's been a hard day's night!"*

Julia follows with, *"I been sleepin' like a dog!"*

Jamie turns to me. "Maybe I shouldn't be Paul McCartney."

"Well, we can't really switch now," I say, and have Adam hold Will so I can light the jack-o'-lanterns. Jamie's has a wicked grin. Daniel's is smiling. Adam's is eerie. I didn't do one, because I was working. Julia's is a simple capital J.

"But I don't—I already wore this to the school Halloween party." The Friday before, Jamie had gone off to school as the lone musician amongst a vanful of otherworldly creatures with superpowers. I didn't mention that the Beatles have more collective power than Spidey, Batman, Mutant Turtles, and Ninjas.

"You look great!" I reassure him.

Jamie's eyes well up. "But I don't look like a Beatle."

Adam's about to launch into the tirade of making one's bed and lying in it and how we have to go and can't he just take a picture of all the kids, and then Daniel offers, "Do you need to have my guitar, Jamie?"

Jamie, touched by Daniel's generosity, calms down and sighs. "I think I'm just going to be a ghost."

Which is how, ten minutes before we trek out into the suburban dusk to beg semi-strangers for candy (could we think of a worse tradition in terms of teaching kids safety?), Jamie comes to be wearing a pillowcase. This is not just any pillowcase. This is my survived-four-pregnancies, extra-long, body-pillow-shaped pillowcase that I have sacrificed and cut into— another marker of leaving that part of my life behind. The child-bearing. The pregnancy. The belly supported at night by a pillow that hoarded mattress space and competed with Adam for rights to touch me.

"Are you sad you're cutting it up?" Jamie asks, remembering how his mother used to cling to the pillow.

I twist my mouth and draw circles where his ghost-eyes will be. "About the pillowcase? Not really. But it's weird to be done with that part."

"Maybe you and Daddy will make more babies," he suggests, his words muffled as he tries to twist the case over his Paul McCartney garb.

"I think we're all set," I tell him, and I mean more than the costume.

Now we're on the porch, all six of us ready to go. Amidst the clusters of pumpkins and fall mums, the leaves tumbling in the windy yard, three Beatles and one ghost of Paul McCartney are set to go. I wear Will in the Bjorn and by the time we get to the second house, Adam is schlepping one of the guitars (Julia can't manage her candy bag *and* the instrument she insisted on bringing) plus I have the drumstick in my hair that Dan gave the kids from his practice set back in Indiana. When everyone finds out what Daniel and Julia are, Jamie begins to lose interest in his costume. By the end, his ghost-eyes are twisting to the side of his head, and he's stuck in the case, so we take it off.

"Let's see . . ." The woman at the door studies the group. "Guitars, turtlenecks . . ."

Julia giggles, unable to contain her excitement. "We're the Beatles. He's John Lennon who got shot but he's just pretending now and Will is George Harrison but my mom's carrying him and Jamie was a ghost but now he's back to being Paul McCartney and I'm Ringo."

The woman is slightly agog.

"Trick or treat," Daniel says. When the woman at the door offers the bowl of candy, the kids actually remember to say thank you (after a multitude of reminders) and we cluster-walk home. People are usually split into two camps when they see our big brood out and about, particularly if I'm alone with the kids or Adam is. Response from people in the market or on the sidewalk or the doctor's office is either—Wow, don't know how you do it/strong woman kind of thing, or else it's a look of sheer pity and the general notion that I am/we are nuts. But tonight, a parent with two kids eyes us and says, "Big crew!"

"Yeah," Jamie says. "We're the Fab Four."

"You've got the perfect number for that, don't you?" The parent goes off in search of treats for his own kids. And we all—Beatles, former ghosts, and parents—make our way back home for treats.

Salmon Risotto

This is not a fussy dish—in fact, you can swap chicken for the salmon or use asparagus instead of broccoli, add in a few handfuls of baby spinach or chopped red pepper at the end, or use up leftover cheese ends you have around.

In a heavy-bottomed pot, sauté in a splash of good olive oil:

1 large onion, chopped

1 clove garlic, minced

2 cups Arborio rice (or Carnaroli or barley)

Do not let it brown. When translucent, add:

1 cup good stock (fish, vegetable, or chicken)	Hearty splash of white wine

If you have the time, add one cup (or ladleful) of stock at a time, waiting until each is absorbed before adding the next, until you've put in about 5–6 cups and the rice is mostly cooked.

If you want the quick method, stir as you add and continue stirring until first cup of liquid is incorporated into rice. Then pour in 5–6 more cups of stock. Bring to a rapid boil. Cover immediately. Reduce heat to a simmer and do not lift the cover.

When the liquid is absorbed and the rice mostly cooked (you want a bit of bite to it), take the cover off and add in whatever you like. I used some wild salmon that I pan-cooked and then cut into bite-size pieces for the kids, but you could cook whole fish and place it directly on top for a nicer looking dish.

Some ideas for additions include:

Sautéed leeks (serve this topped with white, flaky fish such as cod) and baby spinach (it will wilt when added and the pot is covered while you set the table)

Fresh corn from the cob (or frozen) with asparagus spears or baby bok choy

Leftover roasted chicken with caramelized onions

Frozen peas and prosciutto

Arugula and crumbled Gorgonzola

Mushrooms, shallots, and venison (You don't have venison lying around? Me neither!)

Bits of cheeses—mozzarella, Brie, sharp cheddar, and so on

Late-Night Snacks

Back from yet another trip to London to comfort my dad and help with Min, I'm in the kitchen with the kids having them sample some foods from my youth.

"These are Jammy Dodgers," I say, and show them the red-and-yellow sleeve of cookies.

"Oh, cool, a heart!" Julia sticks her small finger into the jam-filled hole and then licks it.

"These are so good." Daniel rubs his belly.

"Jammy Dodgers!" Jamie puts on a fake English accent. "These are so much better than the dog-food sticks you gave us."

"They weren't dog food," I explain for what feels like the twelfth time. "They're called Twiglets, and they're yummy. Or at least I think so." Twiglets are my favorite chip-type snack from England. Knobby and brown like, well, twigs, they are salty, but more than that, they are richly flavored with—and I know this isn't the best ad copy—yeast extract. If you've tried Marmite and loved it, these are the snacks for you. My friend Juliet sends them to me along with Curly Wurly bars, and my recent trip produced many a new food item to share.

Min is living day to day, her quality of life impaired by a massive stroke, and my days in London were spent holding her hand, talking to her, keeping my dad company through his lonely and painful hours bedside, and—for breaks—walking the aisles of the local food shops. No matter what is happening, everyone needs to eat. I would forage for snacks and bring back to my dad miniature sugar-encrusted waffles, crisp Lady apples, sharp cheddar sandwiches. So the kids try Twiglets and Jammy Dodgers, Duchess ginger biscuits and Bird's Custard, which is nice over berries or cut-up banana. The younger kids are asleep and I've chosen to keep Daniel and Jamie up a bit late tonight.

"At some point I'll make you guys my favorite English dessert. Sticky toffee pudding." Their eyes grow wide. They are not well-versed in pudding, because I don't buy prepackaged pudding cups and have only made from scratch butterscotch, vanilla, and coffee a few times. "It's not *pudding* pudding," I try to explain while contending with the hollow sadness of jet lag, of travel, of bringing only bad news home. "Sticky toffee pudding is more like a butterscotch brownie with sauce."

But I don't make that for them this particular night. Instead, I tuck Julia into bed and bring the boys downstairs to the kitchen. It's Tuesday and Adam is working late. I sit Daniel and Jamie down at the kitchen table and hand them paper and pencils.

"Listen," I say, and my voice starts to waver. "You know I got back from seeing Min not too long ago . . . but I'm going to go back in a week or so."

"Again?" Daniel's mouth is open.

"Wait. Let me tell you something." I crouch down so I am eye-level with them. They wait patiently for me to explain. "This last time, I went to keep Grandpa Rick company."

"Because he's sad, right?" Jamie asks. He fiddles with the pencil until I go on.

"He *is* sad. When I go next week, I'm going for me."

"How come?"

I sigh. "To say good-bye." The boys look at each other. They look at me. Adam and I have discussed this, and we both feel that the kids are not old enough to see just how sick Min is, to deal with the flights and the fact that she can't really speak above the occasional whisper, and she's lost her ability to walk and cannot eat for herself. Being in her hospital room with her I was struck—am struck—by the intimacy of feeding someone who is ill. And how different from feeding a baby. Min would open her mouth and I could fork in whatever the tray had on it—her favorite was smoked trout, though this was not a dish she craved prior to her illness. Maybe the smoky flavor and salt tasted good. Maybe it was easy to chew. She would pat the back of my hand and ask for more, or whisper for a drink. As I wheeled her around dank, dark-at-three-in-the-afternoon Marylebone High Street, London never seemed so off-kilter to me, but then we'd stop for cappuccino and she'd want me to spoon in the frothy foam and a quiet calm would settle over everything. But the kids do not need to see this. Even though we have been open with them about the gravity of the situation and Min's impending death, we would rather they keep in mind her vitality, the walks and long lunches in Italy.

"Three months ago we were in Italy eating gelato with her," Jamie mumbles. We take a few minutes to talk about her, about Italy, about what we did there, about what we ate there. Jamie starts to talk about making hummus with her and then stops.

"I know. It's so hard, sweetie." I take his hand. "It's really important when you love someone to tell them how you feel. It's important for them and for you, for your own heart." Jamie nods. "So what I thought we'd do tonight is have you both write Min a letter."

"Because we're not going to see her ever again?" Daniel says, and starts to cry because it's not so much a question as it is an acknowledgment.

"Right," I say. "This is a good-bye letter. You don't want someone to leave without a chance to say good-bye, so we'll write to her."

"Will you read this to her when you see her?" Jamie is poised to write.

"If you want me to, I will." They nod. Jamie begins immediately, his breath a bit jagged, his mouth lined in jam and crumbs. I sit at the table and take the pencil from Daniel. "Tell me what you want to say and I'll write it."

"No," he says and takes the pencil back. "I want to write it all." He thinks for a minute. "I know how to write 'love,' you know." He writes his memories all by himself, spreading them out over page after page, only able to fit one word per page with his careful printing. "See? I can even do 'I love you' without any help." He pauses, gripping the pencil. "But how do you spell 'I will miss you'?"

Coffee-Vanilla Custard

My grandma Ruth showed me how to make coffee and butterscotch custard in her house in Maine. I remember sitting in her sunroom with my own ramekin and trying to make the custard last as long as possible. She also made steamed puddings for me—chocolate-coffee (based on the recipe in The Joy of Cooking*) and prune. The sweetness of the vanilla cream is heightened by the addition of espresso or coffee.*

Let 1 vanilla bean, split down the middle and scraped, sit overnight in 1¾ cups cream, 1 tablespoon cold espresso or strong coffee, and 4 tablespoons sugar.

The next day (or two days later), in a medium-size saucepan, bring the mixture to a boil as you whisk and turn off the heat. Meanwhile, mix:

> 5 egg yolks and ¼ cup
> superfine sugar together

Add (and dissolve in):

> 1 tbsp. instant coffee
> (for kids, use decaf!)

Slowly add the hot cream mixture to the egg yolks, whisking well as you go. Once combined, put mixture back into the saucepan, heating on low and continuing to whisk. This will cook the yolks through but not so that they look like scrambled eggs. When the mixture is thick enough that it coats the back of a spoon, let it cool partially, and portion into ramekins. Dust with cinnamon or grated chocolate before serving.

This dessert can be enjoyed alone with a book or a view. It is also easy to feed to someone else.

In Transit

The following are questions posed to me during the morning and afternoon shuttle runs:

"Mom, can you change what you think about God, or do you have to pick one way and keep it like that?"

"Mom, what's an A-hole?"

"Mummy? What's your favorite dessert ever?"

The above is a succinct explanation of why we will never (*never!*) install a DVD player in the car. You've got everyone contained under one roof, all within earshot, with nowhere to go, able to avoid eye contact if they're embarrassed or want to talk without a confrontation, trapped for the hours' long drive in their own seats, and you're going to put on a *movie?* No, thanks. I'd rather sit in silence, listen to music, fight over which music to listen to, and most of all, talk. But back to the above questions. My answers were, in order:

One. "You can think whatever you want about God. You can feel whatever you want about God. And you don't have to make up your mind now or ever. It can keep changing. There isn't a rule about it. Most things in life you don't have to decide about right now. Even grown-ups can change their minds about things."

Two. "You mean what does it stand for?" Nod from nearly nine-year-old. I approach this the way I have other queries—simply and honestly. "It stands for asshole, honey."

Follow-up question one: "And what is that, exactly?" [giggle] "I mean, it's a swear, that I know."

"Well, it isn't a very nice word."

Follow-up two: "But is an A-hole actually on your body?"

"Um, yes. It's in your bottom. Where the poop comes out." I take a sip of morning coffee and wonder what on Earth is coming next.

"And what does it mean if someone says someone's an . . . you-know-what."

"Sometimes people say someone's an A-hole if they're being rude. If someone's a jerk. Or just a mean person. But it's not something I hope you'll say."

Jamie shrugs from the backseat. "Sure. I mean, I was just wondering."

Three. "You know, this a difficult question for me. It's so hard to choose. You know I love good chocolate-chip cookies. And you know there's the chocolate pudding cake. But my favorite dessert is probably sticky toffee pudding. Remember I told you about it before? I used to get it in England at this tiny little pub, the Compasses, in the countryside where I'd go with Grandpa and Min after a really long hike with Grandpa."

"I want a compass," Jamie says.

"Me too." Julia perks up.

"I want to try sticky toffee pudding." Daniel grins.

And so, without further ado, I set out to buy the ingredients for this warm, sticky, delicious dessert and realized I had all of the things I needed already in the pantry. But that's because I like to snack on dates. If you don't like to snack on dates, or you're not eighty-five years old, chances are you won't have dates in your house on a regular basis and will thus have to make a trip to the store. But it's worth it.

My dad and Min had a cottage in Lower Chicksgrove (Don't you just love the English and their names!) that was about the size of an American closet—that is, tiny but absolutely cozy and beckoning. In my pre-marriage, pre-kid, pre-now days, it was a place to go on weekends, sometimes with friends in tow, other times just for long walks with my dad. Either way, the nights weren't complete without a stop at the Compasses for this rich dessert.

I use Medjool dates because that's what I have on hand, though I'm sure you could use other ones, and dark brown sugar because the depth of brown is one that stays with me even today.

"You remember that all desserts in England are called pudding, right?" The kids nod, eager after our family dinner to try the sticky toffee pudding directly after I pull it from the oven. The top is steaming, the scent fills the kitchen. Will stops crawling to see what the commotion is.

"Can I be served first?" Daniel asks this when the anticipation is just too much to bear.

"Daddy has to try it too," Julia declares.

Adam looks at me. "You think I'll like it?" We are at the stage in marriage when you can pretty much guess what the other person will order, if they'll like it. It is mainly comforting and only slightly stifling. Every once in a while I'm pretty sure we order something against the grain just to shock and surprise each other, to declare there will always be the unknown.

Daniel taps his spoon on the table. "Tell Daddy about the dates."

I try to ignore this because, knowing Adam as I do, I suspect if he's prepped on how many dates went into this, not even the fact that the dish looks like a puffy butterscotch brownie will lure him back. "Let's just all try it while it's warm," I say.

"But there are dates," Daniel insists. "I cut them myself."

The pub served the pudding individually in brick-colored ramekins, which makes sense for a restaurant (where the goal is to cook only what will be used right away) or for a dinner party because with a dollop of ice cream or slosh of rich cream, the personal portions look fancier, but I have poured the whole lot into an oval baking dish. With the oven mitts on, I place the ceramic onto the countertop and scoop the still-steaming caramel-colored sweetness onto plates.

We all try it at the same time. "Is it like what you remember?" Jamie asks.

"Do you taste the dates?" Daniel asks.

"Daniel, there aren't dates in here," Adam says, giving me the look that suggests Daniel's a bit confused. "Hmmmm." Adam gives a murmur of contentment. "It's good."

"Daniel's telling you the truth. There are dates in here." I try not to smirk. "They're cooked."

"Ohhh . . . Daddy ate cooked fruit!" Jamie says, then furrows his brow. "Wait—dates are considered fruit, right?"

"See?" Daniel's satisfied smirk is half over being correct and half about the plate of dessert in front of him.

I touch Adam's shoulder. "I didn't even know it was made with dates until I'd eaten it a hundred times and asked."

"It's like brownie cake," Julia says, her mouth and cheeks speckled with the dessert.

There's a chocolate pudding cake I make in a similar way—you make the dough and put it in the pan, then pour boiling water on top of it, sprinkle it with sugar, and then bake it. This causes the syrupy liquid—in this case a buttery caramel, in the other a thick chocolate pudding—to sink to the bottom. Either way, the results are wonderful, and can be reheated the next day (or later that night if you are so inclined).

I spoon a mouthful in, wishing I'd thought to get some good vanilla ice cream to plunk on top. Did they serve it with cream or ice cream? The details have faded.

"Yum," I say. The warm taste lingers in my mouth and stomach, not really buttery, not particularly date-y, just good. "To answer your question, Jamie, it is just like I remember."

Sticky Toffee Pudding
(as I remember it from the Compasses)

Mix together:

1½ cups chopped dates (approx.)

½ cup milk

2 tsp. vanilla

1⅓ cups flour

1 egg

¾ cup white sugar

½ cup melted salted butter

Pour into buttered baking dish. Cover with:

2 cups boiling water

1½ cups dark brown sugar

a few bits of butter

Do not stir. Bake as-is in 375° oven for about 35 minutes or until middle is set. The whole thing should appear spongy, but cooked through. Serve plain or with cream of some kind, and rest assured you will not taste the dates.

Note: *Compare and contrast with the following chocolate pudding cake, which makes a great big dessert for a great big gathering and demands vanilla ice cream. The kids tried this first one wintry night and smiled with chocolate-smeared faces as we inched toward a new year.*

Chocolate Pudding Cake

First:

2 cups flour

4 tsp. baking powder

1 tsp. salt

1¼ cups sugar

4 tbsp. unsweetened cocoa powder

1 cup milk

4 tbsp. melted butter

Then:

1¾ cups brown sugar   2 cups boiling water

8 tbsp. cocoa

Mix the first seven ingredients and put into a 9 × 13 pan (it will look scant—do not worry). Mix the brown sugar and cocoa and sprinkle on top. Pour the boiling water on top of the cake and put into oven at 350° for 30 minutes. When the cake is baked, the top will be like a brownie and underneath will be a creamy chocolate pudding. Serve with ice cream.

Note: *If you want to reheat the cake, put it in the oven at about 300°. If you are reheating the next day, you can microwave portions of it or heat it in the oven, but add a little more hot water to the top so the pudding part stays creamy.*

How Done Is Done?

The turkey bobs by itself in a big pot of heavily salted water. I've brined the bird each Thanksgiving for the past couple of years, loving the moist meat that results, the crisp skin, the kids' faces upon seeing the bird—

"Take a bath," Daniel says, pointing to it.

The organic twenty-four-pound hulk is ready for the next step. "Just like bathing Will," Julia says. "You need to wash it and pat it dry."

"And then eat it," Jamie chuckles.

"You mean cook it first," Daniel corrects him.

I prep the turkey the day before while Adam does the furniture arranging and the kids argue over who gets to do the place cards. One year Jamie was acting out as we organized the house for Thanksgiving fun (read: craziness), so I gave him a task. "You be in charge of all the place cards—you can doodle, use colors, make up jokes . . ." He was thrilled and sat busying himself for long enough that I could cook without prying him off of a sibling.

One year, ever-verbal Jamie made personalized haikus (my father-in-law's, for example: Papa Peter eats/before everyone else does/slow down, Papa, wait). This year, Daniel wants in on the action and Julia's determined not to be left out. So I divide the names in half, give each boy a list to copy onto slips of paper, and tell Jamie and Daniel to give a couple of the pieces to Julia for decoration. All set.

I go back to the bird, setting it in the pan and wrapping it for tomorrow, when it will cook for a long time. Brining makes stuffing too salty, so I have to ready all of the ingredients for oven-baked dried fruit stuffing. Adam often is so rapt in the meal he finds himself consuming dried fruit (which is not only dried but also then cooked—a double error in his mind), so I don't hold back on the dried fruit challah stuffing. There are apricots and prunes but also thyme and three different types of breadcrumbs. I always try to have some challah to rip up into the stuffing—it adds a sweetness that plays off of the brined meat.

"When will everyone be here?" Daniel asks, his hands covered in marker.

"Soon," Adam says. "They're on their way." Adam spent last night making the same cookies he's made every Thanksgiving since he first learned the recipe in kindergarten. "Chinese cookies" have exactly two ingredients—butterscotch chips and Chinese noodles (the thin, crunchy, unhealthy ones). Back in the days before cooking at school became a food-allergy lawsuit waiting to happen, Adam's teacher had the kids melt the chips, stir in the package of crispy noodles, and scoop spoonfuls of the coated crunch onto wax paper to harden. Adam did the same thing last night, with Jamie stirring, Julia scooping, Daniel mixing, and all of them, Adam included, eating as they went. We now have a pile of the cookies. They resemble bird nests. Adam tried white chocolate, dark chocolate, and milk chocolate chips, but we've all decided the butterscotch is the best. They are not healthy. They are not gourmet. But they work. "Hey," Adam warns now. "Leave the cookies and stop climbing on the couch. People are coming soon."

"When?" Daniel points to his watch.

We've been hosting Thanksgiving for a few years, and the attendees vary only slightly each time. This year we have four generations of family. The thought is at once heart-warming and groan-inducing. There are food preferences: My father-in-law's instinct is to serve himself before anyone else—a source of humor and frustration for everyone else. There are hearing aids for my dad's parents. There's my mom's tiny ninety-three-year-old mother trying not to be bowled over by the kids yet insisting, "I'm fine! I'm fine! Just let me hold on to this chair. . . ." There's Adam's clever if precarious table arrangement based on a trial run at Rosh Hashanah. There's my mother-in-law's overflow of enthusiasm about everything (as Adam said in a toast to her sixtieth birthday, "My mother is so empathetic, she can commune with inanimate objects"). We have my dad, who has left Italy and London after Min's death and moved back to the States for the first time in nearly twenty years. This is his first Thanksgiving in fourteen years without Min—the first of many firsts without her. We have my Brooklyn-cool brother-in-law, Rob, who needs to have his own personal space, even in places where there's none to be found. My brother-in-law is actually one of my favorite people with whom to cook. Rob and I have very similar ideas about food—about being healthy but having fun, about eating well, and about not being too fussy or strict in the kitchen. We are both improvisational cooks who share tasks well.

The swell of noise peaks Thanksgiving morning while the turkey roasts, the vegetables are prepped, the corn pudding cozies up to the bird. My mother-in-law slides her pies onto the counter—glorious apple so filled with the fruit its crust is dome-shaped, crusted with sugar, and for the first time—

"Lemon meringue!" She exudes excitement from her pores. Then she beckons me over. "Just look at the top—it's really beautiful, I have to say." She is always modest about her cooking, but her baking is wonderful. "I thought it'd be fun to try something new, even if it's not very Thanksgiving-y."

I thank her, then shoot Adam a look that says please get the herd out of the kitchen. The kids are on overdrive, racing in their socks around the rooms, popping here and there, screeching and then sitting on laps until they can't take it anymore.

"Is the turkey done?" one of the kids asks.

"Not yet," I say, and send them back to the living room.

"What can I do?" my grandmothers ask. Bev is eighty-five, Ruth is ninety-three. Grandma Ruth used to welcome us to her home with bowls of what she called chocolate-bit cookies, lemon squares, and fresh pumpkin bread. She would bake it in an old coffee can, and we'd fight over who got to eat the extra end pieces she'd slice off first. When Jamie was in preschool, he shared the recipe with his class and it was so well received that they make it every year. Legions of little kids will continue to taste her sweet pumpkin bread for years to come—one of the nicest by-products of recipes, their unending give. Two years ago, Grandma Ruth brought the pumpkin bread, making it herself and wrapping it in tinfoil, schlepping it on the plane from Florida to here. The kids devoured it. My father-in-law got the first slice. This year, she's reverse-migrated, moving back north and into assisted living. No pumpkin bread from her, but I baked one just so she wouldn't think we were doing without.

"You can sit," I tell them. "Just relax—we're fine here."

They're reluctant to do so, and I understand why. Used to be they were the ones throwing the big get-togethers. At my grandma Bev and Papa's, there was happy chaos, the food secondary, a blending of holidays with chopped liver and celery as the hors d'oeuvres, turkey and the dreaded lime Jell-O mold. Grandma Bev made it every year—a big ring of it—the color of heavily chlorinated pool water and flecked with bits of God knows what—cherries? Lemon rind? Raisins? Papa was the only one who ate it, and finally one year, the production of it stopped. The cousins complained: "But . . . but . . . we always have it!" Grandma Bev had shrugged, OK, OK, she didn't know how much it meant to everyone. Maybe we hadn't known either. But the buffet table without the sickly, wobbling mold felt lacking. In the same way we depended on miniature Milky Way bars in the freezer and Silver Bells (their name for Hershey's Kisses) in the butter compartment of their ancient fridge, we needed that mold that went largely unconsumed but widely loved.

At Grandma Ruth and Grandpa Phil's (who died when I was in college) house, for Thanksgiving there was crisp-skinned turkey rubbed with sage butter, chocolate turkeys wrapped in rainbow foil on each plate from my mother, long walks afterward down by the cattails and duck pond by their house in Maine.

"Something smells good," Papa says. "Is the turkey done?" He walks slowly now—he's eighty-eight—but only retired a few years ago.

"Not quite," I say.

"Lovely family." He nods, even though he and I are the only ones in the kitchen at the moment. "And you're all done now, right?"

I had no sooner birthed Will, pushed him out and into the hospital blanket, than people started asking this question. "Are you done now?" Am I a turkey? "But, you know, done like you aren't having any more?" I knew what they meant, but it's difficult to address the answer when I'm only one day postpartum. The truth is, I thought I'd feel . . . more done. I know. I have four. That's a lot of kids. But . . . the babies! The funny expressions as they grow! The incredible sibling connections and family fun in the yard. But yeah, academically, I guess I'm done. "So, do you feel done?" Heather had asked. She wants a gaggle of her own too, and I think she hoped I'd say, "Yes, absolutely." But instead I said the truth. "I know intellectually that I am, but I don't, you know, feel it. But maybe I will."

Papa putters around the kitchen, eyeing this dish, picking at the chopped liver I've set on the table. "So, it's not quite done," he says, meaning the turkey.

I swallow, thinking about how much I love my family as it is—all six of us—but how there's still that pinch of who else might be a part of it. "Not just yet," I say. "Here. Try some homemade cranberry sauce." I lift the lid, take a spoonful, and put it in his mouth.

"Mmmm . . . good." His white beard is flecked with the red stuff, and he leaves.

My mom always made her own—boiling some sugar, water, and the whole berries until thick, adding this (vanilla pod) or that (orange rind) as wanted. It's very easy, and though Adam adores the jellied stuff from the can, there are others who like the whole berry, so we serve both. My mother always served her sauce in a hollowed-out orange—the cranberries pick up the citrus scent and the colors look vibrant—so I do the same. She'll see it when she comes by later.

"I have to eat that corn pudding now!" Daniel cries when he sees it emerge from the oven all brown-topped. The aroma fills the kitchen air and then blends with the others; the baked stuffing, the roasted carrots and Brussels sprouts, the steamed green beans, the crispy potatoes with shallots.

My brother-in-law slips in, helping me shift trays of food, refill wineglasses, bringing in plates. Adam entertains and kid-wrangles, and arranges seating with Jamie, who holds the completed place cards.

By the grace of the kitchen gods, all of the dishes are ready at the same time, and we ferry them to the sideboard—a veritable bounty of the season from which people can serve themselves. There are oohs and ahhs, the occasional "What?" from the hearing-aid contingent; there is a round of "I'm hungry" from the kids; there is a proud and wistful "I can't believe you did this all yourself" from the grandmothers who once did exactly the same. We each sit with our food and Adam stands to talk. He welcomes everyone, says how happy and lucky we are to have this good food, to be together here. He turns to my dad.

"It would be a mistake, though, not to speak for a moment about who isn't here. Tonight we think of Min and remember her, and note that there is a place missing at the table." We take a minute, a glimpse of her appearing in my mind—I can see it on each of the kids' faces—and then we go forward.

As we tuck into the turkey, the sweet potato with apple and marshmallow, the crispy shallots, the satisfying sweetness of the corn pudding, we take turns saying what we're thankful for. I read a letter from the food bank so the kids understand what we've done—we donated Thanksgiving dinners to several local families.

"So they can have this too?" Julia asks, using her fingers for the carrots.

"Yeah because you don't always get to have this if you don't have any food," Daniel says.

We eat, we laugh, we annoy one another, we elbow when my father-in-law is first in line for seconds. We enjoy each salty, savory, sweet, creamy, crunchy, crispy, tart, rich mouthful. My little brother and his wife come by with my mom, and we reach for a few extra dessert plates. All four generations—of people, of foods we're picked up along the way and others we left behind—are crowded around the table. And we are crowded. But that's fine. It's better than fine. It is.

Corn Pudding

This is a variation on a recipe from my mother-in-law, who got it from her friend who had a hand-me-down recipe from someone else. It's that kind of dish. The original called for much more butter and full-fat sour cream, but honestly, this is so sweet and homey, you can leave it as written here. This is neither highbrow nor hard to make. But it is delicious and very kid-friendly. This is easily doubled or tripled.

1 box Jiffy Corn Mix	1 cup low-fat sour cream
1 can creamed corn	1 egg
1 can corn, drained	½ stick butter, melted

Mix ingredients and put into greased ceramic (or other) serving dish—this makes enough for 9 × 9 or 9 × 13 or a nice oval (which I like because I love the crispy edges). Bake at 350° for 45 minutes or until set through.

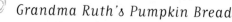 *Grandma Ruth's Pumpkin Bread*

This recipe makes two loaves. You can cook them in bread pans (greased) or, as she did, in a couple of greased coffee cans (the small ones, not the big ones, about 10–15 oz. with paper or plastic labels removed). This bread freezes very well and is good to have on hand for breakfasts or slathered with cream cheese for lunch. This recipe is as she wrote it for me, in her elegant soon-to-be-obsolete script. It includes the following: This is not for every day! So what if it might not be that good for you . . . it will always be delicious.

1 cup oil	1½ cups pumpkin (about one can)
3 cups sugar	
4 eggs	3½ cups flour
1 cup water	2 tsp. baking soda
1½ tsp. cinnamon	1½ tsp. salt
1½ tsp. nutmeg	1 cup raisins

Preheat oven to 350°. Mix oil, sugar, and eggs until smooth. Blend in water, spices, and pumpkin. In another bowl, mix the flour, baking soda, salt, and raisins. Combine and mix batter. Pour into greased tins and bake for one hour. You might also make muffins, which take about half the time.

C'est Parfait

When my husband walks into the kitchen after returning from work he asks the usual: "How's everything?" Then Adam looks around and asks the unusual: "You been drinking with the kids again?"

There are several wineglasses on the drying rack, but contrary to the appearance, I have not been sloshing back a nice Pinot with the four kids.

Earlier in the day, the scene was this: "When I get my pro ball contract," Jamie starts, as he slings his backpack down in the entryway, "I think I'm going to negotiate some tickets so you and Daddy can come to my games." He pauses, brow furrowed. "They'll let me do that, right?"

I adore that he has the utmost confidence not to question that he will, in fact, play Major League Baseball. He doesn't wonder if he's good enough, if his arm will hold out, if he is next on the very short list of Jewish pros plucked from suburban obscurity and thrust into national fame and fortune. He just wonders if he'll be allowed, when he's making "probably, like, twelve million dollars a year, but only really some of that because some I'll donate—and maybe get you a car or something if you want" to bring us to the game.

"I'm pretty sure you'll be able to get us into the games. Even get us good seats," I assure him, and wander around the kitchen and pantry trying to remember what I was doing. Oh, right, searching for food for tonight's dinner.

Jamie looks relieved. Julia pokes her head into the pantry. "Can we have a special dinner?"

The kids ask me this every so often and the words never mean the same thing. Sometimes there's a hidden agenda—*Please don't make cod, Can we get Chinese?, We want sweets.* Other times they are bored with the staple dishes or hoping we'll go out or that I'll whip up something magnificent in the twenty minutes I have free before the cascade of afternoon homework, orthodontist appointments, and touch football overtakes us all.

"What kind of special?" I pick her up and hold her close to me. She wraps her legs around my waist and I tuck my face into the small of her neck, loving the soft warmth of her skin, her disheveled hair, her palms that are sticky with something like jam except that Julia doesn't like jam.

"Special like we don't normally have it or like you have it in a special way." Daniel weighs in from the kitchen, where he is playing at the sink with his "water-living creatures." This is his name for the motley crew of plastic seahorses, manta rays, sharks, fish, whales, which go together, and his frog, giraffe, and diver that don't. I let him keep them in a small bowl by the sink and he will pull a kitchen chair over, add a drop of bubbles to the dish, then splurt some water in and amuse himself with animal/fish dialogue and sea scenarios for a good twenty minutes.

The meal is getting more and more complicated. "I'm not sure about what to make," I say. If there's too much pressure on it, any meal will fail, so I shrug. "Maybe I'll just make something I used to make before you were born."

"On the boat?" Jamie asks. He's ready for school now and by the door.

I nod. "On the boat."

"Because you used to be a chef," Daniel says, and hops down, the front of his shirt wet.

"Yep—I did." I swivel around the pantry, checking for ingredients, and take the masses to school.

I used to work on a boat. It's one of those postcollege stories that involves dropping out of graduate school, following a boy to a remote area, and generally scaring the crap out of my parents while learning skills that would ultimately serve me later in life. This was after college but before trekking to India, before returning to graduate school, before hiking in Iceland and before writing books. Before meeting and marrying Adam.

In short, I had a life that didn't involve my kids. My own parents never really experienced this. My older brother was born when my parents were twenty-one years old and I (and then my younger brother) followed a few years later. There was not much exploration pre-marriage. My parents stayed married a long time (think: decades), moved abroad, and ultimately divorced and remarried. But their early histories were all entwined. In fact, most of the people I know from my parents' generation followed the pre-plotted graph—sliding right from school into marriage, often marrying while in school, then having kids and careers. While my mother had a few notebooks from classes she took in her twenties, a gardening journal, and maybe a letter or two, she didn't have the storage bins Adam and I have sorted through.

We came together armed with pots and pans from living on our own, outdated textbooks and crinkled love letters. Photos in which we are embracing other people. Places where we'd ventured with no thought of each other or of the children we would someday have.

I think it will be interesting to see what this means for our offspring. I can remember prowling around my parents' closet (nosy child!) and the attic looking for things—evidence, I assume, of who my parents had been before I'd arrived. Maybe I wanted to snoop—read a mushy missive—or maybe I desired some peek into the adult life that seems so remote when you are a kid who still needs to ask permission for something as basic as a snack.

Back to the boat. It's a long story that I will freely pull out of my pre-marital suitcase when and if I am asked when the kids are teenagers or adults. The work was tough—physically challenging with literal burns and bruises, and emotionally difficult with figurative ones. Despite the bumps and rocky seas, I got an education that is every bit as valuable to me now as my graduate degree. There were very early mornings spent cooking on a diesel stove. There were wondrous sunsets and rainy days with seals chucking around the boat's edge. There was no crying over the real burn I got on my wrist from a skillet, but very real tears over the captain (did I not mention the boy I'd followed was the proverbial captain to my cook?) and his rather loose definitions of fidelity.

But I learned to cook. To be fair, I had taught myself a lot about cooking while living on my own and at college (I used to roast chickens twice a week at Oxford, shoving the raw, albeit wrapped-up, birds into my backpack and scootering home, determined to sort out how to make stuffing without aid of a book or recipe). But this kind of cooking—chef work—was altogether different. Cooking for fifteen people three meals and one high tea a day, six days a week, and forty people for weekly parties, teaches different kitchen skills. I forced myself to make haddock chowder while baking molasses bread and whipping up giant salads with homemade bleu cheese dressing. I planned meals for the week and packed them, in order, in an ice chest, always starting with the most perishable item—fish—and ending with a fabulous brunch, complete with hash made from leftover beef tenderloin.

Like the old love letters, the photographic remnants of previous heartaches, I keep with me this memory of the systematic kitchen.

So tonight, while I have neither time nor employer to impress with deglazed beef medallions or throw together anything with the word ganache in its title, I do want to revisit the past. The past with a twist.

"Whoa . . . what is this?" Daniel's mouth is agape when he enters the kitchen. He is refusing to wash his hands, claiming he "just did about two hours ago!" I've got other fish to fry so I shrug it off.

"We're having wine?" Julia is incredulous.

"This is your special dinner. It's called parfait," I explain.

I serve them each a red wineglass. The bottom layer is about a tablespoon of homemade granola. The next layer is organic vanilla yogurt, followed by a few slices of banana, some slivered red grapes, more granola, more yogurt, some melon squares, a sprinkling of chopped apple, more yogurt and crunch and a dollop of yogurt to finish on top. In the center of the table is a platter of vegetables—broccoli, baby carrots, cucumber slices, leftover asparagus spears. Each child gets a toothpick to use with the vegetables.

"I can't believe we get to eat out of these glasses!" Daniel makes a face as though participating in something illicit, which is a bit how I feel. Sharing my old past with my present, seaming together disparate parts of my life with one dish. I served it on the boat but only as granola—not parfait—and I used to add dried fruit, which is actually quite sugary, so I tend to leave it out most of the time.

"We get toothpicks!" Julia yelps with glee. Such happiness from a box of ninety-nine-cent wooden sticks.

"Did you used to make this on the boat?" Jamie asks. He is shoveling the food in at a rapid rate so the words smush together. He reaches for a broccoli spear.

"I did," I tell them, thinking back to the rocky motion, the tiny galley, the remoteness of my pre-them memories that, while I'm glad they exist, seem incredibly small. Or rather, my present-day kitchen with all of us in it seems to swell. "I made it." I watch them spoon mouthfuls in, see the pleasure they experience with each mouthful. "But not like this."

Granola

This takes all of twenty minutes to make. I make a large batch and store it in an airtight container (or an oversize Ziploc). Funnily enough, because I introduced this at night, I rarely serve it at breakfast. Sometimes it's a quick weekend lunch. Other times, a cool summer dinner. For housewarming or holidays I sift the cooled granola into canning jars, add some chopped-up dried fruit (see below) and tie with a bow for an easy gift.

Measure oil first—this way the honey will slide out easily and make for simple cleanup.

¾ cup canola oil

¾ cup honey

big splash vanilla extract

1 tsp. brown sugar

5½ cups rolled oats (not the quick-cooking ones)

3 cups bran buds (Grape-Nuts)*

handfuls of dried fruit (golden and brown raisins, cranberries, blueberries, chopped apricots, dates, etc.), optional

fruit for layering (bananas, apples, grapes, cantaloupe, honeydew), optional

Note: *The second time I made this was the start of the Great Melon Revolt in which Jamie declared "wet fruit in parfait is the worst thing ever." This has since waxed and waned, but it does haunt an otherwise easy meal.*

Preheat oven to 300°. Heat oil, honey, and vanilla for about 1 minute in the microwave or 2 minutes on the stovetop. In large bowl, mix warm ingredients and add in dry (except for dried fruit). Stir gently until combined. Pour onto a parchment-lined cookie sheet and spread into one layer. Bake for about 25 minutes, shifting/mixing granola a few times. If you need to leave, turn off the oven and it will be fine. If you're home, take it out. You can't mess it up unless you burn it, which I have certainly done both on and off the boat. *Let granola cool completely* before testing or doing anything else to it. The crunch comes only upon cooldown. Once cool, add dried fruit if desired or mix into plain yogurt for a healthy lunch. Feel free to add toasted almonds or sunflower seeds if you like.

---

* This is my normal ratio, but you can add in more oats or cereal—it's not an exact science. I also recently tried adding in my favorite FiberOne, and the results were stupendous! Another point for FiberOne. Really, can I have the endorsement deal, or what? If you want to add in this dose of fiber, just sift a cup or so into the mix—you don't need to alter the wet ingredients at all.

Anchovies, Our Invisible Friends

Julia is on the phone, her small chin nestled against the receiver, her hands gesticulating. "Well, because you know what? That's fine. I get it. I get it." She is spot-on with her mimicry of some of the grown-up phone calls she overhears. Rather than dominating the call, she's just doing all the responses at once. "That's fine. OK, sure. I love you, mwah mwah bye bye." She hangs up.

"Who was that?" I ask while rummaging through the pantry. My mind sifts through possible ingredients for tonight's dinner, the time in which to prepare it dwindling each second as Will's afternoon nap wanes.

Julia looks at me as though I should know better. "Shevago." She waits for me nod, which I do. "You know, Shevago."

Actually, I don't. Shevago appeared this summer rather suddenly one evening when Adam was working late. As I fed Will in his room, the boys played some version of indoor baseball/try to bonk each other, and Julia meandered in and watched the baby nurse for a minute and then reached for the phone. I'd moved it from my room into Will's room based on past experience—inevitably, the phone is silent until I am nursing or changing a wildly explosive diaper. "Can I call someone?" she asked. "Sure," I'd said. "Real or pretend?"

She paused. "Pretend. But I want to press the numbers."

Will gurgled and clutched my shirt. "That's fine, Jules, but don't press the number one." She nodded. I figured that would keep her from actually placing a call. She dialed with purpose, swiftly, and after a few seconds smiled at me and said into the receiver, "Hi!" as if she knew exactly what pretend person was on the other end of the line.

Though my mother tells me I had "a gaggle" of them, I don't remember specific imaginary friends from my own childhood. Adam and I have watched in wonder and amusement as the kids have had their own invisible friends pop up and suddenly recede. Jamie had a plethora of creatures—Bing-Bang was a bird prone to flying in at inconvenient moments, Ging was harmless, and Gayng was Ging's counterpart. Jamie's number-one sidekick was Plum, whom Jamie described as a doctor who worked in an ambulance and ate tofu. It is relevant to point out that Adam was, at the time, in his medical residency and not around as much as he'd like (read: not much) and his schedule was erratic, particularly when doing rotations such as transport, when he rode in, yes, an ambulance and moved patients from one hospital to another. Maybe Jamie's little mind was making sense of the confusing world of parental appearances and disappearances, and perhaps even punishing his father, because Adam loathes tofu. Or maybe Jamie just liked hanging with a guy named Plum.

None of the kids' fake friends have been the kind my little brother Jon had, the sort that sits in the chair next to you and demands to be served a dish of pasta too. Julia's are clearly relegated to the phone and the occasional play date or pretend party ("Bye! I'm going to a party at Shevago's house!") whereas Jamie's zoomed in and out without warning, never stopping for a meal.

Daniel shucked conventional pretend friendship altogether, focusing in on . . . the blender. We have a red Waring blender that was one of my first grown-up, out-of-college-and-in-my-own-apartment, purchases. It was on sale. It had a mark on its base. It made a vaguely worrying burning smell upon use. When we moved into our current house, the red blender took a perch on the pantry shelf, up high out of reach of little hands, its cord wound tightly to avoid the instinct to pull it down. Adam and I noticed that at various points throughout the day, Daniel would slip away—from the living room, from the kitchen, from upstairs. "What's he doing down there?" We'd wonder and, eventually, when we checked it out, we were both surprised, amused, and mildly disturbed by the results.

"He's, you know, talking to the blender," I said to Adam.

"Define 'talking,'" he'd said, every inch the pediatrician looking for clues.

"He says 'hi' to it, and who knows what else."

Adam thought. I thought. We watched and smiled. When you watch your kid making chitchat with an inanimate object, the first response is to laugh. The second response is to worry. After all, there's a fine line between cute and cuckoo, and there's no one better to demonstrate this than a three-year-old kid.

"Daniel?" We'd called him into the living room, casual, not wanting to upset him. "So . . . you like to talk to the blender, huh?"

Daniel nodded, his cheeks bright pink. "Yup."

Adam's voice was soft. "So, what kinds of things do you like to say?"

Daniel thought for a minute, his mouth poised. "So . . . ," he began, his lisp strong, "sometimes I wave to it. Or I say, 'Hello, red blender.'" He studied our faces for signs he was doing anything wrong. We remained neutral. "Or just, I tell it about my day, things like that."

It was sweet. It was charming. It was weird.

"Daniel." Adam slipped into his examination routine. "Now, that's nice that you can talk to the blender." Adam looked at me and I tried not to laugh. "After you talk or say hi, does the red blender ever talk to you?"

Daniel's eyes traveled from mine to his father's to the floor. Oh my God, my child is engaging in two-way conversations with kitchen gadgets! Daniel raised his eyebrows. "You know, Daddy, blenders can't talk."

Good point. Sigh of relief. After our questioning, Daniel didn't give up his friendship with the Waring. Instead, he became more vocal, less secretive. "Hi, red blender!" he'd shout to it on the way to preschool in the morning. "See you when I get back!" The blender was like a big, red, stationary dog. Clifford with a blade. In the middle of playing Candy Land, Daniel might pop up and say, "I'm just going to tell the red blender I got a double yellow." We could hear him reporting the info in the pantry. Then Daniel would zoom back in and resume the game. I hardly used the blender for its true purpose, and it occurred to me more than once that Daniel probably had no idea of its function. That to him, it was a mythical creature, a statue or robot, looking down on us all.

The imaginary-friend phase, in my experience, doesn't last too long. Toward the end of Daniel's blender camaraderie, Adam and I had some errands to do. We took the kids to Linens-'N-Things for shoe holders or hangers or plastic storage boxes, or something useful that would magically solve our clutter problems. On the way, I thought about the shopping trip, about wrangling Jamie and Daniel and our then-infant Julia. "We need a new toaster," I'd declared. I pictured the kitchen section there and Adam must have considered it at the same time, because we burst out laughing. "If we take Daniel to the kitchen section"—Adam got out of the car while cracking up—"he'll be surrounded by . . ."

I continued, "Blenders."

In fact, when we led Daniel around the store, I felt it my duty to warn him. If you were suddenly ambushed by an army of your imagination, you might get freaked out. "There are special things here," I told him. "And some of them look like the red blender." Daniel nodded, his lips pursed, his eyes solemn. Maybe he wouldn't react at all. I mean, they were just appliances after all.

Daniel neared the cookware, passing the pots and pans, the ladles on hooks, the glass storage jars. Then he stopped short. In front of him were rows of them. Two full shelves stocked with blenders of every description. "There's silver!" he shouted. "And white!" He pointed to a fancy Cuisinart blender. "And a giant one. Hi, blenders!"

"It's like a family reunion," I said to Adam. We watched Daniel roam around. He was amazed and began to laugh the kid chuckle of surprise and fear and wonder all rolled into one. "There's so many!" He looked some more.

"Do you think our blender is here?" Jamie asked him, playing along.

Daniel shook his head. "Don't you know that ours is at our house?"

He was correct, of course, and able to point out the specific rules of pretend play that are known only by the instigator. As a six-year-old now, Daniel has no pretend friends. He willingly goes along with Julia when she wants to pretend, but Daniel's gaze in the pantry has nothing to do with the red blender (more to do with the pretzels we keep in there). If I ask him if he remembers talking to it, he nods and grins. "Yeah, that was funny."

As odd as it was, I treasure that perspective. The way that Daniel looked at an ordinary object and was able to make it extraordinary. Just when the red blender became a mere ordinary object (How boring—a blender that only blends!), Julia (then twenty months old) became fascinated with her own object: the fan in the kitchen, the one in the stove's hood, stainless steel and apparently very friendly. "Well . . . it looks as though this is genetic," I e-mailed my in-laws. "For the past few weeks, Julia has been very focused on the fan in the kitchen—the silver one attached to the stove. Often, she will say hi to it in the morning. Today, her love was made clear when she asked me to do 'Ring Rosy' (ring around the rosy) and while we did, shouted, 'Hi, fan! Look! We do ring rosy!'" Since then, all kitchen apparatuses have returned to their standard functions, but it was fun while it lasted.

"Shevago's gonna call back," Julia informs me. "He needs to drive to New York." I love that Julia's friend has such an unusual name. I'm not sure of his background. If he's of French descent, he would be *Chevageaux*, but Julia has said that he speaks Hebrew, so I am spelling it Shevago. Then again, Julia tells me he's from Indiana, so maybe I'm making him more worldly than is warranted.

"You let me know when you want to call Shevago back," I say when I hear a slight cry from upstairs.

"OK." Julia looks at the phone and presses some numbers, then stops. "You know he's with Shev-Shevago, right?"

I nod. "Sure." I mean, I wasn't aware of this beforehand, but why not? "How did Shevago and Shev-Shevago meet, anyway?" There is clearly a family tree I've yet to unearth that explains the Shevs.

Julia lifts her shoulders and drops them hard. "Because they both know you."

So they are mutual friends. Recently, the two have made friends with Tay-Nay and He-ma-nay (these are, of course, the phonetic spellings). In fact, Julia recently attended a party with them in her room. I was the chaperone. There was no alcohol served.

"They're going out to dinner tonight in New York," Julia says as I slide open a wire shelf in the pantry and examine jars and cans.

"Sounds like fun." I settle on diced tomatoes and then swap them for crushed when I notice we have cellentani pasta. If I were making a food doll, cellentani would be the perfect hair; big taut ringlets that look special and do so well with any sauce. We have boxes of it from a dinner party we had a few weeks back—grown-ups, games, good food and wine—a great weekend night.

"What is that?" Julia reaches for the tube in my hand.

"Anchovy paste," I tell her.

She studies it. "It looks like toothpaste."

"It does, but it's actually made of fish."

She wrinkles her nose, about to complain. "Is it for dinner?" She holds the phone still but sticks it under her arm as though she's carrying a baguette.

I head to the stove, glancing at the clock and listening for sounds of a waking baby. I have long ago given up on monitors in the house—we can hear just as well without them, and often the little grunts and groans or tiny bursts of crying only resulted in me waking a baby or startling myself out of bed, so it's back to good old-fashioned hearing. "It's part of dinner. But you won't taste it."

She looks skeptical, which is Jamie's cue to enter the room with Daniel, both breathless from playing football outside. Jamie takes in the information and processes it quickly. "No way am I going to eat mushed-up fish." He reads, "Anchovy paste." He looks at me. "Baby fish?"

"No, just small ones. They're very flavorful." They're like the imaginary friend of pasta and salad and fish. There but not there.

Jamie flails his hands. "Gross. I mean, why can't you leave it out? We're having pasta, right? Just don't put that on it."

"Yeah," Daniel agrees. "Just so you know, you need to keep that stuff away from the rest of the dinner." He points to the paste.

"This little tube?" I display it for them. "This tiny little thing is causing all this fuss?" They nod and begin more protests. "Enough. Shush. Don't wake Will," I say. Daniel sits, practicing his letter-writing while Jamie does his homework.

"Wait a minute." Julia shakes her head. "That's the phone. I better get it."

"Is it Shevago?" I ask.

"He wants to talk to you." At first I had no idea Shevago was a boy, then Julia told me. She hands me the phone.

"Hi, Shevago," I say with a normal voice. I try to treat her pretend scenarios with respect—no baby voices unless she wants me to pretend to be a fussy baby, just regular pitch and regular subjects. "Really? Hmmm. That sounds interesting." I hand the phone back to Julia. "Shevago wants to know how you make pasta." This is our usual routine. It started one night as we were folding laundry. I talked for a second and then passed the phone to Julia with a specific question from Shevago. "Shevago wants to know how you fold a washcloth." I figured this would amuse her for a little while. Her explanation, however, was better than I could have imagined: "First you smooth out the washcloth so it's a square and then you fold over the edges so it's a rectangle and then a square again."

After this, I decided I'd keep throwing ideas out, help her figure out how to describe things while she enjoyed her imaginary play. She's explained how to pack for vacation, how to make a baby stop crying, the best way to enjoy a picnic, the rules of baseball, and so on.

I bring Will downstairs and let him play on the kitchen floor with a few baby toys. He's in the great stage of being able to sit up but not being able to crawl, which means for the time being he is content with playing on his mat.

Julia answers the question, telling Shevago, "You have to see what you have in the pantry or fridge. Maybe you have macaroni or maybe you have shells. Then you heat it up on the stove and add some olive oil and then you have food for dinner."

I do just as she says but when the pasta is nearly cooked, I drain it and toss it back into the pot. I slosh a bit of olive oil on it, add the crushed tomatoes, squeeze in a healthy dose of the anchovy paste, dribble in a splash of cream, and toss in some steamed broccoli florets. Will fusses, so I pick him up while I dish out the food into white bowls. Julia gets forks for everyone and brings them to the table. Will tries to reach for the hot pasta, so I put him in his baby saucer, where he bounces so hard it looks as though he's trying to propel himself into space.

"You didn't add the gross thing, right?" Daniel sits down at the table with hands he claims he's washed but the blue marker on them suggests otherwise.

Jamie's fork is in his hand before he's seated. His appetite is furious these days. "She didn't, Daniel. You can tell because you can't even see it."

Julia tests a big ringlet. "Yum. Shevago loves this dinner."

I lean on the counter. "Do you want to give some to Shevago?" Maybe Julia will break the trend and bring her friend to the table. I remember many a dish being served, chairs reserved, for my brother Jon's "buddy."

Julia sighs, annoyed with my incompetence probably. "He's not here! You can't give him pasta if he's not here."

"So he's just on the phone?"

"Sometimes I see him, but not right now. And this is good." She slurps a mouthful, her lips ringed in sauce.

Jamie finds Julia's friend amusing. "Maybe Shevago doesn't even like pasta." He smiles at me.

Daniel buys into Julia's invisible friend much more. "You know what,

Julia? Shevago could have this if you go visit him. Or maybe after dinner you can call him and tell him that it tastes good as long as you don't use fish toothpaste."

"You know what, guys?" I take the squeezed tube from the fridge. "I *did* use the gross stuff. But you can't taste it, OK? So many people think anchovies are disgusting but the truth is, they're in lots of sauces and they add a kind of salty richness to things."

Jamie's bowl is nearly empty. "So you just used it anyway, even though we said not to?"

"Yes," I admit. "Did you see it in there? Did you know it was there?" They shake their heads. "But it is, and maybe next time you won't worry about it."

Julia shrugs and peers deep into her bowl with her small face. "I can't see it at all. Are you sure it's there?"

Red (Blender) Pasta

1 lb. cellentani pasta	splash of cream
broccoli florets and/or other green (spinach, peas)	1 tablespoon anchovy paste
olive oil	pepper
1 can crushed tomatoes	

Cook pasta in well-salted water (you can steam the broccoli in there too) until nearly cooked. Drain water and put pasta and broccoli back in pot. Keep on low heat. Drizzle a bit of olive oil in. Add crushed tomatoes. Add a splash of cream and anchovy paste and a bit of pepper. Mix well. Cook for about five minutes until pasta is al dente and sauce is hot. Serve with imagination.

If at First You Don't Succeed, Thai, Thai Again

I've been on a Thai food kick. Yellow curry. Rice-paper rolls. Pad Thai. I learned the hard way that of all the foods I am able to cook, that I enjoy cooking, that I am thrilled about experimenting with, Thai is not one of them.

I purchase yellow curry paste; lemongrass; coconut milk; a host of vegetables including carrots, zucchini, bamboo shoots, and broccoli—even sugar paste, but to no avail. I simmer the coconut milk, add a dollop of paste, and wait for the magic smells I'm used to from our local takeout.

"Basically," I say to Adam after my last failed attempt, "I suck at this."

He eyes my wilting greens, the pot of milky curry. "It looks good," he offers.

But it does not taste good. And yet I crave the flavor. Need the sticky rice.

Nearly all of our family dinners are made at home, but every once in a while we'll go out or, even less frequently, bring in. I drive five minutes to Thai Mango Kitchen, which I discovered when I was pregnant with Will and which, when yellow curry cravings struck, I visited weekly. I bring back lots of foods for us all to try: fresh rolls, some filled with shrimp, others with tofu; crispy spring rolls with shiitake mushrooms and glass noodles; beef and chicken satay.

"Do we pick it up?" Daniel asks when the satay is in front of him.

"Just hold it by the stick," Adam says, and eats the richly marinated beef.

"They soak the meat in coconut milk and curry," I say, and serve the red and yellow curries, nodding at Adam as he consumes a food that ends in "y." Satay might not be berry, but it does show growth.

The whole spread is on the table so the kids can see, smell, and taste for themselves. "Just be a little careful, because the curries are spicy."

"How spicy?" Jamie asks, always wary since his jalapeño encounter years ago.

Daniel takes a spoonful of the yellow curry and explains: "It is so, so, so spicy! But it's also so, so, so good." He eats more of it, showing Jamie the pineapple. "It's sweet, too. But you need to do this." He guzzles milk.

Jamie takes the tiniest bird beak full of curry. "It's too hot for me."

Julia's game and tests the red and the yellow. "I can't tell which one I like more."

"Me either," I say, and spoon the yellow sauce onto a pile of sticky rice. The chewy texture soaks through with the coconut milk and curry flavors, creating a warm and penetrating spice I find irresistible.

"Try this." Adam serves himself some crispy pad thai and offers it to the kids. "It's special Thai noodles called pad thai."

"Daddy always gets it when we have Thai food," I say. "There's also crispy pad thai over here."

They all indulge in both. "I like the regular," Julia says but pronounces it reg-a-li-ar.

"I like the crispy!" Daniel announces, happy with the meal. "And these are so good." He doesn't rush through his spring roll, he savors it, tasting and dipping the roll into the curry sauce.

Jamie surveys the table. "I thought you didn't like tofu, Dad."

"I don't." Adam, matter-of-fact, tries a fresh roll. "But I'm going for it anyway." A thin layer of tofu is wrapped with crunchy fresh lettuce and julienned carrots in a cellophane-thin sheet of rice paper. On the top of the roll, directly under the paper, is a sprig of mint that looks like decoupage.

"Try dipping it in the sauce," I suggest. He does. "Still don't like it?"

"Not my favorite."

"How come we brought in food, anyway?" Jamie wonders.

"Because I sold a book today," I tell them.

"We're celebrating Mummy," Adam says.

We like for the kids to celebrate not only their own accomplishments and achievements, but to share in the significant moments for us, too. Birthdays are great, but everyday life deserves mentions too. Maybe they will learn from us not only pride in a job well done, but to take a minute to enjoy it.

"I did. I wrote a book and worked hard, and now it's going to be published."

"Which one?" Jamie asks, always curious about the stories. "The restaurant one or the novel set in the 1930s?"

"A different one," I say. "One about food."

"Well, then it's a good thing we're eating dinner!" Jamie smiles.

"Congratulations, Mom," Daniel says, and chews his fresh roll. He has plucked out the mint leaf, which I do, too, thinking that they look better than they taste. I will try to cook this again. I will not be put off by failure. And yet I will also, after the third time, learn my lesson and when the craving strikes, go back to Thai Mango Kitchen rather than spending twice the money for something that tastes half as good. I am confident about nearly every other cuisine I've attempted, and it's OK to accept this as a no-go. I tell the kids about my tries and losses and then I go back to the reason for the celebratory dinner.

Adam raises his glass of fizzy water. "Congratulations!"

"Yeah, Mum, good job." Jamie claps like I'm nearing home plate.

"I love these noodles." Julia is not eating noodles but rather a mound of bamboo shoots. "If you sell another book, can we have this again?"

I take a bite of spicy yellow curry, feel the searing heat on my tongue, and take in the newness being ingested by my family. "I'm so glad you like it," I say. "And sure, we can have it again sometime." As long as I don't have to make it.

Rainbow Thai Salad

Assembling this salad doesn't take long and the colors brighten any table. One of these days, I'll take a Thai cooking class, but until then, this dish will suffice. Serve with chicken or fish steamed in coconut milk.

2 tbsp. lime juice

2 tbsp. olive oil

1 tbsp. sesame oil

2 tbsp. coconut milk

1 tsp. sugar or honey

1/4 tsp. Thai chili sauce (optional)

big handful of bean sprouts

4 big leaves romaine lettuce, chopped

1/2 Chinese cabbage, sliced

1/2 purple/red cabbage, sliced thin

a few leaves of basil

1 bunch scallions, sliced

1 clove garlic, crushed

red and yellow pepper, sliced thin

salt

pepper

sunflower seeds or nuts, roughly crushed for topping

Whisk liquids and sugar or honey together. Mix vegetables together. Pour liquid over vegetables and toss, sprinkling salt, pepper, and nuts on top before serving chilled.

Winter

Split Opinions

"I don't like lentils anymore," Jamie announces as though he's declaring his political party.

"Oh, really?" I ask. Normally this wouldn't faze me, but as I am in the process of making lentil soup, it is rather inconvenient.

"Really." Jamie peers into the pot. His blond hair dips down onto his forehead, covering his eyes, very teenagery.

"Well, then I guess you won't like this." I stir the soup with a wooden spoon, moving the lentils around before I add tomatoes.

"So, I don't have to have it then." He drops his shoulders, relieved.

"Here—open this." I hand him the can of fire-roasted crushed tomatoes. "You don't have to, but that's what's for lunch." He grits his teeth both at me and the can. He has only recently learned to navigate our old and annoying can opener. I should replace it. Or someone should.

"Well, just to let you know, I only like split-pea soup. Not lentil."

I roll my eyes at the pot as he slinks off until lunch is ready. The lentils are tender enough now that I can add the tomatoes (acidic things slow the cooking process) and once they are fully incorporated, I will add a big bushel of ripped-up chard. I bought the rainbow chard, drawn in by its incredible bursts of color. Seeing the sunset hues of pink and red, the golden yellow and orange all in winter made these stalks hard to resist. All I did to prepare them was wash them in cold water, chop off the stems midway up, and rip up the rest of the leaves and veins. I pile all of the greenery into the pot on top of the lentils and put the cover on. I will check back in a few minutes to see if the leaves have begun to wilt.

"Mom?" Jamie calls. "Want to play gin?"

I check my watch. I probably have time enough for one hand of gin before I need to stir and finish the soup. "Sure. You shuffle and deal."

Jamie is trying to learn how to do the bridge shuffle and asks me to demonstrate again. "It's one of those skills," I say to him when we're both perched on either side of the coffee table. He needs the floor space to look at the cards; he doesn't feel he can adequately hold all ten of them. "You just suddenly know how to do it. I don't remember learning. I remember wanting to learn and practicing but not actually being able to do it."

Jamie eyes my hands, the easy folding of one card onto the next and nods. "Six of hearts. Do you want it?" I shake my head. "I do. I'm almost winning already. I'm only looking for one card." He sorts things out under the table. He's a very skilled game player and holds his own without any adult having to throw the wrong card. "The soup smells good. It smells like split pea. I wish it was split pea."

"It's not." Jamie's moaning is partially because he is afflicted with a syndrome known in these parts as being eight and a half and also because we recently had, and I don't usually boast about my food, really incredible split-pea soup. The best split-pea soup ever. And if my words mean nothing, let's just say for the record that Daniel tried it. And ate it. Granted, halfway through he sort of realized the entire thing was made of peas, and even though he'd been chanting the mantra, "Wow—maybe I do like peas. I mean, I like this soup," he left the rest of the bowl uneaten. But the rest of us—Adam included—ate bowl after bowl. The recipe was based on one I'd made when I was pregnant. I'd gone to my friend Judy's house in our old neighborhood for a book club meeting. She prefers drawing-room books, those English Austen-type tales of social conceits and dowagers and tea, talking animatedly about social foibles and intrigue between characters. Judy traveled often to France and made such good salads that our book group requested that she bring only that dish to our gatherings. However, as book group was being held at her house, as host she'd been in charge of the main course and chosen to serve soup.

Once I eat something that strikes my fancy, I will often try to eat or buy it right away—the next day, the next afternoon—soon. I'd called Judy after eating the soup she'd thrown together and demanded (nicely) to know exactly how to make it. I was pregnant after all, which is a handy catch-all for all your food cravings. Judy kindly listed some ingredients and left me to figure out the rest of the meal on my own. The key to the fantastically creamy soup is that there's no cream. No butter! No nothing! Just soup! And you have to add, in Judy's words, "A good slug of shitty brandy." Which is how I came to be at six-months pregnant, in the liquor store, asking, "What's the smallest amount of the worst brandy you have?" The guy behind the counter looked as though he didn't know whether to pity me or show me the warning labels on the bottle, but for exactly ninety-nine cents I purchased a nip of brandy and tucked it in my pocket for the soup. When I'd made the whole pot of split pea and it emerged bubbling and creamy from the oven (It cooks for a while in there, so you don't have to tend to it on the stove. Another plus!), the whole family was enticed. That's how Daniel ended up trying it. He heard Adam's ohhs and ahhs, saw Julia scooping it up and Jamie's glee, and suddenly his plain lunch didn't seem so appealing.

"Well, we finished that soup, Jamie. The pea soup is gone." I tap the table. "And it's your turn."

Jamie chews the edge of his striped turtleneck. "And I have gin!"

I show him my cards, the runs and three-of-a-kind, the ones I needed. "We can play again after the lentils are ready." Jamie groans.

Back in the kitchen, the chard has sunk enough that I can stir it into the thick soup. I prefer lentil soup without much broth, and very flavorful, with the lentils still holding their shape, which is why I'm using du Puys, the green French lentils. "It's ready!"

Jamie takes another look at the soup. "It really does smell good. Too bad it's not—"

"Yeah, I know. I get it." I seat him at the table with one of Will's bowls filled with soup. "See? I'm only giving you the smallest amount."

Jamie lifts his spoon, the steam rising from the mound of lentils, the chard and onions and tomatoes poking through. Rich and smoky, the bite I try is wonderful. The perfect lunch on a winter day. The soup is thick enough that you could use it as the base for a piece of roasted cod, placing the cooked fish directly on top of the legumes.

"Mom?" Jamie swallows and drains what seems like his fifth glass of milk of the day. "I think it's split-pea soup I don't like."

I raise my eyebrows. "Are you sure?"

He furrows his brow. "It's one of the two but I don't know which one."

I transfer the lentils into a glass container so we can enjoy it for the rest of the week. "Well, you let me know when you decide."

French Lentil Soup with Chard

The amounts below are, like most dishes I make, entirely flexible. You can change the amount of lentils or tomatoes, but just make sure you aren't adding too much water as you go.

2¼ cups French lentils (the small, greenish ones)

1 large Spanish onion, roughly chopped

olive oil

2 cups stock or very good bouillon

4 cloves garlic, peeled with ends trimmed, but not cut

one 12-oz. can fire-roasted crushed tomatoes

1 tbsp. Marmite (Really, buy it! It's so helpful!)

1 big bunch chard (rainbow or other), trimmed of ends and half their stalks and ripped into large pieces

salt and pepper

Boil the lentils in about 5 cups of water for about 20 minutes. Don't let them get too soft. Drain water and beany scum, but don't wash lentils! Keep lentils in strainer for a few minutes while you sauté the onion in a drizzle of olive oil until just before the onion browns. Add lentils. Add the stock or about 2 cups of water to the pot with bouillon cube. Let this come to a boil. Turn heat to medium and add garlic, tomatoes, and Marmite. Let this bubble away while you prepare your chard. Rip chard and throw all of it on top of soup. Cover. Let it sit for a hand of gin, or about 10 minutes. When you return, stir the now-wilting greens into soup. Add salt or pepper or both or neither. Serve hot.

Note: *This makes a lovely base for roasted fish (a thick cut of cod, for example) or lamb.*

The Best Split-Pea Soup Ever

(Adapted from Judy Kramer's excellent version)

Some soups demand a fireside, others require a summer afternoon. This soup defies seasons and tastes just as delicious in the summer as in the winter. Perfect for dipping into with a hunk of brown bread, or satisfying alone. The addition of whole peas and Pecorino at the end makes for a fulfilling sweet/salty finish.

In heavy-bottomed big pot or Dutch oven (I use a Le Creuset that my mother and grandmother had) sauté the following items, all sliced, in a splash of olive oil:

2 leeks (washed and trimmed of much of the green)	2 onions
	8 cloves garlic (peeled)
5 or 6 big carrots (peeled and trimmed)	5 celery stalks with leaves

Add:

1½ lbs. rinsed split peas	1 veggie bouillon cube (one of the rectangles—such as Rapunzel's vegan with sea salt—or 2 smaller cubes)
2 quarts organic chicken stock	
2 cups water	
Big slug of bad brandy (a slug here means one of those bottles you might get on a plane)	2 bay leaves

Bring to a boil, stirring a bit as you go.

Once boiled, turn flame off. Stir. Put pot into 350° oven for 2 hours with lid open a crack. Add 1 or 2 additional cups of water as time goes, stirring as you add.

After about 2 hours (could be less or a bit more) remove bay leaves, and blend soup in a food processor, blender, or with hand-held.

Add bag of frozen peas (thawed briefly) to very hot soup right before serving; serve with shredded Pecorino Romano.

Remember?

"'Member that thing you had that one time, I want that for lunch." What to do with the ambiguity here? I beg for specifics. Daniel gestures wildly, his palms in front of his face. "You know, that place! And the sandwich."

Sandwich. We are making progress! "Do you know where we had it?"

Daniel looks annoyed. "*I* didn't have it. That's the whole point. *You* had it."

Obviously, I should know that. "So I had a sandwich . . . ," I start, and hope he can feed me some info about it.

"And it had that sweet thing, but also then you said we could have it sometime at a restaurant but we never did. How come you said that if it wasn't true?"

So now I'm being accused of motherly misconduct in the form of an unkept promise, and all for a sandwich I don't recall. "Danno—please, just . . . what was in the sandwich?"

Daniel shrugs and twists his mouth up. "I have no idea."

Armed with only these few details, there is little I can say except, "Sorry, Daniel, but I just can't make that for you because I don't know what it is." My vision of a random fuzzy sandwich floats off into space.

"You have no idea about what?" Adam asks. We tell him what we know. He, too, is at a loss.

"What don't you know?" Jamie asks, his cheeks a shade of scarlet from his last weekend of soccer, pushed very late this year due to a seemingly endless loop of rainy Saturdays. The afternoon is a wash of grays, wet leaves chucked to the ground and trampled on; the kind of charmless pre-snow day that demands crawling into bed mid-afternoon. Not that I've done that in a decade.

"The kind of sandwich Daniel means," I say to Jamie. Daniel proceeds to tell his older brother exactly what he told me and Adam. Will sits on the kitchen floor, annoyed with his own toys and interested instead in my shoelaces.

Jamie grabs a cup for himself and glugs water, matter-of-factly spitting out, "He means the mundy leano."

I laugh. As if this explains it all. "What?"

Jamie wipes his mouth on his sleeve. "You had it at that place that time. . . ." I nod, having heard this before. But then Jamie continues. "It's like all this stuff inside and has powdered sugar on it. Mopey chino?"

They wait for me to figure it out. "You mean Monte Cristo!" Daniel bolts upright in his chair. I clap my hands.

Daniel is relieved and thrilled to be understood. The power of sibling communication. Even now, I can call my brothers and say something along the lines of "Remember that thing with the weird woven wood?" And they'll say, "That porch swing on the Cape? Yeah, it really pinched your fingers." My brothers and I have a collective memory, and I love seeing one build for my own children.

"So can we have it?" Daniel asks.

"Sure," I say. I don't warn them about the fact that sometimes "the thing you had at the place that time" doesn't translate in the present. Fried clams eaten while overlooking the Atlantic taste one way, but quite something else when made at home amidst piles of bills. Sometimes our memories of food are better than re-creating it. "But I've never made it before." I look up Monte Cristo sandwiches online and am hit with multiple variations—some with jam, some without; some with turkey and ham, some with Canadian bacon; some with Swiss cheese, others with American. Some kind of coating is the only uniting factor.

A few days later, I am armed with supplies.

"Are you making pancakes?" Julia pulls a chair over to the counter. Will rolls a ball around the floor and alternates between chasing it and chewing on it, cleverly avoiding the batter I am splattering on the floor. I hand him one of the teething biscuits I made for him in an attempt to feel virtuous. They are the color of squirrels and about as tasty. He chucks the biscuit onto the floor, disinterested.

"It's the outside of the sandwiches," I explain, doubtful as to how they're going to turn out. Overwhelmed with choices and recipes, I made my own version. I was tempted to substitute prosciutto for the ham, but as Daniel requested to have the dish the way I'd had it and let him try it "at that place that time," I bought ham for one of the first times in my life (I don't like it). I also bought Muenster cheese (poor Muenster—so often overlooked!), and Swiss, and thick-cut bread and made sure I had the ingredients for some sort of coating. Some recipes boasted deep-frying the sandwich. Others insisted that dredging in black pepper and flour after an egg bath would give the sandwich a real kick. A kick that would be way too much for the kids.

I layer the meats and cheeses, make the batter, cut the sandwiches, dip both sides of each triangle into the batter, and put them into a frying pan with a drop of oil and a small pad of butter. Once they are slightly browned, I transfer them to a cookie sheet and finish them in a hot oven. The smoke detector only goes off once—a small victory.

Tonight is Tuesday, another late night for Adam, but the sandwiches will keep until he comes home. As the table is set and the kids take their seats, they are slack-mouthed as I dust the tops of the sandwiches with powdered sugar. I let them tap the sifter over their own plates. Julia immediately puts her fingers into the sugar and the others do the same.

"Some people serve this with jam," I say to them, "so I put a little pot of it in the middle of the table just in case."

"Should we dip it in?" Jamie asks.

"If you want to," I say, and spoon mushy peas into Will's mouth. He is agreeable about his baby mush, but looks at his siblings' plates with what I interpret as a bit of food envy: Things to chew! Muenster! Uneaten jam! No one touches the jam except to move it away from their plates, but each child consumes his or her oversize triangles of joy and declares, "Really, really good."

"It's funny because it's salty and sweet," Daniel says. "But I knew I'd like it because I had it that time." I love sharing my food with the kids, especially in restaurants when it's a dish they've never heard of and see me enjoying.

Julia eats the whole first half and then says, "You know what? I'm taking this out because I don't like it." She extracts and then waves a floppy piece of ham. Will reaches for it as she waves but doesn't succeed in capturing it.

"Me too," Daniel says. "I don't want this part." Ham removed.

"I hate ham," Jamie says, even though he ate part of it in the first half of his Monte Cristo.

"Would prosciutto be better?" I ask. Julia thinks so.

"I think it's better just with turkey," Daniel says, and takes a big bite.

Jamie concurs. "But maybe we have to give it another name."

Monte Cristo Sandwich

(The Way We Had at the Place That Time)

For batter, mix together:

⅔ cup water

1 egg

⅔ cup flour

1¾ tsp. baking powder

½ tsp. salt

Set batter mixture aside. Have ready:

8 slices thick-cut bread

4 slices ham (to potentially later be removed)

4 slices Swiss cheese

4 slices Muenster

4 slices turkey
(I used roasted)

confectioners' sugar

bit of oil/butter for frying

I think this works best when the meat and cheese are fairly thick-cut. Layer a slice of bread with ham, then both cheeses, then turkey. Repeat until you have four sandwiches. Cut diagonally and dip into batter, making sure to coat all sides and surfaces. When pan is hot and butter melted, add drop of oil and fry up all the triangles until browning, then transfer to 300° oven until ready to eat. They will puff up slightly. Dust tops with powdered sugar and serve hot.

Nibbles

Adam is at the gym, the slush is slushy outside, Will and Julia are napping, and Daniel and Jamie and I have exhausted the board games and are starting in with the "bored games," which involves the two boys taunting each other and responding with pokes or punches.

"Enough!" I command, and for about two minutes all is calm and pleasant. Then the swatting resumes.

"You don't even know how to spell antidisestablishmentarianism," Jamie spits out.

Before I let it slip that he, too, might not get this word entirely correct, I go to the pantry and grab a few items.

"What're you doing?" Daniel asks me.

I shrug. No big deal. "Not sure."

Jamie's interest is piqued. "Can it have oranges in it?" Many things these past two weeks have had oranges because every year for the holidays my husband receives a gift box of citrus fruit from Florida. In past years, we've pushed grapefruits halves and splotchy oranges on the kids, but this year they are eating them quickly. I used a few oranges with a roast chicken, sliding the slices under the skin, adding sage or rosemary.

"It could, if we have any."

Jamie goes to look in the blue bowl to see if we're out. There were so many to begin with, I had to divvy them up between the fruit bowl in the kitchen and the blue glass bowl in the living room, which is really just for show. For the weeks that the oranges have invaded, the sideboard on which the bowl sits has looked very pretty, as though we're expecting company, which we are not.

"Two. That's it." Jamie holds up his findings.

I take a cookie sheet and rip off a piece of parchment paper to cover it. I have Daniel dump some rolled oats onto the sheet and slide it into the oven to toast while I heat some honey in a pot on the stove. Daniel wants to use the hand grater, which he thinks is "the funnest tool in the kitchen," so I let him use it to zest one of the oranges onto a plate. Then we squeeze the fresh oranges, carefully plucking out the seeds and any big bits of pulp. Afterward, we add the juice to the honey, drinking in the sweet aroma, the bright citrus.

As if on cue, Jamie jostles Daniel aside for a better look into the pot. "Now what?"

I hand him a small bag of Tate & Lyle caster sugar from England and tell him to dump some in. "Everyone back up," I say so I can look at the oats. They are toasty but not brown. I take the tray out of the oven and let the oats cool while the sugar dissolves in the honey.

I combine the oats and some flour, the zest, and some baking soda— maybe I would have used baking powder, but we are out of it and I keep forgetting to replace it. We mix everything with a splash of vanilla (though any liquid would work) and stare at the gloppy dough.

"It's kind of runny," Jamie says.

"Can we eat it raw?" asks Daniel.

"No," I say, but I'm not exactly sure what to do with it either.

"Have you done this before?" Jamie elbows Daniel and they laugh at my expense, which is better than insulting each other.

I have to say I have no idea what I'm doing. I could add in an egg, but it seems like this might actually work as-is. Sort of like lace cookies. "I say we bake them."

Daniel claps his hand, ever the eager eater. "And have them for snack?"

"If they're ready," I say. We line two sheets with parchment paper and dole out big spoonfuls of the slightly drippy, oaty dough without crowding. "I have a feeling these might spread out."

Twelve minutes later, we take them from the oven. "They're huge!" Daniel cries. "We should only have one for snack, not two."

"These are really orange-smelling," Jamie says.

Adam gets home from the gym. "I'll go get Julia," he says, grinning and sweaty.

I wake Will while the cookies cool, which they need to for a long time, and then we all try them.

"Blech," Julia says. She could be post-nap cranky or maybe she doesn't like them. She eats a clementine instead.

"What can we call these?" I ask, and sample one. The first tray came out a bit too soon; they are still too chewy despite having cooled. The other tray cooked for a minute longer, and that made all the difference. "Flat cookies?" Daniel shakes his head. "Orange oaties?" Another shake.

"I don't know," Daniel says.

The boys enjoy their snack and their work. "I squeezed out our last oranges for these," Jamie says.

"That must be gratifying," Adam says.

"Spell that." Daniel kicks Jamie's chair while they chew the flat cookies.

 Orange-Oatey I-Don't-Know Cookies

1 cup rolled oats (not the quick-cook kind)	juice from two oranges (about ½ cup)
¾ cup honey	

½ cup caster sugar (also called superfine—it melts faster than regular sugar)

1 tsp. baking soda

orange zest from one small orange

1 cup plus 1 tbsp. wheat flour

dash of vanilla

Preheat oven to 350°. Lightly toast the oats. Heat the honey and orange juice on the stove. Add the sugar and let heat until melted and the juice is incorporated. Mix toasted oats, baking soda, zest, and flour together. Add liquid. Mix and add dash of vanilla. Spoon onto lined cookie sheets, well-spaced, and bake for about 12 minutes. Let them cool for about 8 minutes before peeling them off parchment paper. Enjoy alone or with vanilla ice cream. You could also crumble them up and sprinkle onto frozen yogurt.

Note: These are quite sticky, so I ended up cutting squares around the parchment paper and storing them directly this way, so each kid could pick out a square and peel off a cookie when it was time to eat.

Upon reflection (and subsequent tastings), the kids decided that they liked a batch without zest better. For adults, the slight zest flavor heightens the experience, but for kids-only, I would vote for leaving it out, especially because it is very tricky for them to avoid the bitter white pith.

Pasty Pastries

My mother used to run a B&B in Cornwall, England. As a result, my brothers and I were fortunate enough to see (or subjected to seeing, depending on the day and on our moods) many tiny villages, drive on many narrow lanes, and generally absorb the country atmosphere of England's very far south coast. Our experiences ran the gamut from lively black-tie dinner parties at historic estates to getting lost in the expanse of rooms and grounds of said estates, to hiking along the steep cliffs, body surfing in unbelievably cold water (even though it was the height of summer), to the nearly tragic Christmas Day when I went into severe anaphylactic shock. The last was your basic nightmare; think adults who'd had a fair bit of wine and a tiny village where on a good day there might not be any medical care available—and this was Christmas Day—so when we phoned for an ambulance, none came. I survived, and of course I've been tested for allergies to everything known to man, beast, and mineral, and the unfortunate fact is that my reaction was idiopathic. That is, there is no known cause. Adam's medical school professor taught his class the meaning by stating, "Idiopathic, from the Greek *ideo*—meaning 'We don't know' and *pathic*, meaning 'What the hell is going on?'"

And the even more unfortunate fact is that I have had this happen since and have passed this random gene down to Daniel, who has gone into shock too, also from causes unknown. Suffice it to say, we are never without multiple EpiPens.

I would be dishonest if I didn't say the Darth Vader Incident as we came to call it (due to how my voice sounded when my throat was closing up) didn't at least slightly lessen Cornwall's appeal. That said, I have kept with me some very good memories from there: the B&B's cozy living room with its huge fireplace; the bizarre feeling of being an American with a paper party hat on my head, champagne glass in hand, tromping around a castle in a midnight dinner-party parade; and seeing light green hops buds draped over the rafters in the kitchen at my mum's B&B.

While roaming the aisles of my local Whole Foods in search of dinner inspiration, I come to the tinned vegetable section and find my eyes glazing over. I spy a can of Heinz's baked beans, but the English version with the light blue wrapper. The sauce is not brown-sugar or molasses-based as the American version is, rather it is tomato-based and not sweet. It's nothing fancy, just delicious comfort food. My favorite breakfast in England is fried eggs with beans and cheese on toast. If it sounds like a mess, it is. A savory, melty, just-crisp-on-the-edges mess that is best eaten with friends or the Sunday paper or both. Sometimes I make it for dinner just for myself and I'm brought right back to those lazy mornings in England. I keep moving, heading to the meat counter in the hopes that something strikes me. I'm bored with chicken. We don't really eat pork. I don't feel like buying steak. We just had turkey. We eat fish a lot. And we've had so many vegetable-based dinners recently that I am ready to cook something else.

"Could I have a pound of buffalo meat?" I ask with a shrug. Of course the kids haven't ever tried it and neither has Adam, and I have no idea what I'll do with it, but at least it's different. By the time I reach the check-out line, I have a plan.

I throw together an easy short-crust dough when I get home—cutting the butter into the flour, dashing some water in, and wrapping the well-formed ball in plastic wrap and stashing it on the cold windowsill in the kitchen. Then I get to cooking the meat, which I do in a big pan with chopped-up onions and a bit of salt and pepper. I take from the fridge some leftover mashed potatoes. From the freezer I take a bag of corn and a bag of peas.

"Are you making hamburger, macaroni, and peas?" Jamie asks, longing for the great blend of salty meat, easy elbow macaroni, and the sweet, toothy peas.

"No, but I can see why you'd think that," I say to him, and keep moving the meat so it doesn't get too brown.

"What is it, then?" Daniel dashes in, his hat and mittens still on.

"Take your hat and mittens to the basket please," I tell him. In a last-ditch effort for winter organization, we have one single catch-all basket in the entryway where the kids are supposed to toss hats, mittens, and gloves immediately upon arriving home. Daniel shouts from there, and I rush to shush him. "Don't wake Will!"

"Then tell us what it is!"

"So, you know I used to live England."

Nods.

"And there's a lot of different foods there."

Nod.

Daniel rubs his belly. "I love those Jammy Dodger cookies. Can we have those?"

"No. Anyway, there's a place in England called Cornwall, and there's a thing they make there called Cornish pasties."

Daniel is wide-eyed. "Pastries?"

"Pasties," I repeat, knowing this word mix-up could result in a huge meltdown.

"Paste-eze?" Jamie says, clarifying.

"Pasties, like the past," I tell them. "A long time ago, there were a lot of people whose job it was to work in a mine . . . ," I start, wondering if it's worth the history lesson.

Jamie interrupts. "Getting stuff like ore or coal."

"Right. In this case, it was tin. Tin mines. And the workers would head off early in the morning for a long day of work." I mime this like I'm in a drama skit, and they watch, half-amused, half-bored. "They needed to take lunch with them, and they needed to keep warm."

"So just . . . what are you making?" Daniel taps his foot on the rung of his chair.

"I'm getting to that. Hold on." I turn off the heat. "Jamie, can you turn the oven to three-fifty?" He does it, proud he's allowed (with supervision) to do so.

"So these guys went off to work in the tin mines . . . ," I say, remembering when my mom explained the backstory to me.

"And got black lung!" Jamie announces, always glad to pull from his well of random knowledge. "I read all about this. It's really bad. You get really, really sick, Daniel." Dan looks worried.

"I'm not serving anything that will make you sick. OK? So, these pasties are pretty big . . ." Daniel lights up again. Big is good. "And also warm. Some people used to tuck their pasty into their overalls and keep warm way down in the tin mines." I clean and then flour part of the soapstone counter, which is great for pastry-making because it stays cold. "They used to get tin all over their hands, and tin is really bad to eat. Even then they knew this would be dangerous. So"—I roll the dough, lay a saucer on top of it, cut out a circle, and repeat until I have five of them—"when it was time for lunch, and they needed a big lunch because they worked long hours at a very hard job, they had a pasty."

I scoop up some mashed potato. Traditionally, Swede was used in the mash. Swede is also known as Swedish turnip. It's rutabaga, or yellow turnip. During World War I, Swede was one of the few vegetables around. As you can imagine, people grew quite tired of it, and its reputation is not stellar. However, it is still, like most of the roots, a workhorse that's hard to mess up in the kitchen. Some people mixed mushed-up Swede into jams during World War II when anything sweet was hard to come by. The mash stretched out the pot of jam. In Sweden the vegetable is sometimes known as cabbage root, in Scotland sometimes "neep" as in short for turn-eep, in other parts of the world it's called snadgies. The point is, pasties call for a winter root vegetable that is not expensive, and easily mashed. I don't have any Swede handy, but I do have leftover potatoes. I show the kids how to layer the potato into the center of the circle, add on the meat and onions, then the vegetables.

"Oh, no! Please, no peas in mine!" Daniel shrieks. Will wakes up.

"I'm putting broccoli in yours, Daniel. Don't worry." I go back to layering, putting one final dollop of mash on top of the vegetables to keep them from falling out. "Now, see how I'm bringing the edges together here? This makes a kind of envelope. With a crust."

"I love crust," Jamie says.

"Well, the reason Cornish pasties have a crust is because the workers had nowhere to wash their hands, so they gripped their pasties like this." I demonstrate. "They held the thick crust with their tin-covered hands, ate their way through a nice warm meal of meat, starch, and veg, and then they dropped the dirty, tinny crust to the ground without ever eating a bite of it."

"So they were healthy!" Jamie said. "That is so smart."

"I would want to eat the crust." Daniel shakes his head.

"Good thing you're not a Cornish miner," I say. I finish the rest of the pasties, slide them into the oven for a while, tucking the newly formed and perhaps first-ever wild buffalo pasties away someplace warm.

It's so easy and nice to serve a whole meal that's contained in one semicircle. All the kids enjoyed this. Adam said it was really tasty and wondered what kind of meat it was. "Because you didn't like it?" I asked. "No, because it was rich but lean," he said. I told the kids by playing a round of "guess which animal you ate last night." After naming the usual (chicken, cow) and moving to the disturbing (porcupine, penguin), I finally revealed buffalo. "Weird," said Jamie, "but I loved it."

Cornish Pasties

I will say right off that you can make this easy, short-crust pasty dough recipe in the same amount of time it takes to use far-inferior, pre-bought dough. That said, if you have some pizza dough and feel that you must use it up, go for it. I know it's not techni-cally Cornish, nor is it as flaky as the one below, but it would work.

SHORT-CRUST DOUGH:

½ cup cold butter cut into pieces

1 cup all-purpose flour (wheat, white or a combo—your call)

3 tbsp. very cold water (I used directly from the tap, but it's winter. In summer, use iced.)

Cut butter into flour until crumbly. Add water. Form dough into a ball. Keep in ball in a cool but not cold place—the windowsill in your kitchen, for example.

FILLING:

1 lb. ground meat—lean beef or buffalo!

1 onion, chopped

dot of butter

salt and pepper

1 cup or more mashed potato (you might also mash a Swede, but potato is easier to come by)

handfuls of peas, corn, or other small veggie

1 egg, beaten, for sealing pasty

Heat oven to 350°. Sauté meat and onion in pan with dab of butter and some salt and pepper. Turn off heat when meat is cooked through and on-ion is transparent.

Roll dough onto a floured surface until about ¼ inch thick. Using a saucer or small plate as your guide, cut circles from the dough. I made five, though this recipe is probably best used for four portions. Arrange a thinnish layer of mashed potato in the center of each circle. Top with thawed frozen peas and/or corn. Add layer of meat and onions. Top with another layer of potatoes to act as glue so everything doesn't spill out. Brush edges of the circle with beaten egg. Bring edges up to center of the circle and crimp or press together firmly, folding over as you go. Bake for about 35 minutes or until pastry is golden brown.

Note: *The nice thing about these is that you can stuff them with anything, as long as you use some mashed something to lock it all in. I've tried mashed carrots, mashed cauliflower (which Adam loved but the kids didn't like), and leftover sweet potato from Thanksgiving. In fact, a lovely American pasty would be to layer cranberries, stuffing, sweet potatoes, and turkey . . . perhaps next year!*

Eight Nights of Lights

1.

It's Christmas circa 1982 and my brothers and I are standing agog in front of a nine-foot-tall pine decked with white lights, ornaments and, upon further inspection, a piece of red paper onto which is pasted a photograph. In our pajamas, we pad closer for a better look. It's a picture of a basset hound, a puppy, all droopy-eared with folds of baggy skin and floppy paws. "Turn around," the card reads, "I'm right here!"

We pivot and sure enough, there are my parents, peeking out from behind the corner with our very own new puppy. All this, and we've yet to open our felt stockings or the presents under the tree.

And also, we're Jewish.

Growing up, we had an enormous Christmas tree. My dad and a few of the kids would drive to my grandparents' place on Cape Cod, chop down a fir, and haul it back to Boston strapped onto the top of the station wagon. We'd decorate it Christmas Eve, place homemade ornaments on the boughs—sprinkle-coated foam cups, chains of green and red paper—and then awake Christmas morning to find our felt stockings bursting with trinkets.

I am Jewish. My parents are Jewish. Their parents are Jewish. And so on. And yet . . . the tree. My grandparents say they started celebrating Christmas because, growing up in Brooklyn, even Jewish immigrant Brooklyn, Christmas didn't appear to have much to do with religion. At least, not theirs. But it had lots to do with being American. So up sprang the tree and in flew the stockings by the fireplace and so dwindled the menorah lighting and consuming coins made out of chocolate.

Adam grew up celebrating Chanukah, and when we got married, we'd decided together that Christmas was not a holiday we were going to have in the house. No hard feelings, Xmas, but we were going to be Jews; the kind who looked at lights, dealt with the holiday shopping masses, but in the end, a family who did all of the eight nights of Chanukah and nothing else. So I go to the produce market and pick up eggnog not only to drink but with which I will make eggnog pancakes, and purchase pounds of potatoes so we can make the traditional Chanukah food.

2.

"Are we having latkes?" Daniel asks, snooping in the pantry for gelt. I've hidden the chocolate coins on a high shelf until later.

"Of course," I say. "What would Chanukah be without potato pancakes?"

"I'll open the door." Adam smirks, making a reference to the smoke detector that will inevitably go off during the potato-pancake-making. This year we're making a variety: sweet potato, zucchini, and the gold-standard regular potato. Part of what I've come to realize about shrugging off my childhood traditions (the tree, the stockings) is that it's wonderful to start our own, new ones; decorating the dining room with stars of David, designating one night of Chanukah as gift-free so we can decide as a family where to donate the money from those gifts. Some things each year are the same (we serve sour cream with the latkes, even though Daniel and I are the only ones who'll touch it) and each year brings different tides. So much about holiday traditions involve food, and Chanukah is no exception.

This year, Chanukah is early and because I have a book coming out that focuses on the holiday, I need to leave the kids and Adam for two of the nights and head to New York for some promotional events. It's the first time I'm leaving Will, and neither of us is prepared. Julia plays a made-up game involving all of us, ordering each person to be "a baby" or "the mother."

"Now you be the mom," she tells me, and I nod. "And you're going to New York." She pauses. "And you're seeing Heather and reading to people." I'm sure she envisions me tucking the book-reading public into bed with a story.

This is fairly easy to pretend. "Sure," I say. "I can pretend that. Just let me grate some food while we pretend." Julia is satisfied with this.

"I can grate if you want," Jamie says, eyeing the heap of potatoes all scrubbed and set in the metal bowl. I show him how to hold the unpeeled potatoes at an angle against the grater. He gets to work, brow furrowed, lips taut as he grips the spud. "Ugh—this is so hard. No way am I doing all of them." Fearfully, he looks at the bowl. Even I realize I've bought too many: Unless I plan to serve latkes until Lent, we'll only need a fraction of what's in the bowl. I show him how, after each potato is grated, we need to put the gratings into a bowl of cold water to get the starchy redness off.

"My hands hurt," Jamie moans.

"Just do a couple more, OK? I still have to do the onion."

"Why don't you just use the blender?" Adam asks. He means the food processor, but I shake my head. "It's too easy. Then the pancakes are too perfect, you know?" He doesn't know, so he shrugs and removes/unclenches Will, who has been tugging on Adam's eyebrows, using them to try to pull himself up.

"OK, I did it," Jamie says.

"I want to try," Daniel announces, and I set him up in Jamie's spot, and

Jamie heads off to examine the Chanukah presents. In an attempt to be ecologically minded, we've wrapped only in newspaper this year, something we did quite frequently growing up, using the comics for their color. This year, we've used the sports section, or funny advertisements facing up.

As Daniel grates another potato, I try to figure out how many eggs to add in this year. It's always a little bit of this, a bit of that for me—some egg, some salt, some meal or crumbs—or not.

"I'm bored of grating," Daniel says mournfully, his small arms still working but very slowly, as though he's paid by the hour regardless of his production rate.

"Me too," I tell him, and wince as I hand-grate several large onions.

"Grammie's gonna love this," Julia says. We have family scattered into the Chanukah schedule—my dad one night, another night my grandparents will stop by, my mom on the night Adam's working late, my in-laws over the weekend and two nights when I'm away. Finally, everything is grated and the kids have officially lost interest in the drawn-out process and have wandered into the other room. I drain the cold, water-soaked potatoes and then dry them in some kitchen towels, then transfer them to a bowl and add eggs and salt. I heat some olive oil in a pan but don't let it get smoking hot. Then I drop smallish batches of the potatoes in and fry them up, pressing them nearly flat and lowering the heat once they begin to brown, turning them over once. Piled up, the pancakes go into the oven to keep warm. I repeat the process with zucchini (which doesn't need to be cold-rinsed) and with sweet potatoes, which, when cooked, produce latkes the color of embers.

Adam rummages through his bag and displays an extra-special treat for the kids. "Flu shots!" he announces, and the kids magnetize to the kitchen, already overlapping with anxieties and answers.

"You didn't tell us tonight's the night!"

"You know not everyone gets flu shots, right? How come we do?"

"Because it keeps you from getting all the sickness stuff that germs have."

"Can we at least have latkes before?"

"Let's do this now and then eat," Adam says. He offers each year to have the nurses at his office do this, or the kids' regular pediatrician, but they always ask for their father. Who better to inflict pain?

"I'll go first," Julia volunteers, her small shoulders shrugging. She pulls up her sleeve and sits calmly on a kitchen chair with Adam next to her. He rubs alcohol onto her skin, his soothing voice explaining it all. "So that was to clean your skin. Now we get the shot ready—see how small the needle is?" Julia looks and nods. "And here"—Julia winces—"it's all done."

She cries for all of two seconds and then hops down. "All done!"

Jamie is all bravado, whipping his entire shirt up ("You can't reach my arm unless I do that") and determined to watch Adam stick the syringe into his skin.

"Jamie, why don't you look the other way," Adam says.

Jamie shakes his head. Then he starts to scream. In previous years, we were finished quickly—each of us pricked and placated with a hug—but this year, my impending departure and the sudden shots have set the boys on edge. Will begins to wail even though he's the one who won't be having his shot tonight, having already dealt with it at the doctor's office.

"No! No! Please help me!" Jamie screeches, leaping from his chair and running into the living room.

We turn to Daniel. "Julia did it, Danno. You'll be OK," I tell him.

Daniel's eyes fill up. "But Jamie didn't even . . . I can't . . . No!" He bolts.

Adam fetches them from the other room and insists they sit down. "The sooner we do it, the sooner it's over with," he says as though this is more than just logic.

"Obviously," Jamie says, glaring at us.

I check on the food, turning the oven down so the latkes aren't over-cooked. "Dinner's ready—as soon as you guys are," I say.

Adam holds the black-and-white syringe up and demonstrates again. "This is a very small needle. It'll hurt, but only for a few seconds."

The seconds turn into agonizing minutes of Jamie's fit-throwing and Daniel's mimicry of his older brother's protests.

"I already did it!" Julia throws her hands up. "You just sit down and let Daddy hurt you."

I shoot Adam a look. He rolls his eyes and preps, finally sticking Jamie and Daniel, who immediately giggle while they cry, murmuring, "It's over. Wow. I thought it was . . . oh, OK . . . it's OK. I'm fine!"

We sit down and serve the latkes to sore-armed kids. We set a dish of applesauce on the table and another one of sour cream and say the prayers over the candles. Then we open some presents—tonight everyone happens to get books—and each kid has a gold-wrapped coin and is feasting on the plastic-tasting chocolate.

"I'm so glad that's over," Jamie says, relief apparent even in his stride.

"Can we have more latkes tomorrow?" Daniel asks on the way up to bed.

3.

As my mother takes a bite of crunchy latke before returning home to where she and Dick have set up their big Christmas tree, she tilts her head at the kitchen walls. "This is a very nice yellow."

"Buttercream, I think it's called," I say, and spoon applesauce onto her plate.

"See how nice the wood trim looks all painted white."

Before I can protest her disdain for the dark woodwork in our Victorian house, I hold up my hands. "I know, I know, you hate the trim in my bedroom."

"I don't hate it . . . It's just . . . you must find it very dark in there, that's all," she says. I wait for her to go on, but sensibly, she drops it, leaving the travesty of my bedroom alone for the time being. The truth is, I don't love the dark trim, I just haven't gotten around to painting it.

"Delicious." She takes another bite. She gets the kids' attention. "Did you help make them?"

The kids nod, lips slick with oil. I love having people over, feeding them, particularly my mom, who fed me, despite her continuous suggestions for how I might improve my house.

Holidays and traditions are what you make them. The big tree that towered over my youth gave way to the hand-painted menorah Jamie made one year, and it is every bit as bright. We will visit my mother's tree, but rather than feel as though we're missing out on the twinkling lights, the one day of gifts, the red and green everywhere, we'll enjoy our stay and head home. Last year, Daniel pointed to the crèche and asked what it was. I explained the Wise Men, Mary, the manger, the baby Jesus, and that they were special to Dick, and Daniel understood. At the time, I was pregnant with Will and Julia was fascinated by babies, so she peered into the manger for a closer look. Daniel put his arm on her shoulder, explaining but missing the point. "That's the baby, Jesus!"

My mom gives everyone small gifts, sings the prayers with the kids, and helps me put them to bed while Adam works. She takes a latke home for Dick, who can eat it in front of the Christmas tree lights. Now, that's American.

4.

I heat some zucchini latkes for the kids and make some simple chicken and broccoli while I clutch Will, knowing I will miss him so much while I'm gone. Not only will his small hands not touch my face and his grin make me ripple with joy, I also have to do without his mouth, which is very useful for nursing. I dread pumping in between meetings, but that's life. I leave food and notes for the kids, nurse Will once more before leaving him with a babysitter, and head for the station.

Sure enough, I get to New York, and after a four-hour train ride, I am about to burst. Heather meets me at the hotel so we can have a moms' night out—a book-reading sleepover—but the hotel isn't interested in my nursing needs.

"So you're saying there's nowhere for her to pump?" Heather's not taking no for an answer.

The guy behind the desk says, "Well, my wife had a baby eight months ago and she dealt with it."

The room isn't ready, and despite my offer to nurse in an unmade room, they've told me I can go stand up in the bathroom or wait a few more hours. My calm maternal instinct slides away and I am instead the angry woman with rock-hard boobs who needs, needs, needs to "get to work" before she can get to work.

"Look," I say, "I can't stand up in the bathroom and do this, and you won't give me a room or a meeting room, so here's what I'm thinking . . . " I eye the big lobby and point to two large cushy chairs that face the Christmas tree and the check-in desks. "Why don't I sit right there, take my shirt off, and pump? I'm sure the people in the lobby would get a kick out of it." I do not smile.

"If that's what you want to do, then go ahead," Mr. Personable says.

Heather nudges me. "What an asshole," she whispers, and I concur. Then she adds, "We're right near really great Korean food."

This produces a smile from me. "Perfect," I say. "Let's have that after I explode."

"I got no rooms available," the guy says, his arms crossed over his chest. I want to do that, but can't because my breasts are now bowling balls. Or water balloons.

I ask for the manager, repeat my plan of stripping down in the lobby with the frankness I use to offer the kids dinner—I am not budging. The manager hems and haws and—magically—produces a clean, vacant room.

After I'm relieved, we head out for a nontraditional Chanukah Korean meal, walking past myriad places to eat, soup and noodle bars, past the 24-hour massage and body scrub place. (I find it oddly comforting that if I were to wake up at two in the morning and really want to be scrubbed, I could walk back here. Not that this is my plan.) We stroll past the bakery with its milk buns and sesame-paste sweets on offer in the window, the bubble teas.

HanGawi is a traditional Korean place, and when we enter, they have us take off our shoes. We stash them in tiny cubbies that the kids would love, and walk in our socks up a few steps to the seating area. Each table is low to the ground and is in its own small section, complete with pillows. We order bibimbap, a bowl of hot rice traditionally topped with small portions of carrots, spinach, bean sprouts, some form of meat or tofu, zucchini, and gochujang—red chili paste. HanGawi is a purely vegetarian restaurant; they add sesame leaves and freshly made tofu. Heather orders the kimchi stone pot.

"So, how's Clementine?" I ask, remembering the way Julia and Clem held hands in Indiana, how they played in an indoor tent during the torrential rain.

"I went to work yesterday," Heather says, "and I told Clem I'd be downstairs writing for an hour. She asked, 'How long's an hour?' and I told her, 'It's a little while.' Then Clem asked, 'Well, how long's a frickin' hour?'"

We laugh over the sponginess of our kids, how they suck up our vocabulary, our traits—good or bad—and we share the small bowls of Baechu kimchi, which is whole cabbage mixed with ground pepper, garlic, ginger, and fish paste and then cut into smaller pieces. We pass the small white square bowl of shredded daikon, sharply flavored and spiced. When the bibimbap arrives, we let the rice sizzle in the stone pots, add the red chili paste, and talk about writing, about getting our families together again.

"Oh, I brought you something," I tell her, and reach into my bag. "Here." I hand her a container of the roasted fava beans I'd brought to Indiana. She reciprocates, rummaging in her bag for a sack of dried Bing cherries, the unsweetened kind I love to add to my salads and which Heather gets at her food co-op where she works long shifts.

"Indiana was so fun," I tell her. "The kids want to go again."

Heather opens the beans, sneaking one. "I can't resist." Then she puts the rest away for later. "Come visit us here," she says, scraping the crunchy rice from the side of the stone pot bowl. I let my rice crisp and sizzle for a long time so it becomes nutty brown and chewy, and when I scrape the bowl's sides, it is nearly caramelized and perfectly crisp.

"Come on," Heather urges. "We're staying east this Christmas. If you guys come on the twenty-sixth, maybe it will feel less weird."

I ponder and then nod. "Well, Adam's working Christmas, but we could get in the car on the twenty-sixth. . . ." I drain my Norwegian fizzy water and smile.

A plan is set in motion. We'll come visit after Christmas.

Heather comes with me to my book-launch party, and then, with milk stored into iced freezer bags, I leave the enormous Christmas tree in Rockefeller Center, the continuous loop of holiday jingles piped through speakers in the stores, and head home to Latkeland, inspired to take the kids for Korean food.

5.

My dad comes over for Chanukah dinner. It's the first year he's ever been in this country at this time—another first to get through—and he shows up happy, with arms full of Chanukah gifts, his nose searching for a potato pancake. I serve him a crisp one on a plate with a dab of applesauce but then warn him, "We're all kind of sick of the latkes by now, so we're taking a break from tradition."

From the oven I pull a large oval baking dish that is stuffed with pasta, four cheeses, and vegetables we had in the house.

"Daniel, you just have to deal," I tell him as he eyes the mixture.

"Everything's combined," he says.

Before he can protest further, we're seated in the dining room and Daniel is left to sort out his own peas from the dish. Eventually he just shrugs. "You can't taste them as much as I thought."

My dad tells everyone how glad he is to be here with us, and we don't find ourselves glancing at any empty chairs. Instead, we savor the richness of the dish, the end-of-the-day fatigue, and the warmth that washes over us.

"Mmm, you can really taste the Pecorino," Dad says, momentarily transported back to the patio in Italy, the long lunches. The savory nuttiness of the cheese lingers in each bite. "This is just right."

I scoop more for my dad, giving him extra spinach, and more for Adam, leaving more out. He likes spinach in things but doesn't love heaps of it the way I do. Will nurses while I eat my dinner and then wriggles free, exploring the floor vent while we finish up.

"Let's call this something funny," Jamie says.

"Let's call it good," Daniel says while he exiles each pea from the pasta to the side of his plate.

"Hey, how come Grandpa got to have a latke?" Julia asks.

"We've had them every day," I tell her. When her face falls to a frown I remind her, "We'll make them again tomorrow, OK?" She has a fondness for the sweet-potato ones.

The kids eye the gifts my dad has brought, and eat their dinners, trying to hurry through so they can do the candles and then the presents. "Let's call this Now You See It Pasta," Jamie says.

"How come?" I ask, even though I know.

"Because now you see it"—Jamie shows his fork, then eats a mouthful and says, his cheeks bulging—"and now you don't."

Jamie, now old enough to light the candles, strikes a match, his eyes filled with terror.

"It's OK," I tell him. "You're doing fine."

"It's just weird, you know, to like, light a match." He tries again. The flame takes and we recite the prayer, starting with *Barukh atah Adonai, Eloheinu, melekh ha'olam*, with everyone saying it, singing it.

6.

I have to head back to New York, this time to a different hotel, where my room is ready right away. Before going out, I find notes from Adam and the kids in my luggage and then walk uptown to a reading from my Chanukah book. I think about the kids reciting prayers over the candles, about Julia spinning around the kitchen and singing and pretending to be a dreidel, and wish I were there. Not even the cranium-size cupcakes my agent and

I share at a nearby bakery reduce the missing. I call them on the phone as I walk the cold streets.

"Hey, Mom," Jamie says breathlessly, "we had . . . some more . . . latkes and now . . . Grandma Bev and Papa Haha brought some sauce . . . I gotta go play indoor football." Daniel shrieks in the background and Jamie drops the phone.

Adam explains that my grandmother made her homemade Kahlúa sauce and that it's waiting for us in the fridge—to pour over ice cream.

"Hello?" I ask into the darkness.

"Hello?" Julia's voice is small.

"Julia, it's Mummy."

"No, Mummy's not here right now."

Granted, it's loud at the house, but still—I've only been gone one day. "Julia, sweetie, it *is* Mummy."

"Oh, *hi!*"

7.

We come home from Adam's aunt Ann and uncle Herb's annual Chanukah party with four exhausted kids. Instead of gifts, tonight we celebrate being together, giving to others. The kids help choose a charity, and we donate money and talk about the cause while we have a family meal. One year, it was Habitat for Humanity, another year, the local food pantry, this year, the Jimmy Fund. Kids can easily understand that not everyone has a warm house or latkes on the table or their health, and they feel good about giving.

"I wish I could share my food with someone who doesn't have any," Daniel says.

We pass latkes around the table, talking about how grateful we are, full of good fortune.

8.

"Get off me now, you stupid dumbhead," Daniel shouts at Jamie, who appears to be body surfing on his brother.

"Boys, quit it," I say.

"I'm hungry," Julia says.

"Well, nothing's ready yet."

"But I already rolled the balls!" Julia wails. She helped make the soufganiyot, jelly doughnuts, but we're waiting for them to finish rising.

"I had no idea about jelly doughnuts," my mother says. She's stopped by for round two of Chanukah fun. She gives me a look that I read as *Why didn't I?*

"I didn't either, Mom," I assure her. "But Julia learned about it at school. It's a tradition, apparently."

"For whom?" my mother asks.

I shrug. "Us, I guess," I say. "Maybe."

I told the kids about my trips to New York, about the train rides, the taxis, the Korean food I ate with no shoes on. I hope we'll take them to a Korean restaurant too. But not now. Now I pry the boys off each other, put Will in his play saucer for a few minutes, and fry up the doughnuts. The kids are momentarily entranced by the sound of dough in oil, the smells of sugar, and the sight of the jam I've left to warm in the kitchen's heat.

They sit at the table, and I say, "Now, there's just one thing." I drain the doughnuts on paper towels and then go to the cabinet where Adam has stashed an extra syringe. I show the kids. "Look, see, we have to use this!" I'm smiling but they start to cry.

"No—not again!" Daniel says.

Jamie's big eyes brim with tears. "But we already had our flu shots!" The injustice fuels the air and before I can explain, I have a full-fledged mutiny on my hands.

"I'm not doing it!"

"You'll have to pin me down!"

"I'm hungry and don't want a shot!"

Will begins to scream because of the screaming.

"Hey! Wait! Settle down!" I wave the syringe like a white flag. "No shot! Relax! I got rid of the needle part." They begin to quiet. "I'm just using the other part to suck up the jam and inject into the doughnuts."

"So the doughnuts get vasintated?" Daniel asks.

"Right," I say, not bothering to correct the vaccination pronunciation. "Watch." I demonstrate, pulling the plunger up as I stick the syringe into a dish of melted strawberry jam. I hold the small doughnut, slide the syringe into its middle, pump it full of jam, and then exit, leaving a small jammy wound.

"Phew," Jamie says.

Tears cling to Daniel's face. "Those look good."

Adam won't be home until past ten, the kids are tired, there are no latkes left in the fridge and none in the freezer, but we have the soufganiyot. My mom and the kids gather at the table. I bring confectioners' sugar and Julia helps me sift the powder on the tops of the tiny doughnuts and we have them with the few remaining latkes, some plain chicken, a mixture of broccoli and carrots, and end this holiday season on a very sweet note.

Soufganiyot (Jelly Doughnuts)

1 package active dry yeast

3 tbsp. granulated sugar

¼ tbsp. warm (but not hot) water

3½ cups flour

½ cup warm milk

2 egg yolks and one white

dash of salt

3 tbsp. butter, very soft

canola oil (for frying)

strawberry, raspberry, or apricot jam or all of them, room temperature

confectioners' sugar for dusting

Dissolve yeast and the granulated sugar in water. Let this sit for five minutes. Mix flour with yeast mixture, milk, whole egg and yolk, a dash of salt, and rest of sugar. Mix by hand or in a mixer (I had the kids mix with a big wooden spoon). Add the soft butter and use your hands to incorporate it until the dough is sticky but stretchy. Put the dough in a greased bowl, cover with a dishtowel, and let it rise somewhere warm for about an hour or a bit more (if you have laundry going, it can rest on the dryer or on the stovetop). Put the dough on a floured surface and roll it out. Use the top of a glass or a biscuit cutter and make circles about 2 inches wide and have kids roll these into balls. Place the balls of dough on parchment paper and cover. Let rise for another half an hour.

Pour about an inch or two of canola oil into a pot (not a pan, because it spatters too much) and fry up the balls of dough for a couple of minutes on each side, until puffy and brown. Set on paper towels to drain.

Using a bulb baster (or a syringe), suck up some jam and insert about a teaspoon into each ball (make a small slit with a knife if need be). Dust with powdered sugar and serve right away.

Now You See It Pasta (Italian Baked Pasta)

6 cippolini onions, peeled and sliced

2 cloves garlic

olive oil

1 pound interestingly shaped pasta (rhombi, cavatappi, chiocciole, fusilli)

baby spinach

1 bag frozen peas

sea salt and black pepper to taste

2 cups of at least two (but more is good) of the following cheeses: Parmigiano-Reggiano, Pecorino Tuscano, goat cheese, cheddar, Bucheron

roasted red peppers

Set oven to 375° and grease a deep baking dish. Sauté onion and garlic in a bit of oil until onions are beginning to brown. Cook the pasta three-quarters through. Before draining, add the spinach and peas to the hot water with pasta. Let sit for 2 minutes and then drain both. Drizzle olive oil onto pasta/pea/spinach mixture and pour into a pan. Add the cooked garlic and onions, as well as salt and pepper. Add bits of cheese, mixing a bit as you go and saving some cheese to sprinkle on top. Before you sprinkle top with remaining cheese, scatter roasted peppers over the whole dish. Top with cheese. Bake until golden brown on top—about 45 minutes.

 ## Eggnog Pancakes

2 cups flour (wheat or white or a mixture)

1 tbsp. oil

2 cups eggnog

2 eggs

1 tsp. salt

1 tbsp. baking powder

Mix all of the ingredients. Make pancakes. Say whatever blessing you want. Or not.

 ## Homemade Kahlúa Sauce

4 cups sugar

1 cup instant coffee

2 cups boiling water

3 tbsp. vanilla extract

1 fifth vodka

Mix dry ingredients together, then add boiling water. Mix until dissolved. Let cool and add the vanilla and the vodka. Put into bottles. Keep for at least a month before enjoying.

In Which India Is Introduced Again

Daniel has spent the better part of our time in Brooklyn in a time-out. An example of why:

But we are leaving New York, having spent our days taking long walks around the neighborhoods, eating Mexican food at a place where they still make guacamole tableside, and playing in a band in Dan's practice room. So far the day has been a fun post-Christmas morning at the Brooklyn Museum with Heather, Dan, Clementine, and Graham. Once we find grown-up Dan, who got distracted and wandered away, we're heading for Indian food in Queens before the whole crew goes to my in-laws' in Connecticut.

"What else do you do in the pouring rain when the kids are exhausted except schlep to Queens for Indian food?" Adam asks as we follow Heather and Dan to the Jackson Diner. The day is gray, save for the slashes of bright color from the saris on display in the shop windows, the vibrant ropes of beads and salwar kameez, billowy traditional outfits in myriad colors. Everything around is us abuzz with shoppers and eaters, music bleating from open-air speakers, languages overlapping, swirling together.

Magically, we find parking and the boys aren't fighting and Will's not yet fussing. Only Julia says, "I think I don't feel well." I touch her forehead.

"She's sick, Ad," I say, but we have to eat before driving the two hours to Connecticut, so we take our seats. The $8.95 buffet is crowded. I nurse Will and take turns with Adam getting plates for Daniel and Julia, though she won't eat hers, preferring instead to put her face on her arms or in my lap. Jamie serves himself, standing on his toes to see what's on offer on the high tables.

"Hey—now we can have mango lassi for real," Jamie remembers. We order the drinks and they arrive, the scent of fresh fruit ripe in the air as we share the cold liquid.

"What *is* that?" Daniel asks, tilting his whole body to get a better view of something.

"Masala dosa," I tell him as we watch a cook prepare it on a griddle. He ladles a bit of oil on and it sizzles, then he scoops a bit of batter on, which he thins with a spatula.

"They're like crêpes."

"But with chickpea flour," the man adds. He fills the dosa with a bit of curried potato and the dreaded peas, then folds the whole thing like a long log. It is far too long to fit on the plates, but I hold it in place as we go back to the table.

Daniel tears off a bite of the outside. "OK, so this part's good." He keeps going. "Nope—I don't like the guts." He points to the peas and potato.

At the other end of the table, Heather and Dan feed Clem and Graham, checking in on everyone every now and then. The place is filled to capacity now, and Will needs to nurse again because he's tired—his sleep schedule's totally off due to traveling and the museum—so I lean over my plate, awkwardly resting my foot on the stroller and getting bumped every time someone lines up for the buffet.

"Check me out," Adam says with a plate of food. "I'm going for the curried goat." Adam and I have discussed in detail that were we ever in a position where one of us had to try something potentially gross, he'd be the volunteer, as long as it's not berries. Adam's competitive spirit outweighs his narrow palate, so were there money involved or team points for ingesting rodents or bugs or something else that our culture frowns upon and yet others enjoy, Adam's the volunteer from our partnership.

I slather naan bread with saag, enjoying the spiciness of the spinach, the crunch of the dosa, the sweetness from the lassi.

"Remind me to make you peach curried chicken sometime," I say to no one in particular, and Julia lifts her head from the table to nod.

When the kids are close to passing out and the grown-ups have shoved enough food in to last the drive north, we go to the cars. Next door to the diner is Delhi Palace Sweets.

"You know you want to go in," Adam tempts me. "Go for it. Just don't be too long."

With great haste, I go to the closet-size store and eye the numerous gleaming treats in the case. Gulab jamun, dough balls in syrup, made from Khoya, a milk reduced to near-solid form. Jalebis—golden red fried pretzel shapes flavored with cardamom, their color induced from saffron threads. Triangles of crushed cashew paste, a giant slab of halvah, and entire green chilis dipped in thick chickpea flour and deep fried. There are pakoras and samosas for a savory treat, but the gooey sweet army of desserts is what lures me. For five dollars, I buy honey-soaked dough balls and some jalebis for the kids to try later.

When we reach Connecticut, the adults are more fatigued than the kids. Jamie, Daniel, Julia, and Clem form a makeshift band in Adam's parents' basement. Upstairs, Heather and I alternate cooking with chasing Will and Graham. By the time the kids are in bed we've fashioned a meal of caramelized butternut squash that mainly got so cooked because we forgot about it, on which we layer sautéed onions and crispy shallots. We serve this with smoked salmon and goat cheese salad, and wild mushroom ravioli.

"Happy anniversary, Mom and Dad," Jamie says in the morning.

"It's not until tomorrow, but thanks anyway," Adam says. Clem and Julia are enmeshed in a make-believe world that involves fairies and a lizard. The phone rings. My grandparents call.

"Happy anniversary!" they sing together.

"Thanks—a day early."

"It's not today?"

"Nope," I say, "Saturday."

"I thought it was today."

"No," I say, and wrangle Daniel from my father-in-law's elliptical machine. "It's Saturday."

The phone rings again.

"Hi, Mum," I say into the receiver.

"Happy anniversary!" she singsongs.

"Thanks," I say.

"What? Your voice is odd—you're not happy?" She sounds concerned.

"No, it's just that it's not really the day—it's tomorrow."

She questions the veracity of what I said but says she'll call again then.

The kids cluster to the table, reaching into the brightly colored box of Indian treats and selecting a couple. We cut a few gulab jamun in half, they are so rich and sticky; and the jalebis are crunchy, nearly seeping with oil. The kids feast but we're too busy chasing them to eat much of it.

Heather, Dan, Adam, and I stay up late playing Pictionary, laughing over our combined lack of artistic skill, happy with the peace that comes when all six children are deep into their slumbers.

"I made reservations," Adam remembers before bed. We will celebrate our anniversary on the actual day at the place where we got married, assuming we can find a sitter. The following day, the kids are in tears saying good-bye. Clem says to Heather, "It's OK if you don't bring me back to Brooklyn. I think I'll just live here."

"So, are you getting ready to go out?" Heather asks when she calls to say she and Dan and the kids are safely back in Brooklyn.

"Still looking for a sitter," I tell her.

"So guess what I'm making tonight?" she asks, but then answers, "The butternut squash. Now, how long do I need to forget it on the stove?"

"A long time," I say.

She tells me her friend Becky is making the flounder recipe I gave Heather in Indiana. "I hope she likes it," I say. I love the traveling element of recipes, the fluidity of sharing foods. "And give me your cauliflower gratin recipe—Julia loved it." We talk for a few more minutes about the next trip, about summer, about them coming to Italy if the house hasn't sold, about whether we'd go back without Min there or if we should all go somewhere new.

Daniel comes into the kitchen in the morning and hands us a note. Based on his earlier works, Adam and I are wary. Will it say "crap"? Or some variation? "Craphead"? "Diyareeeeeaa head" spelled phonetically?

"No, really, it's OK this time," he assures us, his cheeks pink.

We read his note and smile at the words printed in all caps: HAPPY ANNIVERSARY!

(Rumor Has It) Cauliflower Gratin

This recipe is my original, though like many dishes, comes by way of culinary telephone—that is, talked about and misinterpreted and changed until it is recognizable but not the same as it started out. Heather's version was based on her friend Margie's version that she got from their mutual friend Becky, who thought it was based on a Nigella Lawson recipe. I thought it might be Clotilde Dusoulier's, but it turned out Heather and I were both misinformed. Heather had made a loose version of Ina Garten's lovely recipe from Barefoot in Paris. This is neither of those, but contains elements from my mother (the shallots) and from what I had around (the white wine) and the kids (they like cheddar). You can prepare the cauliflower the day before if you like.

1 big cauliflower, cut into florets all roughly the same size

generous ¾ cup compte cheese (or Gruyère), grated

¼ cup cheddar cheese, grated

2 dashes nutmeg

2½ tbsp. butter

1 shallot, minced

3 tbsp. flour

1½ cups milk

1½ tbsp. white wine

salt and pepper

2–3 tbsp. panko breadcrumbs

Preheat oven to 350°. Steam cauliflower until tender (about 10 minutes). Place in baking dish (no need for a gratin dish—any medium-size dish with sides will do). Sprinkle half of the cheese (both kinds) on top of the cauliflower. Dust with nutmeg. In a dab of butter, sauté the shallot over medium heat until cooked but not browned. Add rest of butter, and as soon as butter melts and sizzles, add all flour, whisking as you go. Cook for a couple of minutes (whisking the whole time so the sauce doesn't color). Add the milk slowly at first, whisking to get rid of any clumps. Simmer for a couple more minutes, stirring as the mixture begins to thicken. Add white wine and let cook a minute more so mixture stays thick. Remove from heat—add salt and pepper to taste. Pour sauce evenly over cauliflower, top with remaining cheese. Scatter top with breadcrumbs and dust with nutmeg. Bake for 25 minutes and then under broiler for 1 minute to finish browning top.

Note: *This is wonderful served with a sweeter main course such as chicken or salmon coated in apricot jam and mustard.*

Feta-bulous

I can tell by Adam's grimace that he's beyond dubious about the spread.

"It's very . . . bright," he says, not wanting to offend me.

"I didn't make it, you know," I tell him. "But I think it smells really good." We're in the living room having a picnic dinner, just the two of us, to celebrate our anniversary. We love this kind of meal—baguette and cheeses, sliced salamis and cured meats, roasted vegetables in garlic and olive oil, good wine or, in this case, French pear cider, freshly made hummus, and the bright red feta and pepper spread. Who needs a fancy restaurant? Who needs to schlep out in the wintry mess? Who wants to tack on an additional hundred dollars of babysitting to an already fancy date dinner? We love celebrating our winter wedding by eating like this, clinking our fluted Poiret Granit, all cozied up while the kids sleep upstairs. Also, we couldn't get a sitter.

So we toast our love and the meal while a gentle snow falls outside.

"It's from the Armenian store." I point to the feta. Near our old neighborhood there was an Armenian store, Sevan, highly regarded for its incredible hummus, excellent fresh fetas soaking in brine, and all manner of nuts, seeds, and brittles by the pound. On my way back from Formaggio Kitchen, a store known for its cheese cave, I stopped at Sevan for the hummus but couldn't resist the color of the feta spread. We celebrated the first night of our honeymoon with a huge gourmet fireside picnic. Having been too excited to eat much after the ceremony, we were thrilled with the basket that had been sent by one of my favorite epicurean shops (courtesy of my parents-in-law).

Now we enjoy the feta, which wasn't part of the original spread.

Feta cheese has been made for centuries, originally heavily salted in order to preserve it through the long winter months. Many countries make feta: Greece, Denmark, Italy, the United States, and Germany, although most stores in the United States tend to carry Bulgarian, Greek, or French fetas. Each country has its own recipe—Bulgaria typically mixes sheep's milk and a yogurt culture, Greek law specifies certain percentages of sheep's milk and goat's milk.

My favorite is the French feta. Made from sheep's milk, it is particularly creamy and considerably less salty than the other kinds. The Armenian grocer keeps four or five different kinds of feta on display in vats, soaking in brine to keep it moist or wrapped tightly and ready for purchase. I bought a wedge of French feta for salads tomorrow with the kids and the pepper spread for tonight.

Adam rips off a hunk of baguette and reaches for the feta-pepper spread, grinning. "Here goes." I wait for his "not my favorite" or "you can have it," but he comes back with "I wish you bought more. That is so good!" Adam doesn't like Greek salads, doesn't ever want feta on his food, so it's refreshing to see this reaction. He has a face that would lose money at poker—his eyes stay steady but his mouth betrays his innermost thoughts—the shit-eating grin slips in without him knowing, and his "No, really, it's fine" look is all too easily read. When I was pregnant with Jamie, Adam and I took a major hiatus from fish. No more cod, haddock, trout, salmon. I couldn't stand the smell, the taste, or the thought. I was barely keeping solids down at all, but fish became my nemesis. We once had to switch tables at a restaurant with his eighty-nine-year-old grandmother because the fish scent wafting from the next table over was making me heave. But when Jamie was born, and my stomach back to normal, Adam was ready for fish. I buttered him up with a story about this sour cream and dill fish recipe I'd been fond of. Foolproof, I'd called it. I made it the way I'd always done, but perhaps grew heavy-handed with the dill and maybe didn't cook it that long, or maybe my hormones were still out of whack or maybe it was like other mistakes in the kitchen—they just happen. Either way, I plated it on a bed of wild rice with barely steamed sweet fresh peas. Adam looked eagerly at his plate. I watched him eat the first bite. His mouth turned sour right away but I thought maybe I'd misread it. Then I tasted it. "Oh my God, this is inedible." I spat the mouthful into my napkin. Bits of dill clung to my lips, the mushy fish making my mouth wrinkle.

Adam began to laugh and shoved another mouthful in while his face strained. "I'll eat, it's not . . . the worst . . . ," he said.

"Oh, but it is," I'd said.

"Well," he gave in, "it's not good."

So tonight, when Adam tries and likes the feta, I feel a sense of satisfaction even though I didn't make the cheese myself. Whenever we try something that isn't great Adam says, "But it's not as bad as The Fish." It became the meal against which all others are measured. Probably a boon for me.

The next day, we offer the kids the leftovers: broccoli with pepper flakes, crusty bread, jams we'd bought back in Italy at the Ghiottornia in Pitigliano, which are sweet and savory. Eating the jam is emotionally just a little bittersweet because of Min's death. Julia goes right for the spread. "I love this. I love it!" Her *l* sounds are still tinged with *y*'s so her declaration sounds like "I yuv this."

"I do too, Julia," Adam says. "I thought I wouldn't, but then I did."

Jamie nods. "It's a little salty, but it's really good on crackers."

Daniel tries for a way around the feta spread. "How about I just have the cracker?"

I shake my head. Daniel, ever the lawyer, tries again. "I have a suggestion—you eat the spread, Daddy, because you love it so much, and I'll wait and see if there's any left."

"Daniel," I say, "you don't have to try it, but you can't have the crackers or the baguette, because those are for dipping."

He tries the hummus, which he adores, and dips a few baby carrots in while he watches Julia scarf down the spread. "Can I eat all of this?" she wonders.

"Save some for me," Adam says, and reaches for it.

Daniel starts to whine. "I didn't even get to try it yet!" His voice raises with indignation. "How come I'm the only one who hasn't even had it?"

"No," Jamie proves him wrong. "Will hasn't either." Will looks up from his high chair, his mouth awash with bits of winter squash. He has progressed from soft mush to a very soft dice.

Daniel's eyes fill with tears. "I guess no one cares if I try it."

"One minute you don't want to touch it, the next you're crying because you didn't have any?" Adam asks.

Daniel nods, fighting a smile and more tears.

"So do it already," I say, and push the spread toward him.

He leans in for a whiff. "It smells totally disgusting."

Adam yanks the stuff away. "Are you eating it or making fun of it?"

Daniel sighs and as though he's on a game show and about to eat larvae for money, holds a cracker between his pointer finger and thumb. He first dips a corner into the spread, getting the tiniest dab.

"You're never going to see what it's like if you take that little," Jamie scolds.

Daniel rolls his eyes and grunts, but goes back for a bigger scoop. He puts the cracker and spread in his mouth, chews thoughtfully, and tilts his head. "Whatever."

Feta and Red Pepper Spread

2 large roasted red peppers
(you can do this yourself or
buy jarred)

big hunk feta cheese
(preferably French feta)

¼ cup olive oil

Chop peppers. Crumble feta. Mix peppers and feta together and blend in food processor with olive oil. Add salt and pepper as you see fit.

Side Note

Our picnic would not have been complete without the wonderful roasted wasabi peas from our local place, Fastachi. Fastachi does all their own roasting of nuts, seeds, and peas, and they are extraordinary. Jamie wouldn't try one, due to fear of spice from his surprise jalapeño encounter when he was four, but Daniel and Julia did, and while Daniel rushed for the water to stop the "burning in his nose," Julia chewed and asked for one more before drinking some milk to quell the sensation. Adam didn't want to eat one, but did, and regretted his decision.

Valentine's Day

"What's in there?" Daniel points to the pot on the stove.

"French couscous," I tell him, and get back to shelling shrimp.

"What makes it French?"

"Um . . . ," I start. "A lot of people in France eat couscous. There's a big African population there. . . . Like the way English people are familiar with curry. Tunisia is to France as—" I cut myself off. "I don't know," I tell Daniel. "But it'll be good."

We have the United Nations of vegetables sizzling in olive oil: onions from Spain, peppers from Mexico, shallots from Canada, tomatoes from Italy. But the shrimp are local. Fresh Maine shrimp are at their peak (and their most affordable) in the winter. When I lived in that state, I'd pull over to the side of the road and visit one of the shrimpers. In a white truck reminiscent of a dairy truck, or sometimes just a big old pickup with over-size coolers, the guys would pile pounds of pink shrimp into thick brown paper, and dinner would be a few minutes away. It felt old-school, like hearing my grandmother's stories about when the fishmonger would come to the house and the ice man looked in her window to see the order—a piece of cardboard either tipped on its side for a half-block or standing upright for a full block of ice.

When we first moved into our house, which hadn't been touched in sixty years, the kitchen came complete with an icebox. "Remember, it could only hold one thing of milk and nothing else?" Jamie says when I remind him. He's got a folder loaded with the day's excitement: Valentine's Day cards from his classroom friends, bright reds and cartoon rectangles with newly learned script on the back.

"Is that shrimp?" Julia asks. I nod. "Oh. Can you get the cards I made?"

"Yeah, let's do cards," Daniel yelps.

"I got so many today, Daniel, did you?" Jamie challenges his brother to a competition.

"So, so did I!"

"Get our cards—where are they, anyway?" Jamie demands.

"I can't get them now." I show them my shrimp-shell-covered hands. The wild Maine shrimp are smaller than others and come with their tails and antennae, and I need to work fast while Will is still amused by his drawer of cups. We've designated one of the deep kitchen drawers as a place for any plastic plates, cutlery, sippy cups, cups with baseball players on them, plates made at the paint-your-own-pottery place. The kids have free access to the drawer and can get themselves (or a younger sibling) a drink or set the table by themselves. The drawer also makes for fifteen minutes of clattering—self-contained fun for the baby/toddler set. I prop a plate into the sliding mechanism so Will won't pinch his fingers, and I let him re-move items, practice standing, blow into cups, fling things around the kitchen while I de-tail and de-vein the shrimp. "We can do cards at dinner," I say. "I have cards for you guys too."

They grin, especially Daniel, who blushes like he got his wish. I have cards for the kids, a small gift for Adam, and a nice dinner: shrimp, cous-cous, crisp green beans flaked with confettied red pepper, and strawberry shortcake for dessert. I'm not huge into cutesy food (see: Mummy Nuggets, page 32), but every now and again I get swept up and give in. Tonight, I cut the firm red peppers into large heart shapes, freehand, which hopefully the kids will enjoy and Adam might find sweet. Or cloying. Of course he won't eat the berries, so he can forgo dessert and opt for his gift.

"This is great!" he says when he opens it. I downloaded sheet music for the piano, had it bound, and now we have our own book of favorite songs for him to play and for me to sing. They started out as love songs, but as I found more songs that I knew he'd enjoy I'd think, It's OK if I print David Bowie's "Life on Mars" for Valentine's Day, right?

The dinner goes over well. I add the shrimp to the onions and shallots, careful not to overcook—they only take a few minutes and come up fully pink. The couscous took five minutes—one and a half cups of water to one cup of the grain—only I've used fish and vegetable stock in place of water because this adds flavor during the cooking process rather than having to season it afterward.

"Look—a heart!" Julia says when her pepper appears before her. I've stuck the pepper hearts into the couscous, using it as the anchor, and served the garlicky green beans on the side. Adam gives the kids the folder in which their cards have been stashed—they made them earlier in the week but glue, paint, and marker all had to dry.

With Will on my lap I read my cards and feel fuller than if I'd eaten the whole meal myself—the kid printing, the carefully chosen words, the blobs of color blurring onto the red construction paper.

"I did it blue because, um, I didn't . . . you don't have to use red, right?" Julia looks at me from behind her thick glasses.

"You can use whatever you want," I tell her.

"There aren't rules for everything," Jamie adds in his all-knowing tone. "Thanks for the cards," he says to everyone. Everyone at the table made everyone else a card—except Will. I give Adam a look and thank him for my card, which is every bit as intimate and loving as the best meal, then I ready the desserts for the kids.

"Oh, wait," Daniel says, and dashes to his bag. "I made this." He hands Will a miniature heart with a simple "I love you, Will" on it. Will takes it, chews it, and then waves it wildly in the shrimp-scented air.

Garlicky Green Beans

These are all-purpose—warm at dinner; cold in salads; served with tofu, chicken, fish, or meat; or munched on as a snack. Granted, garlic may not be exactly Valentine's Day material, but true love can ignore pungent breath.

1 lb. green beans	red pepper
4 cloves garlic	sea salt
olive oil	dash of soy sauce
red pepper flakes	

Trim and steam the green beans but make sure they stay crunchy—maybe 5 minutes in just a half-inch of water. Drain. Meanwhile, slice and sauté the garlic in olive oil without letting it brown. Add in a pinch or two of red pepper flakes and cook for 1 minute more. Turn off heat. Dice some red pepper and add to the oil and garlic mixture. Sprinkle with sea salt, trickle with a bit of soy sauce, and pour the whole thing on top of the drained green beans.

The Root of All . . . Evil!

The kids have been dashing around saying the word "evil" as often as they can and for, as far as I can tell, no good reason.

"Stop it," I warn. It's the middle of a slushy February and I can't believe I've turned into one of those people who bemoan winter, but I have. I'm sick of snow. Of being cold. Of lost mittens and hats left at school. Of chapped cheeks and cracked, chapped lips and noses that run marathons.

"Too bad we can't just hibernate like bears," Daniel says. "Or lizards."

Jamie nods over his homework. "I'm doing a report on the American Black Bear. We picked animals out of a hat."

"Do you want to hibernate, Mom?" Daniel asks. I nod.

"Evil!" he shouts, and I launch into another round of why that word shouldn't be thrown around.

Meanwhile, Julia pokes the butternut squash that's cooling on the counter. We cooked it for a while with a bit of brown sugar and now it's about to be made into soup for the masses.

"Squash isn't evil," Julia says absentmindedly.

"No, it's not," I say as more snow begins to fall from the gray sky.

"I think vegetables hibernate," Daniel says. "What happened to the leftovers from the Korean food?"

Daniel opens the fridge, looking, but then shakes his head. "Oh, yeah, I ate them at lunch." Daniel had packed his lunchbox today filled with leftover chop chae, the sweet potato noodles he ordered that came with vegetable slices and shrimp. The meal was a success—a surprise treat for him and Jamie—when I picked them up from their half-day release at school.

"Evil!" Jamie squeals, then slaps his hand to his mouth. "I mean, they don't because they're not animals. And only animals hibernate." He sits up on his knees in his chair. "I might hibernate tonight anyway."

"Me too," I tell him, adding, "I'm done with winter."

Julia nods, her small brow furrowed. "Yeah, except we have to finish the soup."

"And the mash," I say, and point to the nubby lump of celeriac on the counter. My mother fed us lots of root vegetables. Her grandmother had a root cellar that my mother had described in details so clear I can almost picture it: the dusty and old winding wooden staircase, the stone walls and dirt floor, the round barrels and casks filled with tomatoes being pickled in brine, the square boxes made of wood filled with purple-headed turnips, another with carrots up to the brim, parsnips, potatoes, and another where my mother's cat gave birth on a ticking mattress. All of this was tucked away in the cold dark cellar to use in the lean winter months. I didn't have the good fortune of finding the celeriac in my cellar. In fact, if I had, I feel sure that would be enough to put me off eating it, what with the years' worth of mismatching plates, half-broken toys, boxes of shoes and clothing, woodworking tools, and general mayhem of dank muck down there. Instead, I palmed the root at the store and brought it home, feeling empathetic toward the warty, rough vegetable—it is certainly not the food one rushes to because of its looks. However, my mom taught me well.

"Sometimes people call it celery root," I tell the kids. Jamie plays catch with the thing and Daniel watches. Unlike other root vegetables, durable celeriac isn't familiar-looking. Parsnips are, as the kids described, "white carrots," but tougher and sweet. Parsnips are my sister-in-law's favorite, and I think of her every time I roast them. Celeriac isn't pleasantly colored like beets; not firm, purple-striped, and dumpy like a turnip.

Julia reaches for the celeriac. Its exterior is tangled, almost ventricular, with overlapping roots and a brown outside. "We need to cook it." She pauses, hoping we do because it's so unfortunate-looking as-is. "Right?"

"Right." I study the lopsided mass. "Doesn't it look like something a troll would play with?"

"Or some evil creature would use as a weapon," Jamie offers.

"Evil!" Daniel shouts.

My mother roasted this root, occasionally slicing it, but most often mashing it and serving it alongside a roasted herbed chicken or local lamb in the spring near her farm in England. I take a sharp knife and peel the thick skin, but this does not beautify the celeriac any. Indeed, now the thing looks lumpy and naked. I'm half embarrassed for it.

Julia plunks the cubes of celeriac into a pot with a few inches of water in it, and when I've cut up the rest of the root, I let the water boil. The celeriac cooks until it's soft, and then I set it in a metal bowl with a splash of milk (cream is good too) and a few bits of butter and some sea salt. Then I wash mushrooms for some soup.

"And I do the pepper," Julia adds, reaching for our peppermill that only works marginally well. She turns it a few times, and I proceed to start the mashing, which only takes a little work.

"Do bears eat celery-yak?" Daniel asks.

"Cel-air-ee-ak," Jamie corrects. "No."

"Oh, and you know this?" I ask him.

Jamie shrugs. "Probably it's true."

"Bears are hibernating now anyway," Daniel says, and sniffs the mash. We can have it as a side dish with the soup or tomorrow with some fish.

I set the mash aside, and I cut some mushrooms and start that soup and continue on with the squash soup and help Jamie look up information about Black Bears, and serve two soups at once. The smell from both pots soothes us all, the rich taste of the creamy mushroom soup makes Daniel lick his chapped lips for more, and Julia leans her whole body over the bubbling squash soup.

"What's the opposite of evil?" Jamie queries while tasting, and then answers himself. "Oh, yeah, good."

Many Mushroom Soup

It may seem as though you have tons of mushrooms, but they do shrink quickly. I like using lots of them and not quite as much liquid so that the soup is toothy and each bite contains a different mushroom. If you prefer more broth, add more stock or a drop more milk or cream.

any combination of mushrooms, totaling about 2 lbs. (I used oyster, portabella, white, and lots of cremini—trumpet are lovely too)

1 onion, chopped

1 shallot, chopped

butter/olive oil

1 quart vegetable stock

½ cup half-and-half

1 pint half-and-half *or* cream (*or* 12 oz. evaporated milk)

salt and pepper

Wash and cut mushrooms into bite-size but not tiny pieces. In a soup pot, sauté onions and shallot in a bit of butter and a drizzle of olive oil. When translucent, add the piles of chopped mushrooms and cook over medium heat, stirring so they don't brown. Cover and cook for about 15 minutes total. Add stock. Let come to a boil. Reduce heat to simmer and add half-and-half or evaporated milk, salt, and pepper. Heat gently and cook for a few minutes without ever boiling. Serve hot with fresh bread (or use leftovers on top of pasta).

My Mom's Celeriac (Celery Root) Mash

If you like this sweeter, you can try boiling a big carrot or two and mashing that with the celeriac. Parsnips, too, can be added to this mash. If you want to be fancy, put the mash into a pastry bag and pipe it onto a plate and set the meat or fish on top of it. Or eat it right from the bowl.

2 large celery roots	dash of dried mustard
2 tbsp. butter	sea salt
½ cup whole milk or cream	pepper

Peel, cut, and boil the celeriac until soft. Add other items and mash with a fork until mushy but not puréed. If you like, top with apple slices.

Butternut Squash Soup

If you don't have the time to roast the squash beforehand, then cube it and put it in the pot right away with all of the other items and let it simmer until soft and then blend. The flavor is more intense when the squash roasts (roasting brings out the natural sugars), but either way is fine.

2 butternut squash (or other kind), any size	2 tsp. Dijon mustard
butter	pepper—black and cayenne
4 tbsp. brown sugar	salt
olive oil	Worcestershire sauce
4–5 cloves garlic	2 tbsp. maple syrup
3 onions	dash of cinnamon
chicken or veggie stock— about 1 quart	1 diced apple for garnish

Cut each squash in half and scoop out the seeds. Score the insides of each half of the squash (basically draw a couple not-too-deep lines down the length of the squash). Put a pad of butter and a tablespoon of brown sugar in the deep part of the squash. Bake the squash in a 450° oven for about an hour or until the squash is mushy and you can scoop it out easily with a spoon. I don't even use a baking sheet for this, I just put the squash directly on the oven rack.

Meanwhile, in a big soup pot, warm some olive oil and sauté the garlic—either sliced or crushed—and the sliced onions. Cook the onions and garlic over low heat and don't let them get too brown.

Let the squash cool! I have burned myself many times. Scoop the squash out into the soup pot. Add stock so that the squash is not quite covered—about 4 cups. Mix it around. Now you want to purée the soup in batches in the blender—depending on how creamy or thick you like it.

If you want thinner soup, add more stock or broth. Now you add your spices—mustard, a couple dashes of cayenne pepper, some black pepper and salt, a bit of Worcestershire sauce, and some maple syrup, and a dash of cinnamon. Then let the soup heat for a while. When you serve it, you can sprinkle a bit of Bucheron or chèvre on top or a little scoop of plain yogurt. Top with a bit of diced apple if the season calls for it.

Tea Party

If someone were to rifle through our trash this week, the following assumptions might be penned:

- We are a bit incontinent (Julia likes to throw her nighttime pull-up in my trash rather than the bathroom).
- We are a small nation of butter-lovers.
- We are very close to going into sugar-induced shock and/or are trying to kill a legion of diabetics.

These assumptions wouldn't be that far off (save for the diabetics—I have no wish to harm them). Diapers aside, the trash tells the truth: two pounds of butter, five pounds of sugar, pints of milk and cream, and a fortune's worth of whole vanilla beans (from Madagascar and Uganda).

Then again, I am throwing a tea party. Not the kind that Julia and I have with tiny gingham napkins and Lilliputian saucers and cups, the smallest pretend drops of cream and invisible spoons. Rather, this is for grown-ups and all very real. My friend from college is having her first baby, and I offered to throw together a shower. How easy these things sound in theory, months back, before the reality of cooking for ten guests, before the flu strikes every member of the family except for Adam (working in pediatrics, his immune system can withstand great upheaval). Before I was wrestling with the very real feeling of sadness about not having any more babies in our family. I'm glad to leave pregnancy behind (I never was one of those glowing moms-to-be—more like nine months of vomiting so fierce I got to be friends with IV fluids and medication, and a heart condition that was about as much fun). To put it in perspective, my favorite part of pregnancy (aside from being kicked by the baby from the inside), was pushing. But I am sad to say good-bye to the unknown, to the baby smell, to the infinite softness of baby skin, to holding an infant to my chest and to feeling a certain wholeness and serenity that cannot be duplicated.

But here we are celebrating another arrival—my college friend's baby, who is due in eight weeks. Adam shuttles all four kids out for the afternoon while I slide baking sheets in and out of the oven, arrange lemon shortbread baked in a pie plate on a silver tray, dot it with Gerbera daisies for color, and give it a fine coating of powdered sugar. I want everything to be special for my friend—it's her first baby, her first shower, and she should be doted upon.

"Are you saving stuff for us?" Jamie wants to know as he wrestles with his raincoat.

"I'll try," I say as I wonder what to do with the leftover pastry dough. I made a fresh thyme crust for a caramelized onion tart but have enough left for something else. I peer into the fridge as Adam herds Julia to the bathroom and gathers bottle, blanket, books, and other items for his big outing.

"But what if all the tea people eat everything?" Daniel moans.

"Then they eat it," I tell him. I point to the vanilla-bean loaves, their edges crisp and shiny with a vanilla glaze made from water, whole beans, and sugar.

"It's totally not fair," Jamie says.

"When you have a baby, I'll make all this for you," I tell Jamie, realizing I have just enough dough for a rectangular tart. But what to fill it with? I grab some apricot jam I picked up from Le Pain Quotidien in New York, find an egg that wasn't devoted to any of the loaves of bread, and add to the mixture a sprinkling of sugar and half a lemon's worth of juice. I whisk everything together until it's smooth and pour it into the rectangular tart pan. Before I set it into the hot oven, I take six cherries from the bag I bought figuring they'd add a burst of color to the table, and halve them, removing their pits. I place them on top of the tart, cut-side down.

"Bye, Mom!"

"Have fun," I say to Adam. Will, in his arms, tilts his head and says, "Mamamamama," wondering if perhaps this will allow him to remain home. But I shake my head. Too many opportunities to yank down tea cups and generally cause chaos. Plus, if there's anything that detracts from a mother-to-be's attention, it's a baby. "I'll see you soon. And don't worry—there's bound to be leftovers."

I'm even more positive of this statement as I begin to slice the breads and tarts, organize the table: apricot almond bread served with apple butter, vanilla-bean loaf, ginger chocolate-chip bread, vanilla iced scones, lemon shortbread, baby cranberry poppy-seed scones with clotted cream and jam, smoked salmon and cucumber tea sandwiches, onion and thyme tart, and, once it emerges from the oven, small squares of apricot cherry tart. All over the table are baby roses and daisies. With this, I set out my grandmother's tea sets—one pot of jasmine, one of chamomile, and one of Earl Grey.

The shower-goers arrive, the tea is sipped, the plates piled with food. The tart turned out well—the lemon and cherries give it bite while the apricot mellows the tastes. The vanilla-bean loaf takes me back to early days of parenting. The Hi-Rise Bakery was up the road, and I'd walk up there with Daniel and Jamie in the double stroller and buy a slice to have for breakfast the next day. I'd made it once back in our tiny kitchen, but this time I used Amanda Hesser's recipe (based on the loaf from Hi-Rise), from *Cooking for Mr. Latte,* which is pure vanilla love. After the breads are cooked, the recipe calls for coating them in vanilla syrup. I save the left-over syrup to make lavender-vanilla salmon—pan-seared in a bit of olive oil with sea salt, dotted with the fragrant lavender, and finished in the hot pan with a bit of the sweet vanilla syrup.

But for now, I watch the party unfold. We speak of food, of tea, and watch as my friend carefully opens each gift. I've set aside our baby bath for her, some nursing shirts, and purchased some brand-new swaddling blankets. Adam and I printed out a coupon for two sessions of babysitting.

"Oh—an experienced mom and a pediatrician!" she says when she reads the card. "I'm totally doing that."

She is surrounded by friends, by sweet treats, by tiny shirts and miniature outfits, the smallest shoes. As I watch her unwrap the gifts, I feel wistful; I think back to my showers, to the time before I was a mother, how remote that seems now.

"What is this?" my friend asks, resting the package on her dome-shaped belly.

"A sling," another mother says.

"How do you wear it, exactly?"

"And this?" The item is rolled up with a ribbon.

"A hooded towel," I say.

"And you could tell this from across the room?" she asks. I nod. She will be able to tell too. In a few months, she'll be used to swaddling, to feeding, to wearing her baby, to knowing how her newborn likes to be held or soothed. It occurs to me that I still remember all this about my kids, how Jamie liked to be spoken to, a constant stream of words easing his fussiness. How Daniel needed motion—walking, driving. How Julia nursed and touched my hair. How Will needed—still needs—to be held upright, easing his reflux, making it so he can push his whole face into the crook of my neck.

I serve more breads, we guess the mother-to-be's circumference, think of songs with the word "baby" in them, and when the time comes, I pack up goody bags for everyone. I send my friend home with piles of scones for her husband, slices of the lemon shortbread for her, and keep just enough of each dish to share with the kids. Adam gets a slice of vanilla-bean loaf. I hug my friend good-bye, my unpeopled belly touching her populated one, and I do not feel as sad as I thought I would. Instead I feel, if not "done," then full.

Apricot Almond Bread

This bread works well for breakfast or for tea. It's especially good with apple butter on top. I recommend adding chopped crystallized ginger for anyone in her first trimester and feeling queasy.

2 cups dried apricots, sliced	2½ cups flour
1½ cups boiling water	1 tsp. baking soda
¼ cup butter	1 egg
1 cup sugar	¾ cup slivered almonds
1 tsp. salt	

Preheat the oven to 350°. Grease loaf pan. Place apricots in large bowl and pour water over them. Add the butter, sugar, and salt. Stir. Allow mixture to cool slightly. Add flour, baking soda, egg. Mix. Pour batter into loaf pan. Sprinkle almonds on top and press them in a little so they stay. Bake for about an hour, until almonds are golden brown and a tester comes out clean.

Lemon Shortbread Baked in a Pie Plate

This is a recipe I made up while cooking on the boat. It is simple and always comes out well. It has the perfect mixture of sour and sweet. Plus, you can mix the crust and the filling in the same bowl (although not at the same time), and kids can help with nearly all of the prep.

CRUST:

1 cup sugar

2 cups flour

1½ sticks of cold butter in small pieces

FILLING:

2 eggs

1 cup sugar

¼ cup freshly squeezed lemon juice (about 2 lemons)

powdered sugar

zest from one orange

Preheat oven to 350°. Make crust—mix sugar and flour, cut in the butter, and blend with your fingertips until coarse crumbs form. Press mixture into greased 9 or 9½-inch pie plate. Bake about 15 minutes or until golden.

Turn oven down to 325°. Prepare filling by combining all ingredients except powdered sugar and zest. Beat well by hand and then pour right away into baked pie crust. Bake for 15–20 minutes. Let cool until set (this will keep for a day or so in the fridge). Just before serving, pretty up the top with a dusting of powdered sugar and some zest for color.

You may eat this cold or at room temperature.

Note: One of the testers for this recipe had success using Splenda rather than sugar for her diabetic brother. Also, whole-wheat flour works as a fine substitute for white if that's what's readily available.

Mini Cranberry Poppy-Seed Scones

1½ cups flour

½ tsp. baking powder

½ tsp. cream of tartar

1 egg

¼ cup sugar

dash of salt

½ cup milk

1 tsp. poppy seeds

⅓ cup dried cranberries

dash of cinnamon

Heat oven to 400°. Sift all dry ingredients together. Add egg and milk, and mix just enough to blend. Add poppy seeds and cranberries. Spoon into greased mini muffin tins and dust with cinnamon. Bake for 10–12 minutes.

 ## Pastry Crust with Thyme

2½ cups flour

2 tbsp. fresh thyme, chopped

½ tsp. salt

2 sticks butter in pieces

⅔ cup sour cream or plain yogurt

Preheat oven to 375°. Mix all ingredients except sour cream by hand until coarse crumbs form. Add sour cream and stir with a spatula until it forms one ball. Use right away or refrigerate for up to a week. Makes two crusts' worth. Bake for about 25 minutes.

Optional fillings for tart crust:

* 1 egg, ¼ cup apricot jam, ¼ cup sugar, 1 tbsp. lemon juice. Mix ingredients and pour into baked crust. Place halved cherries or other fruits (fresh apricots, a few slices of peaches) on top. Bake for 15–20 minutes at 360° until set.

* 2 large onions, sliced; good sprinkling nutmeg; salt and pepper; ½ cup grated cheddar or Gruyère. Cook onions in a pan in a drop of olive oil until very soft—about 40 minutes. Spread around in cooked tart shell, dust with nutmeg, add salt and pepper, and cover with cheese. Bake for 25–30 minutes at 375° and let rest before serving.

Bananas, Split

The kids are doing their most enthusiastic "Buffalo Soldier," with Julia hitting all the "woy yoy you, woy yoy yoy yuhs" ("oy oy oy," as she says) and Daniel chiming in with his attempts at Rasta. He belts out, *"Buffalo soljahh!"*

And then it quickly dissolves into, "Would a buffalo even eat a person anyway?"

"No, they, like, just stand there being buffalos."

"Hey—we ate buffalo in those Cornish pasty things!"

So Bob Marley, were he to return to this earth and appear in my kitchen, might not appreciate the rendition of his classic tune, but he might enjoy the simple treat we're making.

Jamie asked to try something "flambé."

"What is that, exactly?"

"It means flaming, set on fire," I said as we bagged produce.

"I'm not eating fire," he cautioned me, lest I get any ideas.

"I'm not making you eat fire," I tell him. "Usually you just pour a bit of alcohol, like rum or Grand Marnier on a sweet dish and set it on fire—"

"So we're drinking alcohol?" Jamie's alarm sounds in his voice. "But that's illegal!"

"Wait—let me finish. The alcohol cooks off, and then you have a nice, flavorful dish." Skepticism registers on his whole body, hand on the hip, head cocked to one side, eyebrows raised.

"The stew I made a few weeks ago had red wine in it," I remind him.

"And the shrimp Daddy made has white wine in it . . . ," he adds. "So, fine. Flambé liquor or whatever."

Instead of that, we're making banana packets. All the fun without the alcohol.

"Come on in, inside," I tell the kids. "And shoes off right away." The mud is encroaching on my life, rising from the yard and slinking into the entryway, onto the kitchen floor, where Will finds it with his little fingers and muddies the stair runner.

"Take the tinfoil from the drawer," I say, and one of them listens. I rip off a few squares and have Daniel cut up a few bananas. "Juliet and I used to make this in England." Jules is my oldest friend from London, and we used to make this dessert because it suited our student-size wallets, it was easy and well-received, and because it requires no cleanup. Each child takes a few rounds of banana and places it in the center of his or her tinfoil square.

"Now we sprinkle brown sugar." Which I do, then add a small pat of butter. "You can add an orange slice or a lemon, if you want."

I show them how to crumple up the foil to form a packet.

"Like the pasty." Jamie nods.

"Now it's an envelope, and we'll stick it in the oven and when dinner's done, you'll have a little treat." I put the foil packets directly on the racks in a hot oven. "In the summer we can have these on the grill." If you have a cookout, you can place the packets on the heat right after the last of the other food is done and have the packets sit while you eat. If you like firm fruit, only let it sit about ten minutes, if you are OK with a looser texture, let it go longer; the sugar turns to near-caramel, the butter provides a bit of punch and, should you be in the mood (and over twenty-one), a good drizzle of Grand Marnier or dark rum can't hurt.

"So sweet!"

"Yum—banana pudding!"

Daniel eats his with dedication, spooning it into his open mouth while still humming. "*Buffalo Solider . . .*" He considers it. "It's kind of relaxed, isn't it? Like his other song, the one about the three little birds."

"Yeah," Jamie agrees. "He sounds like he likes to chill out."

"I think he did," I say, thinking of all the posters of Bob Marley that graced the dorm walls in my past.

"I love this," Julia concurs; her *l*'s are now fully pronounced, gone are the *y*'s. No more "I yuve this." For the first time, she's started to say "animal" instead of "aminal" and "table" instead of "tavol." Julia licks her lips. "Do buffalos like bananas?"

Banana Packets

tinfoil	lemon slice or orange slice (optional)
bananas	
brown sugar	rum or Grand Marnier (optional)
salted butter	

Tear tinfoil into square of about 8 inches—one square per person. Slice bananas and put handful into center of each square of tinfoil. Sprinkle with sugar. Dot with a bit of salted butter. Add a lemon or orange slice if desired. Bring top and bottom of squares together to form a packet that you can grip at the top. Place in whatever degree oven you've got going for other foods, or onto grill, and let cook until you're ready to eat (anywhere from 15–40 minutes). Carefully open packets and eat right away or splash with liqueur.

Scenes of Pre-Spring

1.

The kids, gathered at the table with a heap of crayons, books, and plastic frogs, alternate between coloring (Julia), working on alphabetizing his spelling words (Jamie), and playing an intricate game of "frog family" (Daniel). Will, nine months, does his best puppy imitation, crawling under the table, pulling at the kids' pant legs, searching for stray crumbs or misplaced Cheerios.

I pour some liquid in a cup for each kid. "Remember when you tried the coconut?" I ask them.

Daniel immediately giggles and turns red. "You were banging and whacking but it didn't work."

"I don't like coconuts really," Jamie says. "But I like macaroons."

"Well, what about coconut water?" I show them the container. "Want to try?"

A year ago, I probably would have had to convince them. By now, though, they're so used to the idea of trying new things that they just nod.

"Sure." Julia shrugs.

"Even if it doesn't look special or anything," Daniel adds.

Jamie's first to sip the clear water. "Yuck," he says right away and then, not wanting to hurt my feelings, adds, "But I like it a little bit."

I shake my head. "Don't say that for my sake, Jamie, you don't have to feel bad about not liking foods—you tried it, you don't like it, no big deal. Now you know."

He sighs. "Right."

Daniel wipes his mouth. "Well, that was extremely bad and very disgusting."

"I think I'll use that as the title for my next book." I laugh.

Julia licks her lips. "Yum!" She sips more. "I love this."

Adam comes home from work and the kids urge him to try the water too. "I don't like coconut," he says as though this will excuse him. He's been open to trying everything, at least until now.

"So?" Jamie hands him a glass.

"OK, fine." Adam gulps and wrinkles his noise. "No, thanks."

I explain. "They were giving away free samples at the market."

Jamie nods. "Maybe they had to because it's so gross no one would actually pay for it."

2.

I finally give in and buy chocolate soy butter. Normal soy butter is pretty tasty (and when you have a peanut allergy, it has to do as a peanut-butter substitute) and it strikes me as humorous that the "healthy food" store sells the chocolate version, but I guess everyone needs to make a buck. This time, the I.M. Healthy company is taking mine.

The purchase was misguided. I've been dreaming of a sandwich that some friends and I made a while ago: thick, crisped bread with Nutella spread and melted dark chocolate. We'd buttered the bread and toasted the whole thing in a panini maker (I don't own one, but a heavy lid works just as well for weighting it down). So, fantasizing of the melted chocolate oozing over the sides of the chewy bread, I grabbed the chocolate soy butter thinking the kids would find it equally decadent.

But the kids couldn't care less. "How come we're having chocolate at dinner?" Daniel asks, suspicious.

I don't mention I'm premenstrual for the first time in nearly two years and craving all manner of sweets. "When your mom offers you a chocolate sandwich, you don't ask why, you just say thanks," I tell him.

They do, but begrudgingly. Oh, all right, I'll have chocolate. Fine. I'll make do. This is not the reaction I expected. The sandwiches aren't a disaster, just not the fall-down-grateful yumfest I expected. Adam tried a similar experiment. One morning Daniel asked if he could have chocolate milk in his cereal. We don't normally have any chocolate milk in the house, but the milkman had brought some as a gift, and Adam shrugged and said, "Sure." Daniel tried it and was vaguely disgusted, but his curiosity was sated.

I watch them halfheartedly nibble their food.

Julia, chocolate fiend, says, "It's kind of good."

Next time I'll go for the real deal and get out the good dark chocolate, the sandwich weight. "What about chocolate grilled cheese?" I ask.

"Ewww!" Jamie pushes his plate away.

"Not with cheese," I explain. "Just with dark chocolate that you grill. . . ." They all lose interest in my clarification and in the meal. "You all done?"

"It's still light out!" Daniel says. "Let's go outside."

3.

Adam is home on full-day kid duty while I write. I venture downstairs to throw lunch together for myself and find the countertops covered with the day's mail, a bag of bread odds and ends, and a heavy skillet. My detective sense tells me he's making skillet shrimp, a dish he's wanted to attempt for a while. On Wednesdays, my work day, he is home and in charge not only of the kids but of dinner, too.

He buys his ingredients, asking if I need the leftover bread for anything or if it's up for grabs. I'm excited he's creating a new dish. Even though he has a handful of reliable, healthy, tasty meals, he tends to shy away from new dishes.

Later, my cell phone rings right as I'm finishing a meeting.

"Hey, um, so is the food processor broken?" he asks with lids clanging and baby babbles in the background.

"No, it's just very, very safe."

"Meaning I'm not doing something right?"

"Meaning you have to swivel the thing and lock the handle and try to maneuver it and . . ." I try to lead him through the steps. "It's annoying, I know. Until you use it a lot, it's hard to figure out which way everything goes." I can hear frustration building in his voice.

"But I tried it that way and . . ." He grunts and tells the kids to be quiet so he can hear. "This better work, I think I had the top thing too far over . . ." I can imagine exactly what he's doing, trying to get the lid to lock.

"If worse comes to worst," I say, "just use a knife to make bread-crumbs."

"But I want it to be perfect," he says.

That's one of our differences—he likes the perfection (or perception of it) that comes from following a recipe exactly, of taking every step in a manual or guide so the bookcase/dishwasher/overly complicated toy proceeds as planned. I like the mess. But I love that about him. "Wait—here goes." I hear the buzzing. "All set."

The scent of cooked shallots greets me as I open the door. Julia is setting the table.

"Daniel got to last time," she says. Our rule is that whichever kid sets the table chooses where everyone sits, and they like the power associated with that. "So you're here . . . and Daddy's—wait I forgot a fork." She slides across the floor to look in the drawer, standing on her toes to see.

Will chews on a cloth napkin that's fallen from the table. Then he sees me and busts into a giant grin. "Mammmama!"

"He says Mama!" Julia comments.

Adam waves hello from his stance by the stove. "Well, it looks like shrimp."

The kids sit down for dinner.

"Where's *my* vegetable?" Daniel asks, overlooking the big bowl of sugar snap peas in the center of the table.

"You can have those," Adam says. He explains that Daniel can't just have a different vegetable all the time—that we've been over this—he doesn't have to eat it, but that's what's there and there's no more shrimp or anything else unless he eats the greens.

Daniel fights it, then, instead of launching into a tirade, relaxes into conversation.

"This is phenomenal, Dad," Jamie says, inhaling the food. Jamie learned the word when he was three and described his great-grandmother's kugel as "phenomenal," which of course made everyone gush and not mind the phenomenal amount of gunk he'd dropped on the floor and down his pants.

Julia crunches on the snap peas and reaches for more when we remind her she's yet to try the shrimp.

"So, is this good, great, or just OK?" Adam asks.

"Great," Jamie immediately says. "As in phenomenal."

"Good," Daniel says, and Julia agrees.

"I think it's just OK," Adam says, not so much disappointed as matter-of-fact. "Maybe it'd be better with bigger shrimp."

"I think it's great that you made it and that everyone's eating it," I say.

"Guess what?" Adam says when we're cleaning up. "I used a different kind of shrimp than the recipe called for!"

I hug him, poking his ribs. "You? You didn't follow every last order?"

Julia hands me a crayon-drawn swirl. "Look, Mom, it's a flower. Because spring's almost here."

4.

"What a difference!" My mother beams at the newly white woodwork. My bedroom is now the color of cappuccino froth, all trimmed in white instead of the heavy dark wood.

"Yeah, it looks really good, I think," I say, remembering when she'd called the darker trim "a travesty."

"Does Adam like it?" she asks as though that's what really matters.

"Well, he noticed it," I say. "That's a start."

Will agrees from his position in my arms: "Ahrgghh."

"You like it too." She raises her eyebrows at him and then at me. She won't say "I told you so," she has far more tact than that, but it lingers in the air like the key lime pie in the oven.

"Oh, that's Dick's favorite," she says when we're back in the kitchen.

I hand Will over to her and he promptly focuses all attention on her necklace, the single black pearl a baby-magnet. "Do you want to take some home to him?" I ask as I ready the pie cutter.

"Not if you don't have enough."

"I have enough, Mom." I cut a big wedge and wrap it in tinfoil. "Can you make whipped cream?" I ask her, looking forward to the creaminess of homemade whipped cream, the combination of that, the tartness of the key limes, the sweet crunch of the graham-cracker base.

"He'll be thrilled," my mother says, eyeing the kitchen. Sometimes I don't know if she's pleased with what she sees or is silently making a list of household edits. She takes the pie and I keep Will from tugging at my hair. Before she can suggest curtains or more paint, I shuttle my mother out to the porch.

"Can you pick Julia up on Thursday?" I ask. Julia follows us outside. I hand my daughter a wet sponge. She swipes it over the basketball hoop's base, cleaning it and then trying to get it in the basket.

"Sure." My mother smiles, holding the still-warm pie in her hands. Jamie and Daniel dart by, racing around the yard with a Frisbee and a plastic golf club. My mother gets to her car and I watch her drive away before taking Julia's hand and going inside to clean up. The phone rings as soon as I'm back in the kitchen.

My mother's voice comes through the receiver. "Have you thought about redoing the garage?"

5.

Hint: If you're planning a big "International Dinner" in the hopes of continuing to expand your family's breadth of tastes, try not to do it when five out of the six members of the family are struck with the stomach flu.

A can whose contents are unknowable, a freshly prepared mix of herbs, tomatoes, and some untasted cheese, a slab of bread the length of a kitchen table—all these items I purchased but have yet to serve because every time one of us is feeling better, someone else starts heaving.

"Maybe we should postpone the International Dinner?" Adam asks, eyeing the bag of tamari roasted almonds I've put in the pantry.

Jamie's eyes well up with tears. "But I want to have it!" he says, and vomits on the rug.

I may not know everything, but I'm guessing this may not be the best moment to introduce metch, the bulgur wheat and crushed tomatoes rife with scallions and parsley that sounds like a verb, unfortunately rhyming with "retch."

"It's the color of rust," Jamie says when he spies it in the fridge.

This may not be the evening on which to have the kids try soft and puffy Armenian matnakash bread wrapped in thin white paper and baked locally. They may not appreciate Bombay Pav Bhaji, mashed vegetables in a chili butter sauce, or Kashmiri palak paneer, the spinach with cheese curd.

"Who wants Jell-O?" I ask.

Key Lime Pie

If you can get fresh key limes, go for it. If not, I suggest Nelly and Joe's Key Lime Juice. If you like a sweeter pie, use a bit less juice, if you prefer super-tart, add a splash more. Some people enjoy a flaky crust, but the crunch and grain of the graham crust is my preference—its sweetness offsets the tartness of the lime.

CRUST:

5–6 tbsp. butter, melted

12 graham crackers (put in food processor, or put in baggie and have kids smush it with a rolling pin)

FILLING:

5 egg yolks

½ cup key lime juice (you may add a tablespoon more if you love the tart, which I do)

one 14-oz. can sweetened condensed milk

TOPPING:

1 pint heavy cream for whipping

sugar

Pour melted butter into graham cracker crumbs, blend with fingertips until coated and press into a pie plate. Bake for about 8 minutes at 350° while you beat the egg yolks by hand and add lime juice and sweetened condensed milk to them. Whisk a few times until blended. Pour mixture into the partially cooked crust and bake for about 18 minutes or until the first couple of bubbles appear on the top of the pie. Let cool and place in fridge. When you are ready to serve, whip the heavy cream until it is thick, sprinkle with a bit of granulated sugar, and mound it on top of the pie. Cut into slices and serve with garnish of lime twist or just a big smile.

Note: *You might have leftover whipped cream, which makes for a nice topping for fresh sliced fruit or berries, or if you are inclined as Jamie was, pretend shaving cream.*

Grilled Chocolate Sandwiches

These are indulgent, gooey, and leave evidence of consumption in the form of chocolate smears on the mouth or shirt, and a smile. You can try these on leftover baguette, cornbread, or any thick-cut bread (such as the one on page 333).

butter	good dark chocolate
2 smallish slices thick-cut bread (such as Pain de Campagne, baguette, etc.)	Nutella spread

Spread butter on outside of each slice of bread. Place one buttered slice in pan on medium-low heat and put a few squares of the dark chocolate on top. As that begins to warm, spread Nutella on the other piece of bread (the non-buttered side) and place on top of the chocolate that by now is beginning to melt. Once oozing has begun, flip the sandwich to the other side, pressing down with a spatula or weight. Once the bread is crispy and just browned, remove and eat with gusto.

Note: *You might try adding good raspberry jam instead of Nutella, or marshmallow should you feel campfire nostalgia.*

Early
Spring

The Language of Food

"This is the best damn salmon cake I've ever had," Daniel announces, his grin (a—ahem—shit-eating grin) plastered across his face. Upon hearing him swear, I remove his dish and deal with the crying fit that follows.

We have entered the age of the foul mouth, and Adam and I are cracking down. I'd like to state for the record that I never tried swearing in front of my parents until I was a teenager, but I have journal entries that detail my older brother's forays into the land of "shit head" and "asshole" (his) and "dumb idiot damnhead" (mine), which still makes me crack up, even though I wouldn't repeat it.

The cursing has been a slow leak that now has turned to a flood. The first drips started at the end of the summer, right before our trip to Indiana. Jamie and I sat on the porch eating lemon granita, enjoying the icy tartness, the sweet overtones. I'd made it spur-of-the-moment, to break up the "can we have Popsicles" question that was uttered every afternoon following camp or after playing in the yard. Granitas are easy, a traditional

Italian dessert. I love coffee granitas, but the thought of willingly giving my kids caffeine at the end of a tiring summer day seems to defeat the point of having them swim, walk, play baseball, bike, scooter, go to the playground, and splash in the sprinkler. So lemon it was. Fruity zest, chopped and simmered in sugar water, then strained and cooled, some fresh lemon juice added, a quick stir, and into the freezer in a shallow container.

"You have to slosh it around every twenty minutes or so," I told Jamie as he put his lips to the mound of ice. "Kind of scraping the icy stuff so it stays loose enough."

"Like slush," he said. I nodded, tasting it myself.

Jamie's expression said how much he liked it. When the other kids woke up (Julia) or came home from camp (Daniel), I offered it to them, too. Meanwhile, Jamie and I enjoyed the peaceful moments on the porch before Will woke up. Jamie's expression suddenly went sour, and not from the lemon.

"Uh, Mom?"

"Yeah."

"If someone does something you know is wrong, and you don't tell, that's bad, right?"

I nodded. "It's best to tell stuff. Especially if it has to do with safety." I watched Jamie scoop some ice and began to worry. What if someone was in trouble in his bunk? What if he had a burdensome issue plaguing him? "Jamie, you should just tell me what the problem is, that way I can help."

"But I don't want to get in trouble," he said. "Even though I know you always say we won't get in trouble for telling stuff."

I touched his bug-bitten, scraped-up summer legs. "I won't be upset. I'll just try to help." The worry was nagging at me. I envisioned evil counselors, family secrets shared at swimming lessons.

"My counselor is"—Jamie paused, slurping his granita—"teaching me how to swear."

Ah, camp. Money well spent. "Oh, yeah?" Relief rushed over me. Swearing I could handle. "Like what?"

"Like . . . 'hell.'" Jamie giggled, the illicit nature of the conversation making him blush. "Like 'damn.'"

"Any others?" I asked, stacking his dish into mine.

"OK. You promise you won't be mad?" Jamie braced himself for it: "Fok."

I stifled laughter. "How do you spell that?"

"F-O-K. You know, *fok*?" He was wide-eyed with fear, his hand over his mouth.

"It's OK," I assured him. "Those are swear words, and I get why it's funny or daring to learn them at camp. But you just can't walk around saying them, OK?" Jamie nodded, hugely unburdened and ready for Frisbee.

"Can I teach Daniel?" he asked.

I glared at him. "Absolutely not."

And he listened.

For three whole months! And then . . .

The leaking started. Daniel would bump his head and mutter, "Shit." Jamie would get frustrated with his homework and mumble something about "the damn thing." So Adam and I sat them down and told them to stop, and they listened.

For another couple of months.

We made it to the holidays, and at my mom and Dick's, the kids delighted in hearing their grandpa say loudly, "Let's get the damn presents going here."

And hearing my father-in-law slip up when he spilled sauce, spitting out an audible, "Oh, shit!"

And so the leaking turned into a steady stream, confined to home, where it resulted in warnings, then consequences. Adam said things like, "Listen, guys, you know you can't say things like that in public. But if you want to do it when it's just the two of you, and have it be a brother thing, fine." He reasoned with me. "It won't last. They'll get bored of it." I nodded, remembering my journal entries. "Just don't do it in front of Julia," Adam told Jamie and Daniel.

And things were under control until this morning.

Everything was peaceful. Adam and I were lounging in bed, playing with Will, while Jamie, Daniel, and Julia all had breakfast. Jamie had offered to "make it" for his siblings, pouring the cereal and milk, and Adam and I had one of those parental moments where we turned to each other, propped on our pillows, the sunlight streaming in, the whole weekend ahead of us, and smiled. "Isn't this great! They're downstairs and no one's screaming, no one's hitting, no one's fussing."

I took Will into his room to nurse. Adam jumped in the shower. I could hear Julia walk up the stairs and go into the bathroom where her father was. Will's room was right next door.

"Daddy," she said.

"What, Julia?" Adam's voice was cheerful, exuberant about the hours to come.

"Daniel called Jamie a fuckface."

Adam's voice was rigid, filled with heat. "Tell your brothers to get up here, now!"

Despite the day spent atoning for the language sins, Daniel hasn't quite learned his lesson.

"But, but . . . . ," he starts as I take the salmon cakes away and put his plate on the counter. He toys with the bowl of tartar sauce on the table until Adam slides it out of his reach. "I didn't mean to swear." Daniel's small body shudders as he cries. "I like the salmon cakes. And. And. They're good. They're—"

"Don't," Adam warns.

"They. Are. Good." Daniel punctuates with his voice to show he's not swearing.

"That's the thing," I say. "Once you start saying words like that, it's hard to stop. So don't do it anymore."

"Can I have my food back?" He eyes our plates; each one has a couple of salmon cakes—easily put together with mashed potatoes and flaked salmon, served with green beans and wilted chard on the side.

We have Daniel take a few minutes to settle down and make a few more sweeping statements like, "We're done with the swearing" and "How about you watch your language from now on." After all, Adam and I aren't big swearers. We were proud of the fact that none of the kids swore until Jamie was nearly seven. Despite repeated offenses from the grandparents. Their knowledge of curse words was aided by Green Day and Ben Folds, whose music we all like and listen to. On their own, the kids abbreviated the songs and they sing lines with just the letter, as in: "Got s— running through my brain . . . it's a b— if you don't believe. . . ."

I know the kids will grow up and make their own choices about how to speak and we'll make sure they know what to say in polite company, but my honest feeling is that while I won't tolerate having any swear directed at me, the occasional "damn it" here and there isn't the end of the world. It's not where I want to put my energy, especially since so much of it is said to get a rise out of adults.

So dinner continues, swear-free. All the kids finish their salmon cakes, which I'd made a few weeks ago, frozen, and reheated in the oven while I warmed the greens.

"Thanks for a good dinner, Mom," Daniel says, wiping the milk from his mouth on his sleeve.

"These were good, but can you make cod cakes again sometime?" Jamie asks. "With the yogurt stuff?"

"Sure—good idea," I say, remembering the cucumber yogurt sauce, how good it is on a warm summer night. "Cod cakes."

"God cakes," Daniel says, but one look from Adam quells any notion of further thoughts of cursing.

Adam takes the three younger kids up for cleaning, brushing, and bed, and Jamie loads the dishwasher with me.

"Sorry about all the swearing," he says, his blond hair sweeping down over one eye. Jamie's been looking up all manner of words in the huge dictionary we keep in the attic built-in bookshelves. Yesterday, I found the dictionary open to a certain letter that left little doubt as to what word he was searching for. Rather than shouting or punishing him—I mean, hey, at least he's swearing in a literate way—I took the approach my mother always did with me. Straightforward, no nonsense, no room for negotiation. I called him up, pointed to the page and said, "You know, Jamie, next time you look up words like 'bitch' or 'shit,' I wish you'd do me the courtesy of closing the dictionary and smoothing out the pages." His mouth dropped open and he only nodded. No talking back. No justification. No cover-ups. "Um, OK, sure," he said, blushing, and nodded.

Jamie loads the last plate into the dishwasher. "Yeah, it's kind of enough already," I say, letting the water rush over the plates, the remnants of the meal floating toward the disposal.

"When you were little, you made up your own swear," I tell him. When Jamie was two and a half he created "gock." He'd walk around our old apartment saying "Oh, *gock* it all!"

Jamie loves hearing stories about himself, as most kids do. "That is so funny." He tests it out. "Gock it all." Then he walks toward the stairs to head for bed. He pauses, furrowing his brow, unsure whether to say something or not.

I encourage him with my eyebrows and a nod. "Is it about swearing?" I think back to another page of the dictionary.

He nods. "It's just . . . You know, what, Mom? It's not '*fok*,' like I thought at camp. It's 'fuck.'"

I nod, he heads upstairs, and I clean up what I can.

Simple Salmon Cakes

All of these measurements can be approximate. You want the mixture to be firm enough to hold a patty shape, but not dry. You may also try this with other kinds of leftover fish, such as cod or haddock.

cooked salmon (about
1 lb.), flaked, or one 15-oz.
can of salmon with no skin
or bones

mashed potatoes (about
2 cups), with a bit of butter
and milk added so they are
slightly creamy

1½ tbsp. Dijon mustard

dash of lemon juice

1 finely chopped onion

handful of fresh dill sprigs,
torn into small pieces

salt and pepper

breadcrumbs (about 2 cups)

a few dashes of paprika

2 eggs

olive oil (for frying)

butter (for frying)

Mix salmon and all other ingredients except for breadcrumbs, paprika, eggs, oil, and butter. Use your hands so that everything is mixed well. Form into small balls (about the size of golf balls) and pat down slightly so they are semi-rounded patties. Place patties on parchment paper on a cookie sheet. Cover and put in fridge for about half an hour. Combine breadcrumbs with a few dashes of paprika. Beat eggs. Dip patties into egg and then roll in breadcrumb mixture, coating well. Fry for about 1 minute per side in a bit of olive oil and butter until golden brown, then set on cookie sheet to finish crisping in a 375° oven while you finish the rest of the patties. Serve hot with a dollop of tartar sauce (see below), or cold with cucumber yogurt sauce (see next page), or allow them to cool completely and then freeze for later.

 ## Tartar Sauce

Mix together (or have your kids mix):

½ cup mayonnaise

½ cup Greek-style thick
yogurt

2 tbsp. lemon juice

2 tbsp. sweet relish

1 tsp. minced onion

good dash of salt and pepper

Let mixture sit for a day or a few hours and then serve.

Note: *If you don't have relish, chop into tiny pieces whatever pickles you have around and this will suffice.*

Cucumber Yogurt Sauce

I love to have this in the summer to serve with all manner of fish. It's delightful with the salmon cakes, and the kids make it themselves.

1 cucumber, peeled, seeded, and chopped into small bits	½ tsp. salt
	dash of lemon juice
1 clove minced garlic	
	⅛ tsp. cumin
¾ cup plain Greek yogurt (such as Fage)	paprika for dusting top if desired

Mix all ingredients except for paprika. Let mixture sit in fridge overnight or a few hours. Dust with paprika right before serving.

Lemon Granita

Granitas are a good treat and can be made in numerous flavors including coffee, strawberry, chocolate, and this recipe for lemon. For adults, I would add a bit of zest to the boiling mixture, but my kids find this makes the mixture a bit too strong. You can also add a splash of cream to any of the above flavors for a rich, different taste.

½ cup sugar	3 lemons
⅔ cup water	

Heat sugar and water in saucepan until nearly boiling, then allow to cool to room temperature. Add juice of 3 lemons, straining big pulp and seeds as you go. Stir well and then freeze in shallow container (such as metal lasagna pan). As mixture freezes, drag a fork through it every 20 minutes or so at the beginning and a bit more frequently as it gets more frozen. Serve when still slightly slushy.

The kids love when this is served in a wineglass with a sprig of mint on top or a wedge of fresh orange.

Note: If you wanted to make coffee granita, you would substitute brewed coffee or good espresso for the water, increase the sugar by ¼ cup, omit the lemons, and possibly serve with a bit of shaved chocolate on top.

Celebration Dinner

It happens when I'm not expecting it. Jamie's playing baseball and I have the other three kids watching, or more accurately, running around like helium balloons with their strings severed, each one darting this way and that, Will speedily navigating the territory, pulling up, standing unassisted only to plop down suddenly, surprised by gravity yet again.

"Will, want the tennis ball?" Daniel asks, waving the Day-Glo object in his brother's face.

"Not so close," I say, and keep an eye on Julia, who is doing what she calls "bal-la-lay," twisting and spinning, then running and jumping. She asked to take a class in ballet and then, upon hearing that it wasn't free-form, shrugged and said no thank you. "Will, want the ball?"

Will looks up at Daniel and smiles. "Bawll?"

Daniel looks to me. I look back. "Did he . . ."

"Did you say 'ball'?"

Will smiles, drooling and pleased. "Bahlll." He tries it out, forming the word by putting his upper teeth over his lower lip. "Bahl!" He bites the tennis ball to show he knows what he's saying.

My baby said his first word! I want to leap up and shout it to the universe! I call my parents and in-laws and then I just relish the moment.

"Well, he says Dad and Mama," Julia reminds me.

"Yes, but . . ." So it's spring. And Will is talking, and instead of marking this passage into the verbal with any sort of bittersweet feelings, I'm just excited.

The truth is, I had the dinner planned out anyway, but it feels nice to celebrate Will's big step with good food and family. We rarely cook red meat in the house, but I've bought a tenderloin, some Brussels sprouts, and broccoli, and Julia picked out three different kinds of potatoes to roast. I sear the meat on the stovetop in a drop of butter and oil (my mother always taught me that the oil stops the butter from burning and the butter adds more flavor) and then slide it into the oven, remembering all the times I used to make this, how long it's been.

"Pink ones, yellowy ones, and purple ones!" Julia says while watching me wash the potatoes. I cut the fingerlings on the diagonal to increase the surface that can crisp while roasting, halve the bright pink new potatoes and purple potatoes, and put them into the oven while the meat cooks.

"What smells good and bad?" Daniel asks, wandering into the room with his baseball mitt on his head.

"Probably the wine stuff Mummy got at the store."

"It's called port," I tell them.

Adam is working this weekend but will be back in time for dinner, so I ask the kids to clean off the table so we can set it.

"I just want to read," Jamie says.

"It's not going to smell this bad later, is it?" Daniel raises his eyebrows, surveying the countertop. We have cubes of butternut squash for roasting, and I'm slicing the sprouts so they cook quickly.

"No, it's just while the sauce is cooking," I tell him.

"There's apricots in it, Daniel," Julia tries to appease him. "It has raisins."

"What? Raisins? You know I don't like raisins!" Daniel's about to revisit the fits of yore, but I step in.

"It's just to flavor things. If you don't want the dried fruit part of the sauce, that's OK."

"Maybe I'll just have a little on the side."

Adam arrives home and the kids are at once tugging on him but he needs to return a page—he'll be on call overnight. He retreats upstairs to talk to his patients while the kids practice their patience downstairs.

"We're ready to eat," I say a few minutes later.

Daniel stares at his plate but then tentatively forks a piece of meat into his mouth. "This is very good."

The kids dig into the tenderloin, loving every bite.

"See all the potatoes?" Julia points her finger directly onto Adam's food. "I picked them out. Three colors."

"And greens," Jamie says, trying the shaved Brussels sprouts. After slicing them, I put them into a hot pan with some olive oil and sea salt and let them wilt without turning them. When they began to brown, I stirred a bit, and all traces of bitterness evaporated; all that's left is a nutty sweetness with crispy bits that make for a perfect pairing with the meat. The roasted maple squash highlights the sweetness of the sauce, the fruity flavor and the port bring out the meat's natural flavor, and the crunchy, salty potatoes round it all out.

"What a meal," Adam says. He turns to Will and waves a purple-and-yellow striped ball at him. "I heard you know what this is."

Will looks baffled. The kids get worried. "He said it! Really!"

"I believe you," Adam says.

But I want Adam to hear it for himself. I turn to Will. "Can you say ball? Ball?" Maybe he needs it to be a tennis ball.

Will picks up a bit of squash and eats it. Staring at his tray with great interest in the tiny bits of meat and soft potato insides, he ignores the prop but mutters, "Bawhl."

Adam smiles. "Was that ball?"

Will looks up at his dad. "Bahl."

I think about the meat, how I don't use a thermometer often, how I don't always plan out what to add to sauces, what to make with leftover rice or overstock of sprouts. How it just happens. Cooking, like parenting, is sometimes a leap of faith—that the dough will rise, that the tenderloin won't be too rare or too brown, that the wobbly Jell-O will set. That the hodgepodge of items in the pantry, on a shelf, in the fridge, can be fashioned into one coherent meal. That babbles and drool and mumbling baby sounds will form, one day, all of a sudden, into a single word that will alert you to all that lies ahead.

"Ball, ball, ball," Will says, and I am still amazed.

Port Reduction Sauce

2 cups port

¼ cup brown sugar

a handful (or ⅓ cup if you need to measure) each of dried cranberries, diced dried apricots, dark raisins, yellow raisins

dash of Worcestershire sauce

big slosh of lemon juice

salt and pepper

Mix all ingredients in a pot and heat on high. Let the mixture come to a boil, then continue heating on low for about 30 minutes, reducing until syrupy (if you dip a spoon in and the sauce coats it like syrup, it's done). Turn off the heat, covering the pot partially with a lid.

Meanwhile, prepare the meat.

Beef Tenderloin

2–3 lb. tenderloin

salt and pepper

butter and oil

You can use pork tenderloin for this or beef (or even turkey if you like). Generously salt and pepper meat, rubbing both in with your hands. On stove top, sear the tenderloin in a pan—using high heat and butter with oil—until all sides are well-browned. Stick into a 425° oven for about 30 minutes, depending on how well-done you like your meat. Pork tenderloin should be cooked through. Let rest 10 minutes before slicing on the diagonal. Spoon port sauce directly on top.

Note: *If you don't eat any meat, you might try roasting hardy vegetables such as turnips, squash, Brussels sprouts, parsnips, and a tuber—preferably a Yukon Gold potato or two—and serve the reduction sauce alongside those.*

Shredded Brussels Sprouts

Brussels sprouts   sea salt
olive oil

Wash the sprouts. Peel and discard the first outer leaves, and cut off the rough bottom. Slice the rest somewhat finely, keeping a few bits larger for texture. Drizzle olive oil to cover bottom of pan and sprinkle sea salt into the pan. Heat on high. Add the sprouts. Cook for about 8 minutes, lowering heat to medium after 3 minutes, letting the greens wilt and semi-caramelize until bits are brown and toasty.

Mum's the Word

Tonight is the first night of spring. It's the kind of evening that shakes out like a picnic blanket, rolling in with warm air in the afternoon, followed by a temperate and sun-streaked evening. The perfect night to test our new porch furniture.

My mother had stopped by maybe two weeks earlier, all in a dither. "I just think we need to talk," she'd said into the cell phone and, after the year's ups and downs, I'd feared some big announcement.

I met her at the door with a container of dried mango (which the kids tried and universally enjoyed) I was snacking on and at which she'd shaken her head. Instead I gave her a bite of upside-down French toast, which she accepted. Who wouldn't? It's one of the best breakfast (or breakfast-as-dinner) dishes on the planet. "So, what's up?" I tried not to furrow my brow, but she had her hands clasped as though about to deliver bad news.

"Well," she said, "I've been thinking . . ."

Does any good news ever follow these words? My first breakup came after this declaration. "And . . . ," I encouraged. My friend's breast cancer had not returned as we feared, my stepmother's death was now a season past, Will had been delivered as a normal, healthy baby despite my car crash at twenty-three weeks gestation. Now what?

"Now, this isn't meant as criticism . . ." My mother's hands tried to placate me as did her tone. We have a traditional push and pull that often starts in this way. Not a criticism, exactly, more a suggestion. Take, for example, the time she came over to read some of my writing—up in my office—and wound up being unable to concentrate due to what she called "the clonkiness of my filing cabinets." I should mention that she is an interior designer and quite gifted in this realm, but that sometimes her keen visual ideas sidetrack the issue at hand. Like many mothers, mine is capable of simultaneously congratulating me—"Wow! Your first novel, published and in stores!" and being critical: "Are you wearing your hair like that to the book signing?" So when she said, with French toast now swallowed, that she had a suggestion for me, I was wary.

"My hair is fine," I said automatically. She opened her mouth to say no, it wasn't to do with my appearance. (Score one for me!) "And the house is fine, too!" I said.

She knit her brows. "I just was wondering, if maybe—and please don't get upset . . ." Cue my need to do just that. "If I could get Adam an early birthday present."

Suspicion loomed. "What kind of present?" Please don't say hair plugs, I thought.

"New porch furniture. You guys spend so much time out there—and our old stuff is falling apart, and it would be nice if you—"

"Great!" I beamed. We'd been the recipients of castoffs—the old wicker rocker my aunt and uncle didn't need anymore, the white wicker couch from my parents that had been in storage for nearly twenty years and that I'd tried to outfit with cushions to varying degrees of success. "We'd love it. Adam would love it. Great idea." No criticism, no bad news. Was she saying our current furniture was moldy, dirty, unsightly? Probably. Did I care? No.

"Great—you pick it out, have it delivered, and I'll pay for it." You can't ask for more than that. Except perhaps more upside-down French toast, which we had for dinner that night and which everyone wolfed down while the April rain flooded the gutters and turned the front yard into mud worthy of Woodstock.

As Julia and Will napped and the boys finished school, I set about unpacking, unwrapping, and untangling the boxes of our new outdoor furniture. There were bushels of plastic wrap, bubble wrap, shrink wrap, and wads of paper with which to contend. There were boxes the size of bathtubs and crates larger than our bathroom. And all for the two chairs, one couch, and tables we'd ordered in waterproof (no mold!) dark green that matched the shutters of our slightly crumbly Victorian house. I'd arranged them on the porch and disposed of the debris (and by "disposed of," I mean I put everything on the tiny back porch so Adam could deconstruct and recycle it later). The kids had come home from school but gone in through the back of the house.

Now I could call the kids to dinner and show them.

"Kids! Come on to the porch!"

They assemble, each aware of the lengthening days that will continue to beckon us out here.

"This isn't salad!" Daniel's eyes are wide as he focuses on the traditional macaroni salad. We're having turkey burgers with or without cheese, the first corn on the cob (because I'm so longing for summer), and roasted broccoli. The macaroni salad was an afterthought. "I thought you said it was salad."

"It's called macaroni salad," I said, and served the others their plates. "Daddy loves it." Jamie claims the big chair, Daniel and Julia tuck themselves side by side on the new couch.

"I love this new furniture," Julia says. "It's striped!"

Jamie tests the pasta. "How do you like it?" I ask him.

"Not at all," he replies.

Julia refuses it due to its mayonnaise content, Will can't eat it, and though very tempted by the macaroni within it, Daniel can't abide the dish. Adam, however, arrives home and grins. "Hey—great-looking porch. And awesome—macaroni salad!" Adam sits in the other new chair, delighted and forking mouthfuls of that and a few sweet-potato chips while I sing to Will on the rocker.

The next day, I can't help but try again. "Hey, Jamie, want to taste something?" I ask.

He shrugs. "I guess." He opens his mouth and, like he did at six months, all baby-bird ready and eager, waits for me to slide the forkful in. "Yum!" he says. "What is that?"

"Macaroni salad," I tell him.

"Oh, you mean, similar to what we had yesterday?" He is nothing if not eloquent despite overlooking the obvious.

"Yeah," I say. "In fact, exactly the same."

He has another bite and packs some for his school lunch the next day. I take this as some measure of success. Not that I was critical of his not liking it. But more that, like my mom with the new porch furniture, I suspected he'd enjoy it, and it never hurts to ask.

Easy Upside-Down French Toast

This is a surefire hit at brunches or breakfast and easy for entertaining because you can make it a day ahead. An old friend once gave me a recipe she'd gotten from her mother, who'd had it passed to her from a friend. This incarnation is the result of many morphings over the years.

Prepare this the day before you want to serve it.

1 vanilla bean	¾ stick of butter
3 cups milk	¾ cup packed brown sugar

½ tsp. nutmeg

1½ tsp. cinnamon

12 pieces of crusty bread—
French baguette works best,
though any leftover thick
bread is fine

5 eggs

2 tsp. vanilla

¼ tsp. salt

Split the vanilla bean, scrape it into the milk, and let the bean bathe. Melt butter, sugar, nutmeg, and cinnamon in a saucepan on low heat. Pour into bottom of heavy-bottomed baking dish (9 × 13). Place bread on top. Take the vanilla bean pod from the milk and discard. Mix eggs, vanilla, and salt into milk and pour over bread. Refrigerate overnight. Bake at 325° for 40 minutes then 350° for 5–10 minutes more. Turn the baking dish over, inverting onto a tray and serve, or, if you don't have a tray or platter, let people serve themselves from the baking dish.

Note: For Apple Upside-Down French Toast . . . *If you have fresh fall apples, peel and slice six Granny Smiths or other tart apples, sauté them in a bit of the butter but do not let them brown. Continue on with the rest of the directions, melting the rest of the butter, sugar, and spices in, and using the apple layer as the bottom before the bread.*

 ## Macaroni Salad

¾ cup mayonnaise

½ cup plain yogurt

1½ tbsp. Dijon mustard

¼ cup white vinegar

dash of lemon juice

¼ cup sweet pickles (finely chopped)

1 bunch of chopped scallions, chopped

1 stalk of celery, chopped

combination of red, orange, or yellow peppers, chopped to equal ½ cup

salt and pepper, if needed

4 cups elbow macaroni, cooked in salted water, drained, and cooled

Whisk mayonnaise, yogurt, and mustard together. Add vinegar and lemon juice, whisking as you add. Add the pickles, scallions, celery, and peppers. Adjust for salt/pepper and mix into the macaroni. Let sit in fridge, and serve cold while sitting on picnic blanket, sand, or porch furniture.

Bulk

When I see rows of grains or dried fruits; bins of tiny semolina, round Israeli couscous, red lentils, split green and yellow peas, polenta, I imagine all the possibility of what could be. It reminds me of pre-gardening with my grandmothers. How they'd tend to their seedlings or ask me to help plant beets, string beans, onions, or stake the ground for vine tomatoes. Seeing food in its raw state, untouched, gives me energy. I imagine it did to my grandmothers, too. At ages eighty-five and ninety-three, Grandma Bev and Grandma Ruth are no longer gardening, but I think their passion for growing foods, for growing seedlings under lights on racks that took up the den or garage, then harvesting the products, has somehow filtered down to me. A garden, a room, a meal. Grandma Bev grew zucchini and had me root in the dirt for potatoes to steam and slice for warm salads, showed me how to make cold cucumber soup. Grandma Ruth had a flower garden in which I would lose myself amongst the blue cornflowers; orange lilies; black-eyed susans; foxglove; and soft yellow, maroon, and white snapdragons. Both grandmothers grew corn we'd eat barely steamed. Grandma Ruth arranged flowers with artful precision, in spare shallow holders that kept me entranced. Grandma Bev taught me to slice cucumbers thin enough to see through to decorate the top of her cold cucumber soup she'd serve out of big mason jars on the front porch.

The kids mill around the bulk aisles at the store with me today. They tap on the bins, eye the grains, and vie for a chance to use the scooper. We pick up polenta, a big scoop of wheatberries to make into salad, and some flour—we'll make dough tomorrow for some homemade pizza. We buy lots of oats.

I buy oats in bulk—cheaper, less packaging—but we've bought a bit too much today. The excess won't fit in the glass jar I keep on the pantry shelf.

"I could eat them," Jamie suggests. "You think raw tastes good?"

"Just put them in a bowl," Daniel says.

"Or do a project," Julia adds. She's got blue marker on her hands from writing letters, and green paint in her hair even though we haven't been painting.

"Cahh," Will says. He's doubled his word collection, and zooms a car across the floor and chases it.

"Let's just glop some stuff together and make granola bars," I say, and send the kids off to gather the items. "And cook the wheatberries at the same time."

"We didn't get berries," Jamie informs me.

"Wheatberries." I show him the paper bag. He sticks his nose in and looks at me with suspicion. "I'm not kidding. They're called berries." He puts one in his mouth and spits it out. "They taste good in bread. They're the kind of fruit from the wheat grass—the entire kernel."

Julia grabs a handful that seeps through her fingers and dusts the floor. "They're reddy brown. That's how come they're called berries."

I boil some water and pour the wheatberries that aren't on the floor into the pot. The kids and I do a variation on the standard granola, using some ingredients—rolled oats, cranberries, bran buds—but not others.

"So, no honey?" Daniel waves the bottle of it. I shake my head.

"I wrote about the eating habits of black bears in my report," Jamie says while trying to open a jar of brown rice syrup. We have it for pies or other baking projects. "And they like honey, which you know, but I bet they'd like these blocks—or bars—or whatever you want to call them."

Will feels he's missing out on the counter action, so I hand him the container of stoveside utensils—ladles, spatulas, a slotted spoon—while we take turns stirring the rice syrup as it warms. We cut up some dried apricots and toss raw pumpkin seeds, both salted and unsalted, raw sunflower seeds, puffed kamut—which we happen to have, but any puffed cereal would work—dried cranberries, and bran buds with oats in a bowl. Then we pour the goop onto the dry ingredients. When everything's mixed, the kids watch me press it flat into a greased pan. The wheatberries have cooked, so we drain them and begin grabbing ingredients for the rest of the dish.

"Now we wait." Daniel crosses his arms over his chest.

"And then?" Julia wonders.

Jamie swivels in his seat where he's finishing his homework. "Then we eat."

Cold Cucumber Soup

All amounts are approximate—Grandma Bev's cooking has never been exact. Play with the flavors as it suits you, adding a small amount of olive oil to the top before serving if you like.

3 big bulbs garlic

4 large cucumbers, peeled and seeded (reserve some thin slices for garnish)

1 onion

1 scoop sour cream

1 scoop Greek yogurt

½ cup milk

1 cup stock, plus some extra if desired

salt and pepper to taste

handful of dill, chopped

Chop the garlic, cucumbers, and onion. Add the sour cream, yogurt, milk, and stock, and purée in batches. Adjust salt and pepper for flavor. Chill well and serve with a few thin slices of cucumber and a sprig of dill on top of each portion.

Note: *If you like more texture, reserve some small chopped pieces of cucumber to add in at the end, along with a few scallions.*

Crunchy Granola Bars

You can shift around these ingredients depending on what you have around, but these make a satisfying snack or quick breakfast.

3½ tbsp. soy butter (or almond or peanut butter), preferably chunky

3 tbsp. honey

3½ tbsp. brown rice syrup

big splash of vanilla

1 tbsp. brown sugar

1½ cups puffed wheat/rice/kamut

½ cup bran buds/Grape-Nuts cereal

1½ cups rolled oats (not the quick-cook kind)

1 handful (about ⅓ cup) dried cranberries or cut-up dried apricot

¼ cup raw pumpkin seeds

⅓ cup salted sunflower seeds (or a mixture with raw)

cinnamon

Preheat oven to 325°. Line 8- or 9-inch square pan with a long sheet of parchment paper (you want longer ends than the length of the pan). Warm soy butter, honey, brown rice syrup, vanilla, and brown sugar until sugar has melted and soy butter has thinned. Mix dry ingredients in big bowl and dust with cinnamon. Pour liquid on top, mixing as you go. When everything is equally coated, spread the mixture into the pan. Press mixture down with long ends of the parchment paper. Bake for about 25 minutes. When you remove the pan from the oven, again use long ends of the parchment to press bars flat. Allow to cool completely before touching again. When totally cooled and hard, lift the ends of the parchment and put onto a cutting board and cut into longish bars or squares.

Note: *You can add crushed almonds or slivered ones, or toasted coconut if you like, or raisins—golden and brown—if desired.*

Vibrant Wheatberry Salad

The colors in this salad cheer any plate and palate. This salad tides me over as a hearty lunch or works well as a side dish with pan-cooked salmon or baked bluefish for dinner. The kids like the sweetness of the dried fruit. You can add kale or other greens instead of (or in addition to) the spinach. If you have garlicky green beans from page 270 lying around, toss those in too.

1 red onion, sliced	2 tbsp. dried cranberries
1 shallot, diced	⅓ cup dried chopped apricot
1 cup red pepper in thin strips	1 cup wheatberries, cooked in 3 cups boiling, salted water for about 45 minutes until tender
4 tbsp. good olive oil	
½ cup or more zucchini, chopped	salt
1 cup baby spinach, chopped	Pecorino or goat cheese (optional)
2 tbsp. orange juice	

Sauté the red onion, shallot, and pepper in 2 tbsp. of the olive oil until soft, about 5 minutes on medium-low heat. Add in the chopped zucchini and let it heat for a minute, then add spinach—it will wilt. Turn the heat up and add orange juice and dried fruit, mixing gently. Remove from heat and pour over cooked wheatberries. Add remaining 2 tbsp. oil and toss gently, salting as desired. Top with a bit of Pecorino or goat cheese.

Whatever's Left

We are clustered around the kitchen table, two adults and three kids eating, a fourth child being fed. I cut up roasted butternut squash and bits of corn on Will's tray so he can feed himself. He can pretty much do the whole meal himself, save for the pieces that get stuck in his shirt. We listen to his baby noises. He sounds like a bird trying to take flight, cooing and hooting, babbling and saying sounds that will continue to help him expand his vocabulary. He's added "dis and dat" to his repertoire, often using the words as all-purpose, other times saying them when he points to my watch or any button. As the kids eat their fish with neither exclamations of glee nor groans of disgust, I think about the globe of experiences held in the walls of this room. The kitchen has served as cooking classroom, courtroom, clay room, confectionary, and comfort zone. All manner of sibling arguments, marital moments of love and annoyance, meals and talking, all in this one space.

I once started to write a novel that began: *Everything happened in the kitchen.* I can't remember now if it was a comedy or a drama—probably both. I only remember that one line.

So much does happen in the kitchen—in our kitchen. But tonight, it's pretty quiet. No one's complaining or yelping about too much sauce or that a brother is chewing in a gross way or knocking over their milk by mistake. Instead, we are sitting here and talking about dreams, about the warm weather, about the passage of time.

"How come it seems like some things, like, rush by you and then other things, like if you have to practice piano, take so, so long?" Jamie asks.

"That's just how time works," Adam says.

"It's not any different when you're a grown-up," I tell him, and give Will one of my fingers to chew on. "One day feels really long and then suddenly a whole year's slipped by."

"Remember when I wasn't even three and a half?" Julia is amazed, her eyes huge behind her glasses. She corrects herself. "Actually, I'm three and three-quarters. And then I'll be four!"

And then you'll go to college, I think.

Daniel dunks his roll in his corn chowder. "Hey, this time last year Will wasn't even alive and now he's eating corn like we are!" I do not mention that this time last year Daniel wouldn't go near corn chowder. I can tell he doesn't love it even now, but he's not complaining, so I leave it alone.

"'Chowder' is a weird word," Jamie says. He then says it over and over and over again. Adam and I laugh and then ask him to stop.

This corn chowder is simple, easy to make, and easy to turn into fish chowder should any cod or haddock just appear at your door. I always throw in whatever's left in the fridge or pantry drawer—red pepper, onion, potatoes, salmon. Tonight, though, it's a simple bowl consisting of bright yellow corn, onions, potato wedges, some seasonings, all in a thick but lower-fat base. The bread is reminiscent of one I learned to make in my prior cooking life on the boat—a molasses dough that this time I made with wheat flour and into rolls and a loaf. I'll save the loaf for the broccoli sandwiches I want to try later this week—a slathering of mustard or Russian dressing on the thick-cut, sweet dark bread, some broccoli that's cooked but still toothy (or roasted—we'll see), and some grated cheddar and Muenster, a few pinches of Fontina—under the broiler and good to go. But for now, we're eating rolls.

Julia likes to rip up her bread and drop it into the chowder, then spoon it into her mouth.

Jamie shovels the food in as though he's the frontrunner in a competition for speed.

"Hey—slow down," Adam cautions him, tearing open his roll.

"But it's good. And I'm hungry and it tastes like the other chowder you made one time but different, too." I stare at him and watch him swallow. Miraculously he doesn't choke. "You know how sometimes food smells"—Daniel laughs—"no, not like that, Daniel. I mean"—Jamie puts his spoon down—"sometimes you taste something and it makes you remember something?"

"I know exactly what you mean. That happens to me a lot," I say, and swallow some chowder.

They continue testing the soup, deciding if they like it, the heat from the bowls steaming Daniel's and Julia's glasses, Jamie eating fast again.

We talk about how long it's been since Min died.

"That long already?" Daniel asks. He considers this.

"It feels like longer," Jamie says.

"It feels like shorter," Daniel says.

"I agree with you both." I break off a piece of chewy brown bread and hold it without tasting it.

Jamie stares at his chowder. "I'm starting to forget her, I think." His mouth is twisted at the ends, his eyes bracing for tears he refuses to let out. He has reached that age—though he'll fall on the floor crying about Daniel stealing his baseball cards, he holds back on tougher emotions, trying hard to pack it away. I try to encourage him to let it spill out.

"Maybe we should say what we remember about her," I suggest.

Adam nods. "That's a good idea."

Jamie talks with his mouth full. "She had that silvery white-blond hair."

"I remember that she always liked to do her job, which was a painter," Daniel says. "And we walked to the vegetable farm and picked food for dinner ourselves."

"I remember that she took me horseback riding." Julia smiles. "I liked that."

Adam spoons a mouthful in, thinking, and adds, "She was very deliberate in her actions. She was graceful."

Jamie elaborates. "Yeah. She walked like she was trying to get somewhere as quietly as possible." The poetry of kid language is remarkable.

"I remember her voice and her expressions," I say. She could convey sentences in just one glance; how the anger or frustration diminished over the course of our relationship, replaced with understanding and commitment. The clanking of metal spoons, of dishes as we cooked.

We keep eating, the conversation shifting to spring, to short sleeves and Julia's birthday coming up, to whether peppers are really good in chowder or not. "When you make chowder," I tell the kids, "you can decide what to put in it—or not."

After someone leaves you, leaves your kitchen, leaves your house or leaves this earth, what remains of them is really fragments. Shards in the form of memories, glimpses of them from photographs, or sound bites of conversation, everything just nearly graspable—their hand on yours, their gestures, how they held their fork. The scramble of this, the bits and pieces, are painful not just in the loss, but because they undo the whole person and fracture them into whatever's left.

The kids spent much of the year sorting through the grief of their first big loss, and it has taken some time for them—and for me—to move not around Min's death but through it in order to piece back together the good memories.

"Min loved this soup," I tell the kids as they finish up.

"Chowder," Jamie corrects. "She had this?"

I nod. "Once. In this kitchen, in fact."

As I suspected he would, Daniel decides he likes the bread more than the chowder. He casts the bowl aside and eats the crumbs with his fingers.

Jamie mops up the dregs with the last bit of roll he's portioned out for the purpose. Julia has slowed her eating due to feeling full or tired or both. She had a mudpie class (read: kids with clay) earlier in the afternoon, which means she skipped her nap. She's phasing them out bit by bit. By now she is dragging and ready for an early bed. Adam has the night shift tomorrow so tonight I put whatever's left of the chowder into the fridge for him to have as leftovers. The kids clear their own plates, except for Will, who is coated in a layer of squash and corn.

"That was tasty," Adam says, tucking the baby under one arm. The kids shrug and nod.

"Let's go upstairs," I say to everyone and to no one. They dash off, leaving our basic kitchen—a jumble of shoes, plates, baseball cards and books, art and stick-figure drawings and penmanship practice, a red block, discarded peppers, and empty chowder dishes. The stuff of memories.

Chowder Two Ways: Corn Chowder and Saffron Fish Chowder

All the amounts are changeable. If you have only two potatoes, fine. If you have some cooked or uncooked salmon or haddock, add it in! It's a big chowder party here. Using the evaporated milk will give the creamy flavor and color without the heavy fat content of cream or half-and-half. I don't like cubed potatoes—they remind me of a bad experience with Campbell's Chunky Soup (you know, the one you could supposedly eat with a fork). Instead, just chop them into odd shapes and enjoy.

2 onions, in small chunks

3 potatoes, in wedges (purple or red look great)

drop of olive oil

2 bags frozen corn (preferably one yellow and one white) or corn fresh off the cob from 8 ears

1 quart vegetable stock (chicken works too)

1 tsp. Marmite

1 can evaporated milk (2%, whole, or skimmed)

salt and pepper

pinch of cayenne pepper

dash of Worcestershire
sauce

1 lb. salmon or haddock
(optional for version 1 and
necessary for version 2)

2 pinches saffron (version 2)

VERSION ONE:

Cook the onions and potatoes in big pot with a drizzle of olive oil. When onions are translucent, add the corn. Let it warm for a minute. Add the stock and Marmite and bring to boil. Let simmer until potatoes are nearly cooked, about 20 minutes. Reduce heat to medium-low and add can of milk. Season with salt pepper, cayenne, and Worcestershire sauce.

You can stop here or add fish if you like. If you add fish, lay it on top of the soup (no need to cut it into pieces) and simmer the soup for about 10 minutes while the fish cooks. If the fish is leftover fish and therefore already cooked, add it in to warm it through but no need to keep cooking.

If you prefer a puréed type of corn chowder, you can purée half the soup for a textured chowder or the whole thing for a more refined dish.

VERSION TWO:

A wonderful variation is Saffron Fish Chowder. Make as above, adding one pinch of saffron during the onion cooking, and one pinch after the milk is added. Lay one pound of cod or skinned haddock or salmon on top of chowder, cover, and simmer until fish is cooked and flaky.

Serve warm with:

Molasses Wheat Rolls/Bread

These are chewy and satisfying with soups or just on their own. This batch makes a lot, so you can freeze some rolls in a freezer bag or a loaf in tinfoil.

2 tbsp. yeast

3 cups warm water

1 tbsp. butter, softened

2 tbsp. applesauce

| 1 cup molasses | 6 cups whole-wheat flour |
| 1½ tsp. salt | 4 cups white flour |

Dissolve yeast in water. Add butter, applesauce, and molasses. Then add salt. Add flours one cup at a time. Once mixed in, knead dough for about 10 minutes. Put dough in a greased bowl. Cover it with a dishtowel. Let it rise in a warm spot until it's doubled (a couple of hours or however long you need). Punch the dough—it will sink. Either put into loaf pans or make into rolls. Let rise again until puffy and then bake.

To make that roll-shape, put a mound of dough in your palm. You want to squeeze out a fair amount of the dough through your thumb and pointer finger—as if you were making your hand talk (Jamie suggested it looks as if "the little hand person puked up bread dough").

Bake loaves for about 50 minutes at 375°, rolls for about half that time.

Salad Days

Certain words are easily paired with kids—kids and fun, kids and dirt, kids and irrational needs for the red plate not the blue one. But one word that doesn't leap to mind when thinking of kids is "salad."

When Adam announced the menu, planning salad for one Wednesday-night dinner, the kids were semi-perplexed, but mostly annoyed.

"I don't like salad," Daniel said before even coming all the way into the room.

"You don't know that." Adam shook his head and diced peppers.

"You ate a salad yesterday!" Jamie accused me. "Why do you have to eat one again today?"

So we came up with the idea of giving them each a small salad with items they knew and liked like roasted broccoli, colorful peppers, cucumber, and roasted carrots and fashioning the plate with only a little lettuce, which it turns out is "the scary part of salad."

Sometimes we serve the salads alone, or with leek and onion quinoa on the side, once with cheddar cheese and just-picked-asparagus risotto, sometimes with freshly baked bread, once with some quick-made sorbet.

One of my favorite breads, wheat-oat, I learned to bake in graduate school. I lived in a house that my rotating roommates named the Dumpy Ranch House, which is self-explanatory save for the fact that it was in the woods and host to many a fine, simple meal. My friend Julie and I would bake together, kneading rolled oats into wheat flour and mixing in honey or molasses or maple syrup, depending on what was around. The kids and Adam adore the bread now when I make it. We had broccoli sandwiches on it the other night; toasted thick pieces of bread slathered with Russian dressing (Adam, Daniel, Julia) and spicy mustard (me, Jamie), and topped with crisp-steamed broccoli and cheddar and Fontina cheeses melted under the broiler. The sorbet was the result of simply having around some extra lemons and a milk bottle that needed emptying before Larry, the milkman, came the next day. I was tired of running off to the store midweek, tired of plastic buildup from the gallons gulped, so now we have Larry. He delivers milk from a local dairy in glass bottles—it tastes great, the bottles are recycled, and my midweek trips are reduced considerably. At the rate we're going through milk we should have our own cow, but our lawn isn't up to it. The lemon sorbet used up the last two cups of milk we had the night before the delivery, and I whisked it with some sugar and lemon juice and a dash of salt, and we enjoyed a refreshing scoop topped with a raspberry (for all but Adam).

One night when Adam cooked, he made popovers from scratch to serve with salads. "I'm not sure they're going to rise," he said, concerned that he'd made the batter and had to leave it in the fridge while he did the morning drop-offs. But the popovers popped and the kids enjoyed them and ate their greens, and Adam kept his cool despite losing the recipe before he'd finished.

But salads don't require bread or pudding, and as the weeks slipped by, we've had salads again, each time adding a bit more of this (roasted onions, fresh corn) and a bit more of that (baby romaine, butter lettuce). Now, as the spring greens come in, we cook them for just a few minutes in the oven and lace the top of the salad with chopped chard, asparagus, ramps. We add a couple of bright new potatoes. A bit of local goat cheese or fish, left-over chicken or some crunchy tofu.

"A salad is really just a bunch of stuff on a plate," Jamie says when we're all around the table, each of us with a personally tailored salad.

"That's true." I nod.

"But it's also kind of rainbowy," Julia notices.

We crunch away as the spring air seeps in through the open windows.

 ## Quick Lemon Sorbet

½ cup lemon juice	dash of salt
¾ cup sugar	2 cups milk

Mix together all ingredients until sugar and salt have dissolved, and freeze in metal bowl. Sprinkle with orange zest or serve with raspberries on top.

Serves 4–6, depending on size of scoop.

Wheat-Oat Bread

This recipe is a variation from my friend Julie Wade, a wonderful bread baker, who now mainly births babies instead of loaves. She and I spent many a graduate school afternoon sweltering in our Dumpy Ranch House kitchen, kneading, talking, and sitting on the counter waiting for a hunk of good, warm bread.

1 tbsp. yeast	4 cups flour (you may use a combination of wheat and white or all wheat; I prefer all wheat)
2 cups warm water	
½ cup honey or molasses or maple syrup	
	1 tsp. salt
1 cup rolled oats (or cornmeal)	

Let yeast dissolve in warm water with syrup/honey/molasses. Add in other ingredients bit by bit until incorporated. Knead on floured surface for about three songs on the radio, or 10 minutes. Set dough in greased bowl, draped with a thin dishcloth on top, and let rise for 1 or 2 hours (or longer, if you need to go out). Punch down and put into loaf pan and let rise for 30 minutes. Cook at 350° for 40 minutes. Makes one hearty loaf.

You Say It's Your . . .

The yard looks as though we planted mini-people and they've sprouted through the spring earth, blooming into four-year-olds.

Julia, both shrunken and big in her dad's old T-shirt, paints side by side with her friend Jonah, both kids absorbed in their artwork. We go to birthday parties every weekend, it seems, at pottery places, bowling alleys, kid gyms, and batting cages, and while I appreciate the idea of having the party (and cleanup) elsewhere, we tend to host them at our house. Jamie has a summer birthday, and we did a "Backyard Olympics" complete with egg tosses and relays, and the "square of fun" in which kids stood while parents chucked water balloons, drenching the eight-year-olds while hilarity ensued.

"I want to paint at my party," Julia had said a while back.

Adam and I consulted. "I'm pretty sure we don't want ten three- and four-year-olds armed with paintbrushes in the living room," Adam said.

"Can we do it outside?"

We could, only the first time we tried to have the party, it rained. And it was unseasonably cold. So we had to cancel. Now it's a week later and, it feels, a whole season ahead. Sunshine, warm breeze, kids and their parents and siblings playing catch and painting. I bought a long roll of white paper, taped it to the side of the fence in the front yard, and let the kids make their own mural. Adam collected old T-shirts and now the small limbs and frames are draped with his old medical residency scrub tops, or out-of-date tops that announce Y2K or stores now defunct.

"Jonah can't wait for cake," his mom, Julie, says.

I nod, smiling at the scene. Adam juggles Wiffle balls while talking to parents and making sure not too much paint spills on the grass. I stayed up late mixing colors. It was cheaper to just buy the primary ones and white and then concoct the purple, pinks, light blues, oranges, and greens. We put each color into baby-food jars and lined them up on the grass and on tables.

"You know, there isn't any cake," I say, and grimace. I have lofty visions of making cakes, but the truth is, when I do they taste fine (how bad can cake be?) but they tilt. Or I run out of icing midway through the frosting and don't have time to make more, like at Jamie's sixth birthday. The truth is, the kids don't care—as long as their favorite colors are represented—but it's one area in which I tend to eschew homemade and go for the wonderful bakery down the road. Cake somehow reminds me of all the times when cooking goes wrong. One year after Adam and I were married, we went to Connecticut to celebrate his dad's birthday. Knowing I was an avid cook, his mother tried to include me by having me help make their traditional coconut double-layer cake (that everyone except Adam had a tradition of adoring). I followed the directions, blending confectioners' sugar and toasting coconut, and produced more than enough light and fluffy icing to cover the cake my mother-in-law made. My father-in-law blew out his candles and took a bite. "Who made the icing?" he asked. "I did," I said, a small grin appearing on my face. "Oh. I don't like it," my father-in-law said, but ate it anyway while we laughed at his candor.

"No cake for Julia," I say.

"Really? Is she allergic?"

I explain. "Julia's not into cake . . . but you know, Jamie never really liked cake. And I'm kind of lopsided at making them . . . and he's not into frosting. So for his birthday last summer he had make-your-own sundaes." The other mom looks at me with trepidation. "So then Julia asked if she *had* to have cake."

Her exact words were, "Is it a law you have to have cake on your birthday?" And I'd replied no, of course not.

"So anyway, I told her she could pick out whatever she wanted to have since it's her party."

"But it's not cake?"

"No. We have Rice Krispies treats with M&M'S in them," I say, and Julie nods. "They're very colorful!"

Jonah doesn't care that there's no cake. No one does. Julia hides her face in my leg while everyone sings to her, Daniel and Jamie look longingly at the presents, the yard is—at least temporarily—replete with people and colors. The kids' mural is bright with streaks of red and magenta, long lines of wavy blues and yellows, decorating the day. And everyone crunches away on the chewy treats.

"I might have cake next year," Julia says.

Daniel sings the Beatles' "Birthday" to her. "Or you could have cupcakes."

"Or these again," Jamie offers.

One by one the kids depart, a cheek or eyebrow dotted with paint, their hands clutching the "goody bag" that consists entirely of the CD Julia and Adam made last night. Her current favorite songs all in one place.

Adam picks at another treat, and I go to gather the paints before Will finds them.

"I kind of want to keep the mural," I say to Adam. We stand back, admiring it. "I can't believe how big she is," I add.

"I know." Adam nods. "It's fun having all the colors here." Then he pauses. He looks at Julia, at her growing limbs, how she can reach the doorknob herself now to go inside. "Let's leave it up for a little bit."

Rainbow Rice Krispies Bars

You can follow the original recipe on the cereal box and add a few big handfuls of M&M'S at the last stage of mixing, or you can use some colored mini-marshmallows and M&M'S. Either way, the butter, cereal, and marshmallow combo is sticky and yummy and a fine choice for those who don't like cake.

Sublime Coconut Cake

My mother-in-law makes this cake regularly. Her recipe is from her old friend Lew, who passed the concoction along years ago from an old family recipe for a 1234 cake. The cake is moist and fluffy, the frosting light but flavorful. Even for those who don't love coconut, this cake is a crowd-pleaser. Over the decade of making it, I have changed it slightly.

You can make this cake in stages if your timing demands it: Crack open one coconut and grate it into medium-size shavings. If doing this in advance, put the shavings into the fridge. This can be done 2–3 days in advance.

FOR THE CAKE:

1 cup unsalted butter at room temperature

2 cups superfine sugar

3 cups flour

4 level tsp. baking powder

3 whole eggs

1 egg yolk (so 4 eggs in total)

1 cup coconut milk

1 tsp. vanilla extract

Preheat the oven to 375°. Cream butter and sugar. Sift flour once and re-measure, then sift together all dry ingredients. Add eggs and yolk one by one to the butter and sugar mixture and beat after each addition. Add dry ingredients a bit at a time, alternating with coconut milk and vanilla.

Spray two round (9 × 2) baking pans and shake into them a bit of flour (tap out the excess). Insert parchment paper circle on the bottom of the pans and spray lightly and dust with flour. Fill evenly with batter.

Bake for 30–45 minutes until a toothpick placed near the center comes out clean.

FROSTING:

1 lb. confectioners' sugar

½ cup butter, softened

1 tsp. vanilla

2 tbsp. cream of coconut

1 tbsp. flour

3 tbsp. coconut milk (add more or less milk as needed)

the grated coconut from before

Mix together sugar and butter. Mix in the cream of coconut and vanilla. Sprinkle in flour. Add in milk little by little, only enough so that frosting is light and spreadable but not runny.

After cake has cooled completely, frost the top of bottom layer and sprinkle around a bit of the grated coconut to cover the surface. Place the second round on top and frost the top and sides. Spread the rest of the grated coconut around the top and gently pat coconut to sides so that cake is completely covered.

Note: If you prefer the look and texture of toasted coconut, you may put the grated coconut on a cookie sheet and bake it 300° for about 15 minutes, or until just tanned.

Spring Ahead

The kitchen is radiant—one of those afternoons when the spring sunlight coats the walls like honey and the window lets in bursts of warm air that is only every now and then tinged with chill. The morning's slashes of rain and gray produced antsy and nudgey children in need of fresh air, but also brown sugar molasses muffins whose smoky, sweet flavor still hangs about the now-bright kitchen. I'm on a molasses kick because I'd bought a large jar of it, used some for various breads, and wanted to finish it off. I take a muffin to eat as a snack while I glance out the window. The hedges are budding green. Purple crocuses, the electric yellow forsythia bush we planted in the fall, everything is blooming.

And no one is listening.

"Can you pick up your jacket from the entryway?"

"Whose cleat is this?"

"Where's Will?"

"Who moved the pasta?"

The kids are a whirl of activity, playing Wiffle ball and bouncing balls on the porch. Adam nets the last of the brown leaves left over from winter, and I've found the answer to one of my earlier questions.

"Will, what are you doing under the table?"

"Car?" he asks, though he holds in his small grip a crayon someone dropped who knows when.

"Is that a car?" I ask, moving the chairs so he isn't trapped.

"Ball?" he wonders. These are his only words—ball, car, dis, and dat—this last one always a question.

I pull him out and let him toy with one of my earrings (I remembered to put them on today for the first time in months) while I try to answer one of my other questions.

"Hey!" I shout to Jamie and Daniel. "Where's the pasta?"

They give me looks that suggest that unless I'm taking a turn at bat or spewing Red Sox stats, they have no time for me. Julia's about to take her turn at bat, and they're trying to be patient.

"Hold it up a little more," Jamie instructs.

"You're gonna have to pitch much closer than that. She can't hit!" Daniel wails.

"Daniel," I warn him. "You're doing great, Ju."

She hefts the bat up, turns her body the way Adam and I taught her and, in her skirt and sneakers and tie-dyed hand-me-down T-shirt, swings.

"Yes!" she yelps when the bat makes contact.

"Technically it's foul," Jamie says.

Daniel steps in. "Run, Julia, go to first!"

"Great hit!" Adam shouts from the hedges.

Still holding Will, I feel Saturday slipping away already, the weekend half over, the season on its slow climb into summer.

"So who moved the box of pasta?" I ask, well aware that I could be the one who left it somewhere—like the time the teakettle found its way into the fridge.

"You mean this one?" Julia asks from the trees. She's tucked into her fort, a small clearing in the thick brush that separates our house from the neighbors'. Last summer we put a stool in there, some flowers she'd collected, and strung up various colored ribbons in the branches overhead. I didn't know if she'd be interested in it still, but she likes her space. "I put it in my fort." She shakes the box of pasta like a maraca.

Will wriggles free and stands up, trying to walk to Adam. Soon. He will walk and then he'll run and then drive and then visit me in the nursing home. Wait. Slow down. Back to right now and pasta. "I'm heading in to make dinner."

Hanging on the wall of the kitchen is a print Adam and

I bought way back in Orvieto during one of our trips to Italy. To call it a print gives it an undeserved promotion, because really it's just a sheet of wrapping paper but fine quality in that Italian way, white with a cream-colored border. We had it framed in wood. What the picture shows is many types of pastas, each name written in Italian, most of them antiquated or unusual in shape or texture, many unavailable here: *Anelli Siciliani* (Sicilian halos, loops one might fling around a miniature stick), *ballerine* (dancers, which are wonderful with thicker sauces like the wild boar ragu or a dried mushroom and herb), *cappellitti umbri*, *cappello napoletano*, *corni di bue* (ox horns), *crestine* (which look like bass clefs), *denti di cavallo* (horse teeth), *Farfalle tonde* (round butterfly), *Margherita Messinese lunga* (these look like elegant, elongated tools one might use to excavate a garden), *merletti* (meaning laces, but resembling a complicated flower), *Occhi di trota* (trout eyes) also called *occhi di Pernice* (partridge eyes)—apparently the two creatures have similar eyes—who knew? *Radiatori* (radiators, and exactly thus shaped—the kind that hissed and burned and provided the driest air imaginable in my first apartment), *Trottole* (spinning tops, their twists and curves suggesting motion despite being made from flour and water). The list goes on, poetic and playful, and informative. The kids often debate their favorite shape, or which section of the print they would keep if only allowed one, or which would be good for another use—say, pelting one another.

Tonight, fitting with the theme of no one listening, I am making orecchiette.

"Which means what?" Jamie slides into his seat and waits to be served.

"Little ears," I say, and pick one up to show him.

Jamie holds one to his head. "I can hear you!"

Daniel cracks up while Julia asks me to pick her up. Adam leans over the stove and then pries Will off his leg and buckles him into his booster seat, which is now flush with the table; he isn't a baby anymore, but a toddler.

I hug Julia and then deposit her in her seat and sit down myself while Adam scoops the pasta onto our plates. The cubes of butternut squash are cooked but still retain their shapes, the sweetness palatable before tasting. Sprinkled onto the tops of each plate are spiky bits of Parmesan and a pinch of shredded mozzarella. The roasted broccoli everyone loves is piled high onto a serving platter.

"So if you could choose one kind of pasta from here which would it be?" Daniel asks, pointing to the print.

I don't answer first; I let Julia go and then Jamie and Daniel, and Adam, who chooses spaghetti "because someone's got to."

"What about you, Mom?" Jamie asks. His whole body seems to hulk over the table. The shirt he wears was as baggy as a Shar-pei's skin last summer and now it looks as though he borrowed it from Daniel. Next summer, Daniel will fit into it and then Julia. Even Will.

"This is the perfect dinner." Adam sighs as he eats. His cheeks are flushed just from the few hours of spring sun today.

"Not perfect." Daniel shakes his head.

"Broccoli is perfect." Julia munches away.

"Maybe there are a lot of perfect meals," Jamie muses. "How come I like this squash but not the other times you made it?"

I shrug. "Because you change. Tastes change."

We take turns concocting our perfect meals—this one, or others, anything permissible. The truth is, the are many perfect meals and there are none. Or when one is perfected, the next time maybe it doesn't come out exactly the same or your mood has shifted and it doesn't register the same way. Or it's better.

"It's not about the food, anyway," Daniel says with his mouth full. "It's just about, you know"—he looks around the table—"this."

Orecchiette with Maple Squash and Mozzarella

1 lb. orecchiette	2 tbsp. maple syrup
olive oil	1½ tbsp. brown sugar
sea salt	½ cup shredded mozzarella
1 butternut squash, seeded, peeled, and cubed	salt and pepper
	2 tbsp. shredded Parmesan

Cook the pasta in well-salted water until al dente, drain well, and put back into the pot with a drizzle of olive oil. In a pan, heat some olive oil and throw in a bit of sea salt. Add the cubes of squash and let them cook on medium-high for a few minutes so they begin to brown, then reduce heat and keep cooking, only stirring when really necessary, until soft but not mushy (about 15–20 minutes). When ready, drizzle maple syrup on top and sprinkle with brown sugar. Let cook one minute longer until sugar and syrup are bubbly. Add to cooked pasta, and let warm on very low heat. Add mozzarella. When mozzarella has started to melt, season for taste with salt, syrup, pepper, and/or brown sugar. Sprinkle pasta with Parmesan right before eating.

Serve with roasted broccoli for a nice mix of sweet and savory.

Molasses Muffins

2 egg whites

¼ cup molasses

2 tbsp. oil

1 cup milk

2 cups flour (all-purpose
or wheat)

¼ cup brown sugar, plus a
little more for topping

1 tsp. salt

2 tsp. baking soda

Mix everything together until smooth. Spoon into greased muffin tins.
Press a little brown sugar into the top of each muffin. Bake at 350° for 15
minutes, or longer if the muffins are big.

Note: *Should you ever desire your own pasta mold—be it trout eyes, butterflies, dancers, or any other shape, you can visit www.trafileturconi.it. They even have custom
designs—your very own squiggle or toe. Or you can go to www.landucci.it or www
.montoni.com.*

More

"So, guess what?" I say to Heather. She's with her kids in Brooklyn baking bread and I'm with mine making dinner.

"You want to lend me a baby?" she asks. Heather's on a baby kick—her other best friend just gave birth, another is adopting, and she knows it's time to expand her brood.

"You can borrow Will," I tell her, and motion for the kids to keep stretching the dough. We roll the pliable mass of it onto the back of a floured cookie sheet, stretching and rolling it thin, then place it onto a parchment-lined sheet in an uneven rectangle. "But you have to give him back."

Babies and pregnancies are popping up everywhere—and they're not mine! I send *Make Way for Ducklings* and other favorite books, make dinners, hand out babysitting coupons as gifts to the new parents, but I don't feel that tug that Heather does. I expect they'll move forward with their plans for adoption soon or try for another biological baby before the month is up. "No, what I was going to tell you is . . . remember Indiana? Those weird beans?"

"The ones I made with mustard seeds and everything we had around?" Her smile is audible.

"Yeah." I hold the phone under my chin and reach for a jar of fig jam. "I know what they are!"

"No way," Heather says and then, not to me, adds, "No—don't hit your brother with the spoon. Make a drum."

"I think—maybe—they're Valena beans. Sometimes they're called Valena Italian beans—or, as the farmer said—"

"Eye-talian-o."

"Right. You can eat them green like we did or let them dry. They turn tan or brown. My grandma's been researching."

Heather pauses. I pause. "I have fig spread all over my hands," I say. "I can't put the phone down."

"Maybe I'll grow Eye-talian-o beans," she muses.

"Valena."

"Right. On the porch." Heather breathes deeply.

"The days take forever, sometimes," I say, and she follows.

"I know, but then—"

"Then you turn around and Will's talking and standing by himself and Julia's reading and Daniel's writing whole stories and Jamie's making skillet shrimp all by himself."

"He is?" Heather's incredulity echoes into the phone. I can nearly hear her shaking her head. "I gotta have another kid. Like now." I sigh in agreement. "Hey. Have you used the sorghum yet?"

I remember the heavy jar of sticky, dark sorghum, the pamphlet of recipes that came with it. "It's in the pantry—I'm thinking maybe this weekend I'll crack it open . . ." I think about other food items—jams Heather and I haven't tested, relishes that await finding in some state fair or a foreign market—street food we've yet to bite into. More.

We hang up and keep cooking our separate dishes—her bread rises, our pizza dough is stretched thin, perfect for crisping.

"Now what?" Jamie asks, taking the phone for me while my hands are coated from rubbing olive oil and fig spread onto the dough.

Now is when I will cook, and in a day I will visit my friend for whom I threw the tea party baby shower. Her boy, Calum, was born today. For once I will be the one bringing soup and cookies and sweet tidings to the hospital rather than being the one in the Eames-print gown, sore and tired and not just the slightest bit shocked. My friend craves the wild salmon with Asian marinade, she desires greens and baked goods to get her through sleepless nights.

Now is when, instead of wishing *I* were in that hospital bed with *my* newborn, I will dig further into and be grateful for all I have. I will inhale Will's baby smell; his skin and washed hair, the pervasive smell of milk that goes from me to him and then back to me by way of his drooling on my shirtsleeve. I will ingest this until I can't smell it anymore—he is grown or I've forgotten about it one day (those sorts of things seem to happen) and then I remember it only to find the whole, glorious mix of it has faded. But he—we—have meals ahead of us, the scraping of forks, chairs marking the floor, dough waiting to be shaped, vegetables waiting to be cut, conversations waiting to be spoken.

"Mum? Hell-o?" Jamie taps my back.

"Now what?" Daniel scratches his head, waiting.

"Now the onions," I say, and Julia obliges, dropping bits of caramelized onions onto the fig spread.

"Then the cheese, right?" Daniel spreads fistfuls of mozzarella around the sheet. Will reaches for the bits that drop on the floor, but I snake them away from him—no dairy until he's one year.

"And the prosciutto!" Gently, Julia lays out the thin strips onto the top of the pizza.

"And then just these." I slice a couple of roasted asparagus stalks in half—they're in season now and local—and lay them in crisscrosses over the top of the pizza.

"It looks so good." Daniel rubs his belly.

"It'll be even better when we cook it," I say, recalling Daniel's anti-mixture policy that's apparently on leave for tonight.

"I can always peel things off if I don't like them," Daniel says, nixing my prior thought.

Jamie studies the cookie sheet. "It's weird, because you can just keep taking the same things, like cheese or dough or onions or something, and make it into other things you didn't know about."

I think of Heather and Dan's family, of Adam and our brood, of the pantry items—sorghum included—that we've yet to try. I think how we are not quite done.

Caramelized Onion, Fig, Asparagus, and Prosciutto Pizza

This is a lovely combination of sweet and salty and makes for a good dinner shared with friends or cut into smaller lengths and served at room temperature at a brunch. Make or buy a basic pizza dough. I use homemade whole wheat. Let it warm so it is soft and stretchy.

2 large Spanish onions	2 cups mozzarella cheese, shredded
olive oil	6 slices best-quality prosciutto
1 jar of fig jam (or fig and ginger), about 12 oz.	4 stalks asparagus (ideally, roasted)
sea salt	

Slice onions thin and in long shreds. Cook onions in pan with no oil on medium-low, stirring now and then, until fully translucent but not brown and until their liquid has evaporated. Roll and stretch dough so it is as long and wide as a cookie sheet—with no distinct crust. Place dough on parchment-lined baking sheet (this will help when it's time to move and cut it). Rub a bit of olive oil onto the dough with your palm. Scoop some jam onto the dough and, using your hands, spread a layer over the whole thing—it's OK if there are clumps in places. Drop the onions around and sprinkle with some sea salt. Cover with cheese. Lay pieces of prosciutto on top, not covering whole dough, but flinging bits here and there. Slice asparagus in half lengthwise (if you have leftover roasted asparagus, use that; if not, just slice some raw ones). Lay them in an X pattern over the top.

Bake at 450° for about 15 minutes or until cheese bubbles and dough is cooked. Let cool for a couple of minutes and then move to a cutting board to slice into rectangular pieces.

Roasted Asparagus

These lovely stalks make a great side dish, a hearty appetizer (plain or perhaps with a yogurt-dill sauce for dipping), can top a salad, or can be enjoyed standing up as you ponder what to make for lunch. When roasting asparagus, look for thicker stalks. Thinner ones will work, but reduce the cooking time to about 8 minutes.

1 bunch asparagus	olive oil
sea salt	

Trim stalks or peel thicker stems from midway down. Rub baking sheet with olive oil, dust with sea salt, and cook at 425° for 10–12 minutes. Better to have the stalks be crunchy than wilted, so if you remove them too soon, just drape them with a kitchen cloth—they'll steam a bit and be tender when you serve.

Out with a Bang

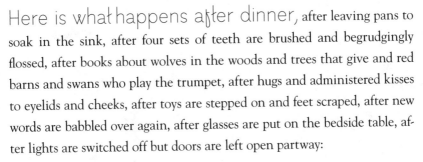

Here is what happens after dinner, after leaving pans to soak in the sink, after four sets of teeth are brushed and begrudgingly flossed, after books about wolves in the woods and trees that give and red barns and swans who play the trumpet, after hugs and administered kisses to eyelids and cheeks, after toys are stepped on and feet scraped, after new words are babbled over again, after glasses are put on the bedside table, after lights are switched off but doors are left open partway:

We sit on the couch.

"And then what?" Jamie asked, arranging himself in his bed with the shade propped open so he could see the night-lighted street. Daniel did the same from his bed, and the two conferred about what they saw outside as they prepared to drift off to sleep.

"And then Daddy and I just talk," I explained. Jamie is insatiably curious about the goings-on of grown-ups. We are a species he wants to track, detail, and write up in a report. Eating habits. Sleeping habits. Perhaps mating. Definitely communication patterns.

"Do you talk about me? Or just, like, mortgages and . . . taxes and things like that?"

"Growing up I thought the word 'mortgage' was very, very adult. I wondered when I'd know what it meant," I told him.

"And I already know it," he boasted. "It's like when you buy part of a house but not the whole thing and then you have to pay the part that you didn't pay before. But with interest." He grinned and raised his eyebrows. "Right?"

I know by now not to be surprised, but I still am. He knows mortgages, income tax, sports trivia from before I was even born, but last night pronounced "prohibition" pro-hibe-ishon (although he knew what it was).

"Mainly Daddy and I just talk about the day we had, or about the next day," I said. "Just regular who-said-what, what happened at work or home."

I kissed the boys good night and left them to their own conversation in the dark, which began with Daniel asking, "Would a killer whale eat a great white shark or the other way around?"

Adam closed Julia's door and I closed Will's and then we went downstairs.

Now we sit on the couch, talking. We do this for a while. All is peaceful. My feet are tucked under Adam's legs, the sky darkens, the streetlight makes the view appear like that Magritte painting, the one in which everything looks normal—a dark house at night—until you realize the sky is daytime blue and the world is a bit off-kilter.

Which is just what happens to us when Adam is cut off in midsentence: "And then I said to him— What the hell was that?"

We both bolt upright. More noise. "It's so loud!" I stand up. "Is it the kids?"

Adam shakes his head and looks up at the ceiling. "Not unless their ceilings are caving in."

"Oh my God!" We are statues, waiting to hear where the crashing comes from next. If we had earthquakes here, I'd gather the kids.

More crashes. Adam rushes to the kitchen and doesn't come back with anything other than a shout. "Em—get in here—and wear shoes!"

I should have worn boots.

When I follow Adam to the kitchen, he only needs to point to the pantry for me to begin moaning.

"Well, that explains the noise," I groan, and realize we have a ton of work ahead of us.

Every shelf in the pantry—from floor to ceiling—has dominoed down to the one below. Each glass jar—of tomato sauce, strawberry jam, preserved cipollini onions, cherries in balsamic—is shattered, its contents sploshed everywhere. Adam and I stare at the wreckage, unable at first to spring to action. Mixed in with the glass and goop are pounds of pasta and their glass containers, cans of corn, organic white beans, boxes of crackers and cereals. The slop has spilled onto the red blender, the food processor, the waffle iron we hardly ever use. The oatmeal tin Jamie had just used that morning wasn't closed properly, and it, too, has belched up its innards. It's as though the pantry has given up, decided on another profession—I think I'll be a coat closet now, thanks—and heaved its contents down in one fatal blow.

"I just . . . I don't even . . . ," I stammer.

"I know." Adam opens the door to the basement, where we keep cleaning supplies. "Where do we even begin?"

But we do. We do what you do in any crisis: We go slowly. We clean up. We move on.

Would molasses mustard peach curry champagne wild boar purée make a delicious sauce? No, it wouldn't. There is little to salvage, but we set aside dented tins, a small pot of red currant jelly and a canning jar filled with Dijon mustard. A half-pint jar from my grandma Bev's gardening days in which I now store sunflower seeds.

The sorghum from Indiana is lost, as is the last of the *marmelatta di prugne* from Italy, the *cinghiali* sauce from Farnese, the cipollini onions immersed in olive oil I planned on using in part two of another baked pasta. All of this is a thick shellac on the floor, coating the walls, the wire racks.

The glass and liquids and sauces have splattered the washer and dryer, crept into doorjambs and the spaces in the original hardwood floor, reached in back of Diet Coke cases and beyond the five-liter jug of olive oil my dad brought back for us.

"At least the kids weren't here—God, can you imagine?" But we can't. Our kids are safe—and, miraculously, still asleep upstairs despite the thunderclaps of noise.

No one is injured, or at least not physically hurt. It takes six hours to clean up. Not to mention the money and time it took to stock the shelves—the various trips to farmer's markets, fairs, country stores. My grandmother's Kahlúa vodka sauce, my mother's rose-hip pancake syrup, the sorghum I wanted to use to make more molasses muffins, all the jars I've saved for a later date—are gone.

And maybe that's part of it—we cannot save it all for tomorrow. I am always stockpiling for the next meal, the next season. I am constantly battling the urge to look back or forward with my kids, to think of how they were or will be, rather than how they are. The task of any good cook, of any parent, is to be present—in the kitchen and out. To taste all the items, absorb each child's day, all those moments, and form them into the day's meals.

"Next time," I tell Adam, "I'll use the sorghum sooner."

"And the spicy red pepper jam from Pitigliano," he says, his tongue and mouth recalling it. "I really liked that."

"It's over there." I point to the corner where bright red sticky stuff has made its way over the windowsill, down the pantry's back wall.

Adam and I crouch in the muck. At our feet, all around us, are scents and sights, a mush of where we've been, what we've tasted, foods we hadn't yet tried.

"Oh, no! My honey—look, the lavender honey . . ." Using the dustpan, I scoop up the massive broken jar—a whole five pounds my dad brought back when he went to close the house in Italy.

"We'll go back someday," Adam says, and begins picking up the big pieces, setting on a plastic bag the few dented cans that survived the fall.

"You think?" I scoop up more goo. It's nearly two in the morning.

"Well, at least the kids weren't hurt," he says, reassuring us both again. The shelves themselves are hanging off their hinges, knocked onto the floor, precariously perched in the window. "I can't believe they didn't wake up."

The thought of their curiosity, the crawling, the small feet, the shards of glass, the temptation of spilled sugar spiked with broken ceramic, is enough to make me press on with the cleaning. So we clean. We mop and wash the salvaged tins. We hulk glass-covered muck into the garbage and out to the cans.

We keep going until the mess is gone, the walls are scrubbed, and the only way to be sure of what we had there, is to remember.

The next day, we're in the yard, and we tell the kids the story.

"See?" Jamie twirls his baseball bat like a baton. "And you said all you do is sit on the couch."

The six of us hang around outside in our short sleeves, playing and talking, chasing one another, and I think about the day's plans, about upcoming meals. Maybe we'll have some finger shrimp—quickly seared in the pan and served with three sauces: currant-mustard, a jewel-colored sauce made easily with two of the remnants of last night's crash—red currant jelly and Dijon mustard—blended with a fork; yogurt-dill, with capers, lemon juice, and a salvaged tube of garlic paste; or honey-ginger. All three a great trio for shrimp skewers. Or maybe we'll grill the fish my mom's friend caught on the Cape, serve it simple with garlic and lemons and salt. Maybe the undamaged sunflower seeds can be fashioned into a new kind of pesto—arugula and sunflower pesto instead of basil and pine nuts. Maybe we'll tear up leftover brioche and plunk the pieces into some beaten eggs and milk, throw some cheese on top and have an egg bake—the simple answer to soufflé. Maybe Heather will send her last jar of sorghum to me, along with the pamphlet that explains how to use it—or maybe we'll have to return to the Midwest and see for ourselves. Maybe we'll go with my dad to a different shop in another country and find sauces and canned vegetables there. Perhaps the lone bag of rice cakes will be the perfect palette for the soy butter that only bounced and didn't break. Maybe we'll use the dented tins of baby corn and bamboo shoots and I'll attempt Thai cooking again. Or we'll scrap using anything from the pantry and order in. Or have a picnic.

It is not my job to choose my children's tastes, to demand that they enjoy certain foods. It is my job to give them the emotional strength to navigate the roads ahead, be those roads intellectual, environmental, familial, moral, or social. To give them the gastronomic tour, lead them with a map, but in the end, hand the compass and guidebooks over to them so they can weave through the culinary landscape ahead.

All four kids are dirt-streaked from the spring lawn, whooping with delight at the warm air with their dad with whom I have built—am building—this life. We are all ready to eat. I hold the door open so we can head inside to the kitchen and see what's cooking.

Arugula Sunflower Pesto

This turned out to be a fresh, spicy bright-green sauce. Wonderful served over any strong pasta.

2 big cloves garlic	1 cup good olive oil
2 cups arugula, rinsed and patted dry	1 cup Parmigiano-Reggiano
1 cup sunflower seeds	¼ cup Romano

Pulse and chop garlic, arugula, and seeds in food processor. When combined and mixed well, add oil in slowly until sauce is thick. Add cheeses, gently mixing as you go. Add salt and pepper as desired.

Note: *This recipe makes enough for about two pounds of pasta. If you'd like to freeze half of the sauce (and it freezes well), do so before adding the cheese. You might also try spooning small bits of the sauce into wonton wrappers, sealing with a bit of egg, boiling them for two minutes, and then sautéing them in a pan with a bit of butter for a ravioli-type dinner.*

Sauces for Shrimp (or cheese, or chicken, or vegetables)

Currant-Mustard

Back in the 1980s in London this was one of the first sauces I ever made. It became an old dinner-party standard—a starter to accompany triangles of fried Camembert. The melting cheese, crisp breading, and sweet tang of currant and mustard not only tasted delicious but looked pretty on the plate.

½ cup red currant jelly   4 tbsp. Dijon mustard

Mix. Serve with cold shrimp as an appetizer or with a wedge of fried brie.

Yogurt-Dill

A standby for grilling or dipping.

1½ tbsp. chopped capers   1 cup plain yogurt
1½ tbsp. lemon juice   1 tsp. minced garlic
1 tbsp. chopped fresh dill   2 tbsp. minced red onion

Mix all ingredients, slather onto chicken before baking or grilling, or serve cold alongside cooked shrimp for summer starter.

Honey-Lemon-Ginger

1 tsp. grated fresh ginger

⅓ cup honey

½ lemon's worth of juice or more

Mix well. Adjust for taste. Serve in small cups (such as an egg dish) with shrimp skewers.

Acknowledgments

The best meals are a collaborative effort and this book is no exception.

Thanks to: Faye Bender for her immediate excitement about this book (and about blueberry jam, Korean food, and fava beans); Ellen Archer for loving this project at first sight, and Sarah Landis for her careful and insightful edits (and willingness to make peach cobbler); everyone at Hyperion/Voice for enthusiasm and hard work—the proof is in the pudding (and the main course).

To the Swainegut family for brilliant meals and even greater friendship.

To the recipe testers: Kathleen Cheng, Liz Haas, Heather Woodcock, Jill Fischer, Jeanée Redmond, Hooter von Binker, Liz Bloodworth, Barbara, Faye, Ann, and Leslie Diamond.

To Lisa Lessard for baseball, patience, and care (not to mention creamed corn).

To my extended family for kebabs, cakes, cookies, and company.

To my parents and brothers, the first to suffer through my tableside questions and, later, to enjoy my recipes. I love you.

To my grandparents for letting me lick the bowl (and praising me for it).

To my kids—my greatest joys no matter what the season.

And to Adam, for tasting everything I have to offer, accepting my food whims, and making all the meals happen. There's no one with whom I'd rather share dessert (or breakfast . . . or lunch . . . or dinner . . .).

Recipe Index